W9-CIR-387

Family Planning Management Terms

A Pocket Glossary in Three Languages

Janice Miller
Claire Bahamon

Family Planning Management Development

Management Sciences for Health
400 Centre Street
Newton, Massachusetts 02158
USA

Cover Design
Linda Suttenfield
Jacki Forbes

Cover Graphics
Jacki Forbes

Book Layout
Ceallaigh Reddy

Printing
Foremost Impressions

Copyright ©1995, 1996 by Management Sciences for Health

This publication was produced by Family Planning Management Development (FPMD), a project of Management Sciences for Health in Boston Massachusetts.

Funding for this publication was provided by the U.S. Agency for International Development under project number: 936-3055 and contract number: DPE-3055-C-00-0051-00.

Any part of this publication may be reproduced without prior permission from FPMD or Management Sciences for Health, provided the publication is acknowledged and the material is made available free of charge. Any commercial reproduction requires prior permission from the FPMD project. FPMD would appreciate receiving a copy of any materials in which the contents of this publication are used.

ISBN 0-913723-34-7

List of Authors, Editors, and Translators

Author and Editor
Janice Miller

Managing Editors—Translations
Claire Bahamon
Linda Suttenfield

Spanish Translators
Eliana Gottschalck
Javier Silva Calderón

French Translators
Isabelle d'Haucourt
Africa Consultants International
Gisele Bisaccia

Editor—Spanish and French Language Sections
Claire Bahamon

Spanish-Language Editors
Alberto Rizo
Edgar Necochea
Susana de Pazos
María Dolores Castro
Judy Seltzer

French-Language Editors
Mohammed Zarouf
Hammouda Bellamine
Linda Lank

Contents

Acknowledgments

This glossary of terms combines the family planning management terms and definitions used in the Family Planning Management Development (FPMD) project's two primary publications: *The Family Planning Manager* bi-monthly management series and *The Family Planning Manager's Handbook*. As the English- and foreign-language editions of these publications were developed over a period of several years, I would like to thank the many individuals who contributed to the development and review of the English, Spanish, and French editions of these publications on which this glossary is based.

In particular, I am grateful to Claire Bahamon and Linda Suttenfield who worked closely with the Spanish- and French-language translators and editors of *The Family Planning Manager* and *The Handbook* to ensure that the translated terms in both publications were accurate and consistent. Linda Suttenfield also worked with me to design this *Pocket Glossary* and managed the production of the final product. I would also like to thank Kim Austin and Ceallaigh Reddy for their careful review and proofreading of various drafts of the glossary, Ceallaigh Reddy for her patience and extraordinary attention to detail in the layout of the publication, and Jacki Forbes for producing the cover graphics. Finally, I would like to thank Jim Wolff who has overseen the development of FPMD's publications and is a constant source of ideas and encouragement.

Thanks also goes to the members of the International Review Boards of *The Family Planning Manager* series and *The Family Planning Manager's Handbook*, FPMD technical staff, and reviewers from our collaborating organizations in the field of international health and family planning. Several individuals, in particular, contributed to this glossary by extensively reviewing and updating various terms and definitions that pertained to their fields of expertise: Saul Helfenbein and David Collins of Management Sciences for Health; Sallie Craig Huber, a consultant to FPMD; Terrence Jezowski of AVSC International; John Ross of The Futures Group; Lynne Gaffikin of JHPIEGO Corporation; Robert Magnani of the EVALUATION Project; and Timothy Johnson and Susanna Binzen of the Division of Reproductive Health at the Centers for Disease Control and Prevention. Their advice and suggestions were invaluable.

Financial support for this publication was provided by the United States Agency for International Development (USAID). We appreciate the interest in and commitment to the work of FPMD in improving management systems and practices in developing-country family planning programs.

Introduction

The Family Planning Management Development (FPMD) project works with managers of public and private health and family planning programs in developing countries to improve their management capabilities and the effectiveness and sustainability of their programs.

In 1991, the project published *The Family Planning Manager's Handbook*, the first handbook written specifically for family planning managers. In 1992, the project began publishing a bi-monthly continuing-education management publication, *The Family Planning Manager*, which addresses specific management strategies for improving health and family planning services. These publications were subsequently published in Spanish and French. Over the past several years, many managers have commented on the usefulness of the glossary contained in *The Handbook* and, more recently, on a glossary published as an issue of *The Family Planning Manager*. This *Pocket Glossary* combines the glossaries of these two publications in one book and links each term with the corresponding terms in Spanish and French.

As more managers engage in south-to-south collaboration and new programs are modelled on those that have proven to be successful—both within and between countries—the knowledge of basic management practices and the use of a common vocabulary is increasingly important. The purpose of this glossary is to improve the understanding of management terms and practices used in managing family planning programs and to promote a common working vocabulary among managers around the world.

Each section of the *Pocket Glossary* is organized in the same way, beginning with the full glossary of terms and definitions, listed alphabetically in the relevant language, and including the appropriate foreign-language equivalents of each term. The glossary of terms is followed by a list of only the terms and their foreign-language equivalents, and ends with a bibliography of family planning glossaries.

We hope that this *Pocket Glossary* will be useful to the many types of managers working in health and family planning programs around the world and that it will help to improve the understanding and use of sound management practices and, ultimately, will contribute to the success of their programs in providing high-quality reproductive health services.

Glossary of Terms

Acceptance Rate: The number of new users who have begun using any method of contraception, measured among a designated population (community, district, program area), covering a specific period of time (month, quarter, or year). An acceptance rate can be measured for all methods or for a single, specific method. *For example, in a clinic, the acceptance rate for oral contraceptives measured over the three-month period (January through March) could be expressed as 100 per 1000 clients, or 10 percent of visiting clients accepted an initial supply of oral contraceptives—a 10 percent acceptance rate during the first quarter of that year. Tasa de Aceptación; Taux d'acceptation*

Accounting System: A system for collecting, recording, processing, and reporting all financially related transactions. Two common systems are cash accounting and accrual accounting. *Sistema Contable; Système de comptabilité*

Accounts Payable (also known as Payables): Money owed by your organization according to bills or invoices already received. *Cuentas por Pagar; Comptes à payer*

Accounts Receivable (also known as Receivables): Money owed to your organization, corresponding to bills or invoices that have already been sent out. *Cuentas por Cobrar; Comptes à recevoir*

Accrual Accounting: An accounting system that records revenue when it is earned, expenses when they are incurred, and costs of using fixed assets such as buildings or equipment (as opposed to **Cash Accounting**). *Contabilidad sobre Bases Devengadas; Comptabilité d'exercice*

Action Plan: Developed by a manager and his or her staff, an action plan lists program goals and objectives, and activities that will be implemented in order to achieve the objectives. An action plan often covers a time period of a year, indicates the person(s) responsible for implementing each activity, shows when each activity is due to be completed, and indicates the financial resources required. (See also **Operational Plan**.) *Plan de Acción; Plan d'action*

Active Users: See **Continuing Users**.

Activities: Actions that will be undertaken by the program staff in order to achieve program objectives. *Actividades; Activités*

English

Activity Planning: The process of defining activities, planning the sequence of those activities, and identifying the resources (human, financial, and material) that will be used to carry out those activities to achieve the desired results. *Planeación de Actividades; Planification des activités*

Advisory Board: A group of external, experienced professionals who are charged with the responsibility of advising the senior management of an organization or program. An advisory board is usually structured more informally than a board of directors but may have similar responsibilities, such as helping senior management to formulate the organizational mission and policies, defining strategic directions, and providing general oversight of the financial health of the organization or program. *Junta de Asesores; Conseil consultatif*

Allocation of Costs: In a cost or fund accounting system, the assignment of costs to different programs, operating centers, or types of services. *For example, the accounting system may allocate 50 percent of the Training Coordinator's salary to overhead, and then allocate 10 percent to each of five different programs. Asignación de Costos; Répartition des coûts*

Appointment Card: A card provided to the family planning client showing the date and time of her next scheduled visit to the clinic, the address (and telephone number, if available) of the clinic, and often the name of a contact person. Using an appointment system helps clients remember when to return for a follow-upvisit, helps the clinic staff to plan and provide services more efficiently, and can help to reduce the time a client spends waiting for services. *Tarjeta de Citas; Fiche de rendez-vous*

Asset: An asset is anything that has value that helps an organization provide its services to clients. Examples of assets include: cash, land, buildings, equipment, inventories (of supplies or goods for sale), furniture, and money owed to the organization (receivables). (See **Fixed Assets** and **Current Assets**.) *Activo; Actif*

Average Lead Time: The average length of time between placing an order for contraceptives or commodities and receiving the supplies ordered. *Tiempo de Espera Promedio; Délai moyen de livraison*

Average Monthly Consumption (AMC): The average number of units of a specific type or brand of contraceptive that are dispensed in a month. The average is usually based on quantities that have been dispensed over a period of six months. *Consumo Mensual Promedio (CMP); Consommation mensuelle moyenne (CMM)*

B **ad Debt:** Accounts receivable that are considered to be uncollectible. *Deuda Incobrable; Créance irrécouvrable*

Balance on Hand: See **Stock on Hand.**

Balance Sheet: The financial report that summarizes the value of the assets, liabilities, and reserves of an organization at a specific point in time. *Balance General; Bilan*

Bank Reconciliation: Adjusting the balance of your bank account according to the bank statement to reflect deposits made and checks that have been drawn but not yet cleared by the bank. *Conciliación Bancaria; Reconcilation (ou rapprochement bancaire)*

Bar Chart: A graph that represents data or sets of data in vertical or horizontal bars so that the relationship between the data can be seen and interpreted more easily. Bar charts can be used to analyze most types of service data and help to show the differences between several different categories of data such as number of contraceptive users, non-users, and discontinuers. *Gráfica de Barras; Graphique à colonnes*

Barriers to Services: National or local governmental laws or policies, professional practices and procedures, administrative regulations, or other official or unofficial rules that block people from receiving services because of age, gender, marital status, parity, financial ability, residence, etc. *Barreras a los Servicios; Obstacles aux services*

Baseline Survey: A survey that is conducted at the start of a project to determine the level of key indicators against which future results are compared. *Encuesta de Base; Enquête de base*

Benchmarking: A technique in which a set of indicators and sub-indicators are established, against which performance or progress towards obectives can be measured. Benchmarking can also be used to compare a service or process in one organization with similar services or processes in another similar organization for the purposes of improving the effectiveness and efficiency of a program. *Técnica de Análisis de Casos Modelo («Benchmarking»); Technique du modèle parfait*

Benchmarks: Established objectives or criteria that must be achieved over a specific period of time. Benchmarks are often set as incentives for a program to reach its short-term objectives which, when reached, qualify the program to receive additional funding or other forms of program support. *Requisitos Previos(«Benchmarks»); Jalons de performance progressifs*

Bin Card: See **Stock Card.**

Board of Directors: Often a legal requirement for a nonprofit or for-profit organization, a board of directors is generally composed of a group of professionals with diverse skills and experience and is charged with the responsibility of overseeing the stability of the organization. Because board members are not employees of the organization and their membership is generally voluntary, boards can effectively and objectively guide an organization since no financial gain is involved. Areas of responsibility include: developing a strategic plan, supporting the leadership and growth of the organization, providing financial oversight, maintaining community and government relations, ensuring that high-quality services are provided, and managing its own board activities. *Junta Directiva; Conseil d'administration*

Brainstorming: A group activity which allows people to quickly generate ideas, raise questions, and propose solutions on issues. *Lluvia de Ideas; Lancement d'idées («Brainstorming»)*

Break-Even Point: The volume of activity at which the revenue from operations equals the operating expenses. *Punto de Equilibrio; Seuil de rentabilité*

Budget Performance Report: A report that compares actual revenues and expenses with those projected in the budget. *Informe de Ejecución del Presupuesto; Rapport de performance budgétaire*

Business Plan: Often developed for the purposes of finding funding for a program or project, a business plan details the goals, activities, income sources, other financial resources, and expected revenue that will be generated from the business or activities. *Plan de Negocios; Plan d'entreprise*

C apital Costs: Costs of acquiring, constructing, or renovating fixed assets such as land, buildings, and large equipment (as opposed to **Operating Costs**). *Costos de Inversión (Gastos de Capital); Coûts d'investissement*

Cash Accounting: An accounting system that records revenue when it is received and expenses when they are paid (as opposed to **Accrual Accounting**). *Contabilidad de Caja; Comptabilité de caisse*

Cash Flow Projection Worksheet (also known as Cash Flow Statement): A projection of cash receipts and disbursements used to identify potential excess and shortages of cash funds. *Planilla de Proyecciones del Flujo de Fondos; Formulaire de projection de l'état de la trésorerie*

Cause-and-Effect Diagram: A tool often used in a continuous quality improvement program to group people's ideas about the causes of a particular problem in an orderly way. This tool is also known as a "fishbone" diagram because of the shape that it takes when illustrating the primary and secondary causes of a problem. *Diagrama de Causa y Efecto; Diagramme de cause à effet*

Central Warehouse: A storage facility which handles and stores all commodities received from sources outside the country. *Bodega (almacén) Central; Magasin central*

Chart of Accounts: The structure, within the accounting system that lists the programs, operating centers, and categories by which the revenues and expenses will be recorded and assigns a number to each line item. *Catálogo de Cuentas; Tableau des comptes*

Chronogram (also known as a Gantt Chart or Project Activity Timeline): A project planning tool that summarizes the major project activities listed in chronological sequence. It shows the month or quarter that each activity will be completed and the person or persons responsible for carrying out each activity. It helps managers to monitor activities and short-term results, keep a project on schedule, and manage project resources. *Cronograma; Chronogramme*

Client Characteristics: Information about client traits and needs that is used for analyzing a program's client base in order to provide high-quality client care based on clients' needs. Client characteristics include: age, marital status, number of pregnancies, presence of sexually transmitted diseases (STDs), literacy, preference for spacing births or ending reproduction, etc. *Características del Cliente; Caractéristiques des clients*

Client/Clinic Data: Summary information about the clients served by a clinic or community-based program. Types of clinic/client data typically include: types of contraceptive methods used by a program's clients (method mix), number of continuing users served by a clinic or program per month or year, number of new acceptors of a contraceptive method in a clinic or program, number of discontinuers of a method or clients who have dropped out of the program, and summary information on average age, marital status, and number of children of the clients. *Datos sobre Clientes/Clínica; Données sur les clients ou sur les formations sanitaires*

Client Fees: Charges made to a client as payment for services provided to him or her, such as the provision of contraceptive supplies, counseling, clinical or laboratory services, and others. Client fees include registration fees collected at each visit, service fees collected for individual services provided, and membership fees collected on a yearly basis. Many programs charge clients a small fee to help cover some of the cost of providing services and to encourage clients to place a value on the services provided. *Tarifas para los Clientes; Paiements effectués par les clients*

Client Flow Analysis (also known as Patient Flow Analysis): The process of determining the efficiency of service delivery operations in a health facility. It is based on observations made of the movement of clients through the health facility and tracks, in particular, the amount of time a client spends waiting to be seen by a provider and the amount of contact time a client has with each of the clinic's service providers. *Análisis del Flujo de Clientes; Analyse du flux des clients*

Client Flow Chart: The chart that summarizes the information obtained from the client flow form. It shows the total time spent in the clinic, including time spent waiting and time spent with staff, as well as the percentage of the total time in the clinic that clients spent waiting for services. *Tabla del Flujo de Clientes; Tableau du flux des clients*

Client Flow Form: The form used to record the information needed to perform a client flow analysis. The form records the client number, family planning method, type of visit, clinic arrival time, and the time and duration of each contact with staff. *Formulario de Flujo de Clientes; Formulaire de flux des clients*

Client Motivation: Information, education, discussion, or promotional activities that serve to encourage a client or potential client to use, or continue to use, contraceptives and reproductive health services on a regular basis. *Motivación del Cliente; Motivation des clients*

Client Profile: A representation in numbers and/or percentages of the main characteristics of a program's clients. A client profile allows managers to gain a better understanding of the types of clients the program serves and (in some cases) the high-priority needs of those clients, so that the program can better serve its clients and potentially attract new clients who have similar needs. *Perfil del Cliente; Profil des clients*

Client Record (also known as Medical Record): The file or form completed for each client containing information on the client's medical and family planning history, health status, and physical exams. The file should include (at a minimum) the name, address, sex, age, parity, reproductive health history, and contraceptive method used by the client. The file is kept at the clinic and is updated by the staff each time a client returns for services. *Expediente del Cliente; Dossier du client*

Client Referral Card: A card given to a client or potential client by a community-based agent, outreach worker, or clinic provider that refers the client to another service facility for specific services that are not provided by the issuing agent or clinic. The referral card provides the name and location of the facility to which the client is being sent, the program or clinic making the referral, the name of the client being referred, and the reason for referral. *Tarjeta de Referencia del Cliente; Carte de référence du client*

Client Satisfaction: The benefits or value of the services (as perceived by the clients) provided by a program or clinic, often measured in terms of the quality of interpersonal interaction with providers, the range of contraceptive choice, and the efficiency and responsiveness to individual client needs. *Satisfacción del Cliente; Satisfaction des clients*

Client Survey: A survey, often conducted through interviews, used to determine what clients' needs are, whether their needs are being met, what their perceptions are of the quality of care, their ability to pay for services, and other characteristics of a given client population. *Encuesta a Clientes; Enquête auprès des clients*

Client Waiting Time: The time clients spend waiting to be seen by providers in a clinic. (See **Client Flow Analysis**.) *Tiempo de Espera de Clientes; Temps d'attente des clients*

Clinic Management: All aspects of managing a clinic effectively, including planning activities and services, organizing the clinic space and work process for serving clients, managing financial and programmatic resources (including clinic and contraceptive supplies), managing information, monitoring progress toward objectives, and supervising clinical and non-clinical staff. *Administración de la Clínica; Gestion de la formation sanitaire*

Clinic Performance: Clinic performance is often measured by counting the number of clients served by the clinic, and/or the number of new acceptors and continuing users served by the clinic over a specific period of time, and is evaluated relative to objectives set for the clinic. *Rendimiento de la Clínica; Performance de la formation sanitaire*

Clinic Protocol: The list of medical standards that staff are expected to follow, which describes in detail the medical procedures and quality of care standards that ensure the safety and health of family planning clients. *Norma (o Guía) Clínica; Protocole sanitaire*

Cluster Survey: A population-based survey technique that allows managers and evaluators to survey small population groupings and use the results to represent a larger portion of the overall population, thereby providing more rapid feedback on the impact of program activities. Stratified sampling techniques, by which the population is divided into different categories that are of interest to the program (such as age, parity, residence, and education), can be used in cluster surveys to improve the accuracy of the results. *Encuesta de Grupos; Enquête par grappes*

Cold Chain Maintenance: The management of a system of freezers, refrigerators, dry ice carriers, and other devices used for maintaining the proper temperature for vaccines from the point of manufacture to the point of administration. *Mantenimiento de la Cadena de Frío; Entretien de la chaîne du froid*

Community-Based Services (CBS): Health and family planning information and services provided to women and couples where they live or through locally-based depot holders. Services are organized through community-based activities where outreach workers, from a local clinic or the community, provide selected contraceptives (usually pills and condoms) to clients, follow up with clients who have questions, complaints, or side-effects, and make referrals to area clinics as appropriate. *Servicios Comunitarios (SC); Services à base communautaire (SBC)*

Community Participation: A critical component of family planning programs, community participation can take many forms; it occurs when members of the community and local government play a significant role in managing the local family planning program including contributing money or materials, or volunteer time, thus deriving a sense of ownership of the program and accepting responsibility for achieving stated objectives. *Participación Comunitaria; Participation communautaire*

Community Survey: A survey of a community that is the focus of a new program or an existing family planning program. In a community survey, interviewers/researchers often collect information on current knowledge, attitudes, and practices regarding contraception. Additional information can be collected as appropriate on the perception of a program's services (whether or not the respondents use those services), their source of services, income, and other socio-economic indicators that will help managers plan or improve the program. *Encuesta de la Comunidad; Enquête communautaire*

Comparison Table: See **Matrix.**

Competency-Based Training: Training that focuses exclusively on teaching the skills, facts, and attitudes that are related to specific jobs. The content of such training is ideally predetermined by the trainees themselves. *Capacitación Funcional (basada en la competencia); Formation basée sur les compétences*

Consolidated Budget: A budget that unifies information on the projected revenues and expenses from a variety of donors, programs, or facilities within the same institution. *Presupuesto Consolidado; Budget consolidé*

Consolidation Stage: The third stage of organizational development during which the organization focuses on developing and refining its systems to increase management effectiveness, including its internal abilities to mobilize and control resources for organizational and program sustainability. (See **Stages of Organizational Development.**) *Etapa de Consolidación; Phase de consolidation*

Contact Time: The amount of time that a client spends with clinic staff during a visit to a service facility. This is one of the elements that is analyzed in a client flow analysis. *Tiempo de Contacto; Temps de contact*

Continuation Rate: The number of users who continue to use any method of contraception, measured among a designated population (community, district, program area), covering a specific period of time (month, quarter, or year). A continuation rate can also be measured for one specific method. *Tasa de Continuación; Taux de continuation*

Continuing Users (also known as Active Users): Continuing users are contraceptive users who are practicing family planning on a given date. They are usually counted and reported on separately from new clients of a program and new users of a method. *Usuarios Continuos; Utilisateurs assidus*

Continuous Quality Improvement (CQI): A structured, cyclical process for improving systems and processes in an organization or program. It involves identifying an area where there is an opportunity for improvement, defining a problem within this area, outlining the sequence of activities (the process) that occurs in this area, establishing the desired outcomes of the process and the requirements needed to achieve them, selecting specific steps in the process to study, collecting and analyzing data about the process, taking corrective action, and monitoring the results of those actions. CQI is based on a team approach, and requires developing teams composed of staff from different functional areas and levels in the organization. It assumes that any system can always be improved and therefore emphasizes a process of constant improvement, which requires long-term organizational commitment and effective teamwork. *Proceso de Mejoramiento Continuo de la Calidad (PMC); Amélioration continue de la qualité (ACQ)*

Continuous (Perpetual) Review System (also known as Variable Order Interval System): A system of inventory control and resupply whereby stock levels are constantly reviewed and orders are placed when the stock reaches or falls below the predetermined reorder level. In this system, the reorders are usually for standard quantities but do not occur on a scheduled basis. *Sistema Continuo (Perpetuo) de Inventario; Système de revue continuelle ou perpetuelle*

Contraceptive Data Analysis Chart: A worksheet used (for each method of contraception) to track the stock on hand and the amount of supplies ordered, received, and dispensed on a monthly basis. This worksheet helps managers to monitor changes in the quantities of stock on a month-by-month basis and provides a summary of the stock transactions over a one-year period. *Tabla de Análisis de Datos sobre Anticonceptivos; Tableau d'analyse des données sur les contraceptifs*

Contraceptive Prevalence: The percentage of all women of reproductive age (WRA) or married women of reproductive age (MWRA), typically age 15 to 49, who are using a method of contraception. Contraceptive prevalence usually refers to the use of all methods, but may be given separately for modern methods (pills, IUDs, implants, injectables, condoms, diaphragms, cervical caps, and voluntary sterilization). It is calculated by dividing the number of WRA or MWRA who are using a method (numerator) by the total number of WRA or MWRA (denominator). *Prevalencia de Uso de Anticonceptivos; Prévalence contraceptive*

Contraceptive Product Cost: Used when determining the cost of services, the contraceptive product cost is the unit cost of a contraceptive product. If contraceptives are donated, then the contraceptive product cost will need to be estimated. The cost normally includes any expenditures on international and local transportation, customs, and taxes. *Costo del Anticonceptivo; Coûts des produits contraceptifs*

Contraceptive Supply Management (also known as Logistics Management): The management of all aspects of the supply cycle: product selection, forecasting, procurement, storage and inventory management, distribution, and use, so that a supply of unexpired contraceptives is available to clients in sufficient quantities when they need them. *Administración de Suministros Anticonceptivos; Gestion des stocks de contraceptifs*

Control Systems: All procedures and rules that guard against corruption, theft, and inappropriate utilization of funds or other resources. *Sistemas de Fiscalización; Systèmes de contrôle*

Coordination: The planned collaboration of the different individuals, departments, and organizations concerned with achieving a common goal. *Coordinación; Coordination*

Co-Payment Scheme: A system of paying for services rendered, whereby the client pays a portion of the fee which is supplemented by a third party such as an employer, an insurance company, or a pre-paid health plan. *Esquema de Pagos Compartidos; Système de co-paiement*

COPE (Client-Oriented, Provider Efficient): This is a low-technology technique to improve services for clients. COPE enables local service delivery teams to assess their own work in order to identify and find solutions to problems in their facility. *«COPE» (Dirigido al Cliente, Eficiente para el Proveedor); COPE (Client orienté, prestation efficace)*

Cost Accounting: The accounting process that distributes costs to designated responsibility centers, such as programs or service departments. *Contabilidad de Costos; Comptabilité analytique*

Cost Analysis: A study of the costs (personnel, products, equipment, etc.) associated with implementing a project, program, service, or other activities. *Análisis de Costos; Analyse des coûts*

Cost Center: See **Responsibility Center.**

Cost-Effectiveness: A method of measuring the relative efficiency of a program by comparing the cost with the impact, using an indicator such as the contraceptive prevalence rate (CPR). One purpose of a cost-effectiveness study is to identify program strategies and operational modes that achieve the greatest impact for the least cost. *Costo-Efectividad; Coût-efficacité*

Cost per Couple-Year of Protection: See **Cost per Year of Use.**

Cost per Year of Use (also known as Cost per Couple-Year of Protection): The cost of supplying an average client with a contraceptive for one year. The cost is calculated using the total cost per visit (personnel cost plus supplies), the average number of follow-up visits per year, and the average length of use of that method. The cost per year of use is a measure of output—the total cost of one couple-year of protection (CYP). *Costo por Año de Uso; Coût par année d'utilisation*

Cost-Sharing: A system of reducing operational costs by coordinating with other organizations, such as joint volume purchasing, sharing storage facilities and costs, and sharing transportation costs. *Colaboración entre Programas para la Reducción de Costos; Partage des coûts*

Cost Variance: The difference between the expected and actual expenditures for a product, service, or program. *Variación de Costos; Variance des coûts*

Couple-Years of Protection (CYP): A measure representing the total number of years of contraceptive protection provided by a method. For each method, the CYP is calculated by taking the number units distributed and dividing that number by a factor representing the number of units (of that method) needed to protect a couple for one year. *Años Protección Pareja (APP); Couple-années de protection (CAP)*

CQI Core Group: Used in a continuous quality improvement (CQI) program, the core group is a group of people designated to lead the CQI process. The group is responsible for planning the implementation of the process, getting it started, developing training materials, organizing and providing training for all staff, and supporting it at all levels of the organization. *Núcleo del PMC (o Grupo Interno para el PMC); Groupe-noyau pour l'ACQ*

Cross-Functional Team: A group of individuals made up of people from different programs or departments, such as nursing, laboratory services, administration, and outreach who work together to achieve a common goal. *Equipo Interfuncional; Equipe à fonctions multiples*

Cross-Subsidization/Cross-Subsidies: The system of using monies generated in one service to support the cost of another service within the same program. *For example, monies generated from sales of contraceptives in one clinic can be used to subsidize the cost of providing services to clients who are unable to pay for services or contraceptives in that same clinic or at other program sites. Subsidios Cruzados; Subvention croisée*

Cross-Tabulation: A table or chart used for simultaneously displaying summary data pertaining to two or more different sets of variables. *Tabulación Cruzada; Tableau croisée*

Cross-Training: Training staff to perform the functions of other staff members, so that when some staff are too busy or sick, other staff can help perform their job functions. *Capacitación Interfuncional; Formation polyvalente*

Current Assets (or Short-Term Assets): Assets that are typically used within the space of a year, such as cash and office and medical supplies. *Activos Circulantes (Activos a corto plazo); Actifs courants ou à court terme*

Daily Activity Register: The daily log of the number of client visits to a clinic, sub-divided into the types and quantities of contraceptives dispensed to each type of client (new or continuing user). The number of client visits and the number of each type and brand of contraceptive dispensed should be totaled daily. *Registro Diario de Actividades; Registre journalier des activités*

Daily Feedback Forms: Evaluation forms designed to give trainers and managers valuable feedback on the trainees' satisfaction with the training, used on a daily basis. *Formularios Diarios de Retro-alimentación; Formulaires pour la rétro-information journalière*

Data Analysis: The process of examining data and finding patterns or trends. This provides managers with new information about their programs and services and helps them to make better management decisions. *Análisis de Datos; Analyse des données*

Decentralization: A process of transferring responsibility, authority, control, and accountability for specific or broad management functions, to lower levels within a organization, system, or program. (See **Deconcentration, Delegation, Devolution,** and **Privatization.**) *Descentralización; Décentralisation*

Decision Tree: A series of questions used as a tool to analyze whether training is necessary to resolve a performance problem. *Arbol de Decisiones; Arbre de décisions*

Deconcentration: In program decentralization, deconcentration means that some management functions, such as developing program budgets, are transferred from the central level to *lower-level field units within the same agency or organization,* but the overall control of the program remains at the central level. *Desconcentración; Déconcentration*

Delegation: In program decentralization, delegation means that the central level transfers the responsibility for specific managerial functions, such as developing and conducting management training, to *organizations or agencies that are outside the regular bureaucratic structure,* and thus these functions are only indirectly controlled by the central government. *Delegación; Délégation*

Depot Services: A type of community-based service, this arrangement relies on having a person in a permanent location within the community who is available to provide information and contraceptive supplies (usually pills and condoms) to community members as needed. Because clients generally come to the depot for services, this approach reduces the number of people involved in delivering services at the community-level. *Servicios de Almacén (o de Distribución Local); Services au dépôt communautaire*

Depreciation: The accounting practice that spreads the cost of a fixed asset over its anticipated useful life. Depreciation may be in the form of an accounting transaction or may be "funded" by systematically depositing cash in a special fund for asset replacement. *For example, a $20,000 truck with an estimated life of ten years will incur a yearly depreciation expense of $2,000. Depreciación; Amortissement*

Devolution: In program decentralization, devolution refers to the transfer of power to newly created or strengthened *sub-national units of government*, the activities of which are outside the central government's direct control. In this approach, the responsibility, authority, and accountability for a program are usually transferred to a provincial or municipal government. *Devolución; Dévolution*

Direct Costs: Those costs that are directly associated with, or attributable to, a specific activity or department (such as training or tuition fees for a training program, seminar, or conference; contraceptive product costs; staff salaries and wages; costs of purchased services, etc.). Such budgeted costs should be clearly identifiable in an activity plan. *Costos Directos; Coûts directs*

Discontinuation Rate: Discontinuation rates can be measured for each contraceptive method offered by a clinic, for several methods offered, or for all the methods offered by a clinic or program. The rate is calculated by dividing the number of discontinuers of a method or methods (for a specific period of time, such as a year) by the total number of users of that or those same methods, including those who discontinued the method(s), during the same time period. Multiplying the result by 100 provides the percent discontinuation of that or those methods for time period chosen. *Tasa de Abandono; Taux de discontinuation*

Discontinuer (also known as Dropout): Someone who was formerly using a method of contraception but, for any of a variety of reasons, is no longer using contraception. A clinic/program discontinuer is someone who is no longer coming to the clinic for services. Although this may imply that the client is no longer using contraception, in some cases the client may be receiving services at another service facility. In order to track numbers of discontinuers, it is important for each program to define (for each type of method user) how long a client can be absent from the clinic after a scheduled appointment (or after the client was due for a resupply of contraceptives) before being considered a discontinuer. *For example, a pill user may be considered a discontinuer if three months have passed since she was due to pick up a resupply of pills. But an IUD user should not necessarily be considered a discontinuer if she doesn't visit the clinic even for an entire year, unless she had an appointment or was asked to return to the clinic for a check-up.* *«Abandono»; Discontinuateur*

Distribution-Based Forecasts: This method of contraceptive forecasting will provide estimates on the number of contraceptives required, based on previous amounts distributed from the warehouse to the contraceptive outlet or clinic. *Proyecciones Basadas en la Distribución; Prévisions basées sur la distribution*

"Doing the Right Things": A modern management motto which refers to the programmatic, strategic, and ethical soundness of a program. Managers who are concerned about "doing the right things" are concerned about the strategic direction of a program or organization and question the mission, goals, and objectives that underlie their decisions. *«Hacer las Cosas Correctas»; «Faire les choses nécessaires»*

"Doing Things in the Right Way": A modern management motto which refers to whether activities are being carried out in the most effective and efficient way. Managers are concerned about "doing things in the right way" when they deal with day-to-day program operations. *«Hacer las Cosas en Forma Correcta»; «Faire les choses correctement»*

Dropout: See Discontinuer.

Effectiveness: The extent to which a program has made desired changes or has met its objectives through the delivery of services. *Efectividad; Efficacité*

Efficiency: The extent to which a program has used resources appropriately and completed activities in a timely manner. *Eficiencia; Efficience*

ELCO Map: A graphic representation of the location in a community or village of ELigible COuples (ELCOs—usually married couples of reproductive age, but the definition of eligible couple varies by country), showing where they live and the type of contraceptive method they are currently using. Generally used by fieldworkers, these maps keep track of each couple's reproductive status and any changes in the contraceptive method they use. *Mapa PAEL; Carte ELCO*

Emergency Order: An order for contraceptives or commodities that is placed out of the normal ordering schedule, usually when stocks have run dangerously low due to an unforeseen increase in demand. Emergency orders are usually placed for a quantity that will bring the stock levels up to a level that will last until the normal reorder time, taking into account the amount that will be dispensed in the interim. *Pedido de Emergencia; Commande d'urgence*

Emergent Stage: The first stage of organizational development in which the primary goal is to start delivering services. This stage is characterized by an incomplete or unclear organizational mission, a simple organizational structure, basic programs and systems, and a high dependence on external financial support. (See **Stages of Organizational Development.**) *Etapa de Surgimiento (o Etapa Emergente); Phase d'émergence*

Endowment: A financial gift or gift with considerable financial value which may be sold or invested to produce additional income through interest, rent, or dividends and then used at a future time for institutional needs for purposes as stipulated by the donor. *Dotación; Dotation*

Equity (also known as Fund Balance): The net worth of the organization, which is calculated by subtracting the total liabilities from the total assets. *Capital Contable o Patrimonio; Capitaux propres*

Evaluation: A study of a program in which any number of different processes may be used to gather and analyze information to determine whether the program is carrying out the activities that it had planned and the extent to which the program is achieving its stated objectives (through these activities). Evaluation results can be used to learn in what areas the program is most effective and what modifications should be made to improve the program. *Evaluación; Evaluation*

Exit Interview: An interview conducted with clients as they leave the family planning clinic to assess how they felt about the services they received. The interview can be an informal conversation or a more formal questionnaire that focuses on a particular aspect of service delivery. *Entrevista de Salida; Entretien à la sortie*

Expenditures: Expense payments made in cash or checks. *Erogaciones; Dépenses*

Expenses: All the costs incurred in operating a program. In an accrual system, an expense is recorded in the accounting system when it is incurred, before cash is paid. *Gastos; Frais*

Experiential Learning: A method of teaching which uses active participation and the applied use of new skills through role playing and on-the-job experience, in addition to lecturing. *Aprendizaje de Experiencias; Apprentissage par l'expérience*

Expiration Date: The date determined by the manufacturer after which a contraceptive or other drug product should no longer be dispensed to or used by clients. *Fecha de Expiración; Date de péremption*

External Audit: An activity carried out by an independent person or group to verify the accuracy of an organization's financial statements. *Auditoría Externa; Audit externe*

External Coordination: The process of identifying the common goals and functions of different organizations and of collaborating among organizations to implement activities to reach these common goals. Frequently, the allocation of activities and responsibilities among organizations is determined by the specific strengths of each organization. *Coordinación externa; Coordination externe*

External Environment: The prevailing conditions in the country or region that affect the development and implementation of the family planning program including demographics, culture, policy, economy, health, market characteristics, and sources of funding and commodities. *Contexto Externo; Environnement externe*

F acilitative Supervision: An approach to supervision that emphasizes mentoring, joint problem solving, and two-way communications between the supervisor and the worker. *Supervisión Facilitadora; Supervision à but de facilitation*

Facilitator: A person who assists, encourages, and supports a group of people in a participative way to work together, make decisions, and resolve conflict for the purpose of achieving a common goal. *Facilitador; Animateur*

Family Planning Activities Worksheet: A form sometimes used in busy clinics as an intermediary form between the Daily Activity Register and the Monthly Summary. The totals from the Daily Activity Register are transferred to the Worksheet each day, then totaled for the month and transferred to the Monthly Summary of Family Planning Activities. *Planilla de Actividades de Planificación Familiar; Fiche de calcul des activités de planification familiale*

Family Planning Commodities: Refers to all of the contraceptives, medical supplies, and equipment needed to provide and deliver family planning services. *Suministros de Planificación Familiar; Produits pour la planification familiale*

Feedback: The process that allows for two-way communication between the field and the office or an employee and a supervisor, for the purpose of modifying, correcting, and strengthening performance and results. *Retroalimentación; Rétro-information*

Fee-For-Service Program: A program that charges a fee for individual services provided by the program or clinic. In a fee-for-service program a different fee is usually charged for each type of service provided, based on the actual cost of providing that service. In such a program, a new client receiving her first supply of pills will generally pay more than a continuing user who returns for a resupply. This is because the new client receives more comprehensive services on a first visit than a revisit client who is only picking up a resupply of pills. *Programa de Cobro de Tarifas por Servicios; Programme de paiement des prestations*

Financial Audit: A formal periodic examination of accounts and financial records of an organization or program, generally performed for the purposes of verifying that funds were used as they were intended and in accordance with standard financial management practices. *Auditoría Financiera; Audit financier*

Financial Management: A process of implementing and managing financial control systems, collecting financial data, analyzing financial reports, and making sound financial decisions based on the analyses. Financial management requires knowing how to read and interpret three key documents: a cash flow projection worksheet, a balance sheet, and an income statement. *Administración Financiera; Gestion financière*

Financial Position: The financial status of an organization at a particular point in time. The financial position indicates the organization's overall financial situation, taking into account current assets and liabilities, and projected income and expenses. *Posición Financiera; Situation financière*

Financial Reporting: An established system for periodic reporting on financial transactions and financial status of an organization or program. *Informes Financieros; Rapport financier*

Financial Statement: The financial reports covering a period of time (month or year) that summarize the income and expenses for the period (Income and Expense Reports), and the assets and liabilities (Balance Sheet) at the end of the period. *Estado Financiero; Etat financier*

First Consultation of a Client: See **New Client.**

First-to-Expire, First-Out (FEFO): A supply management system whereby contraceptives with the earliest expiration date are distributed first and contraceptives with later expiration dates are distributed only after the earlier-dated supplies have been issued. *Primero en Expirar, Primero en Salir (PEPS); Premier à périmer, premier sorti (PPPS)*

First Visit: See **New Client.**

Five-Table System: Often used in mobile, community-based approaches, the five-table system is a program that provides integrated maternal and child health and family planning services at one, temporary location. In this system, a table is set up for each of five services: registering the child; weighing the child; recording the results on a growth chart; providing health information (such as nutrition, oral rehydration, immunization, breastfeeding, child spacing/family planning information); and providing any necessary medical treatment, contraceptives, or a referral to a fixed health facility as needed. *Sistema de Cinco Mesas; Système des cinq tables*

Fixed Assets (or Long-Term Assets): Assets that have a useful life of longer than a year, such as land, buildings, furniture, and large pieces of equipment. *Activos fijos o bien duraderos; Immobilisations*

Fixed Costs or Expenses: Costs that do not vary with the quantity of people served or services delivered, such as main office expenses, insurance, rent, or interest on a mortgage. *Costos o Gastos Fijos; Coûts (ou frais) fixes*

Fixed Order Interval System: See **Periodic Review System.**

Flowchart: A chart used to analyze a process or activity that shows the sequence of activities, steps, and decision points that occur in a particular, discrete process, such as registering a client in a clinic. By defining a beginning and end point for the process and analyzing each step in the process, managers can identify problem areas and potential improvements in order to reach the desired outcome(s). *Diagrama de Flujo; Diagramme du processus*

Focus Group: A planned and guided discussion among a group of participants for the purpose of examining a specific issue or issues. This is a qualitative method of gathering information. Results of focus group discussions are often complemented with or serve to further explain quantitative data collected through surveys or other quantitative methods. *Grupo Focal; Groupe de discussion focalisée*

Follow-up Visit: See **Revisit**.

Formal Training: A course of instruction that has specific learning objectives and is conducted outside the regular workplace. *Capacitación Formal; Formation formelle*

Frequency Table: A chart used to record the number of times a particular event or occurrence takes place in a given time period, such as number of new acceptors and revisits during each month of the previous year, or for each reason cited for not using contraception, the number of people stating those reasons, etc. *Tabla de Frecuencias; Tableau de fréquence*

Functional Allocation: An activity which presents, in chart form, the names of collaborating organizations and their primary responsibilities in various functional areas, for the purpose of revealing duplication of or gaps in services. *Distribución Funcional; Répartition des fonctions*

Functional Responsibilities: The types of work responsibilities that a person or group is accountable for performing, such as planning, monitoring, evaluating, providing medical services, training, etc. *Responsabilidades Funcionales; Responsabilités de fonction*

Fund Accounting: An accounting system that tracks expenses and revenues for different donor accounts. *Contabilidad de Fondos; Comptabilité par fonds*

Fund Balance (also known as Equity): In a nonprofit organization, the fund balance is the net worth of an organization, which is calculated by subtracting the value of the expenses from the total revenues. *Balance de Fondos o Reserva; Bilan des fonds (ou Réserves)*

Fund Raising: The process of seeking financial support from community groups, local or central government units, local or international donor organizations or individuals, and others. *Recaudación de Fondos; Mobilisation de fonds*

"Funnel" Approach: Used to describe an approach to delivering integrated services, the "funnel" approach depicts an agency or organization that separates its various programs vertically at the national and district levels, but integrates the programs and services at the clinic/community level. (See also **"Hourglass"Approach**.) *Integración Tipo «Embudo»; Approche de «l'entonnoir»*

G antt Chart: See **Chronogram.**

General Administration: Activities or, in the case of a budget, expenditures associated with the normal course of doing business, such as postage, freight, photocopying, telephone, utilities, bank charges, vehicle registration, and other usual and customary administrative costs (excluding personnel costs). *Administración General; Administration générale*

Goals: The proposed long-range benefits of the program to the selected population, defined in general terms. *Objetivos Generales; Buts*

Grade: In job descriptions, the standard level or rank on which the salary scale is based. It is determined, in part, by the skills and qualifications required to perform the job. *Grado o Nivel; Grade*

Grants: Funds or donations given to an organization or program for the purpose of carrying out specific programs or services. Grants are usually provided by governments and local or international donors. *Donaciones; Subventions*

Graph: Used in data analysis, a graph illustrates in a picture the relationships or patterns that exist between numbers and sets of numbers, which would otherwise be difficult to see by looking at the raw data. (See **Line Graph, Bar Chart**, and **Pie Chart.**) *Gráfica; Graphique*

Grievance Policy: The standard policy, usually stated in a personnel manual, describing the formal procedure through which employee complaints are submitted, processed, and resolved. *Normas para Manejo de Quejas y Reclamos; Procédure de soumission de doléances*

Growth Stage: The second stage of organizational development. At this stage, organizations develop a clear mission, define strategies for fulfilling the mission, have specific goals and objectives, and develop and use operational plans to achieve objectives. During this stage, as activities and services rapidly expand, the organization's reliance on external resources to support those programs and services also increases. (See **Stages of Organizational Development.**) *Etapa de Crecimiento; Phase de croissance*

H istogram: A type of bar chart used to display data within a *single data category* such as age, which can be grouped as 20-24, 25-29, 30-34, etc. A normal bar chart is used to display data representing *different* *categories of data,* such as users of contraceptives, non-users of contraceptives, city or rural residence, etc. (For more information on Histograms and Bar Charts, please refer to Volume II, Number 1, of *The Family Planning Manager* "Using CQI to Strengthen Family Planning Programs" and the supplement *Manager's Toolbox for CQI.*) *Histograma; Histogramme*

Historical Data: Data collected from past reports, such as contraceptive distribution reports, daily activity registers, inventory cards, etc. *Datos Históricos; Données rétrospectives*

"Hourglass" Approach: Used to describe an approach to delivering integrated services, the "hourglass" approach depicts a combined vertical and integrated program in which staff at the national level are divided into separate divisions for family planning, immunization, infectious disease control, nutrition, and maternal health. At the regional or district level, however, programs are coordinated by one or two individuals, and at the service provider level staff are again assigned to separate programs. (See also **"Funnel" Approach.**) *Integración Tipo «Reloj de Arena»; Approche du «sablier»*

Household Survey: A survey that collects information about the occupation(s) of a couple, the contraceptive method they use and/or have used in the past, whether the woman is pregnant or breastfeeding, recent births, total number of births and deaths, and other information concerning a couple's reproductive health and family planning history that is of interest to the program. Household surveys are used to establish the level or the indicator against which future results are compared. *Encuesta de Hogares; Enquête auprès des ménages*

I **dentification Codes:** A series of numbers or letters used in a management information system to help differentiate specific locations of services (or clinic type), types of visits (first visit, revisit, procedure visit), types of services or contraceptives provided (IEC, IUD insertion, pill resupply), and other categories of data. To be useful, the same identification codes should be used consistently by all people who use the management information system. *Códigos de Identificación; Codes d'identification*

Impact: In a family planning and reproductive health program, the extent to which the program has changed or improved the knowledge, attitudes, behavior, or health of the program participants. *Impacto; Impact*

Imprest Fund: A fixed cash flow set aside for small immediate cash outlays, which is replenished periodically in accordance with the amount expended. *Fondo de Caja Chica; Caisse d'avance*

Incentive Grants: Funds used to reward program performance, the achievement of objectives, or to motivate programs to launch new initiatives. Incentive grants are used to motivate programs and employees to (continue to) meet their objectives and maintain or improve program quality. *Donaciones para Incentivar; Subvention qui contiennent des primes*

Incentive System: A policy that rewards employees for excellent performance or special achievements and motivates employees to meet their objectives and to maintain program quality. *Sistema de Incentivos; Système de primes d'encouragement*

Income Statement (also known as Revenue and Expense Report, Income and Expense Report, and Profit and Loss Statement): A periodic summary report of income and expenses, showing a surplus (profit) or deficit (loss) for the period covered by the report. *Estado de Pérdidas y Ganancias; Etat des revenus et des dépenses*

Indicator: A certain condition, capability, or numerical measure which, when recorded, collected, and analyzed, makes complex concepts more readily measurable and allows managers and evaluators to compare actual program results with expected results. *Indicador; Indicateur*

Indirect Costs (also known as Overhead Costs): The operating costs of an organization which are shared by more than one activity or department (such as building maintenance and utility expenses). *Costos Indirectos; Coûts indirects*

Informal Training: Training that occurs on the job and is often accomplished through personal instruction, guidance from a supervisor, or even by observing co-workers. *Capacitación Informal; Formation informelle*

Information Flow Table: A chart showing the types of information (the indicators) that will be collected, how the information will be collected and reported, who will collect it, to whom it will be submitted, how it will be used, and the level of detail needed. The purpose of the chart is to ensure an appropriate flow of information in the correct sequence and to communicate to staff how the information system functions. *Gráfica de Flujo de Información; Tableau de circulation de l'information*

Information System: A standardized system for collecting, recording, interpreting, analyzing, reporting, and disseminating data so that the data are available to be used for making critical management decisions. In a family planning clinic, this normally refers to collection and reporting of programmatic and financial information connected with providing client services and operating a facility. (See also **Two-Tier Information System**.) *Sistema de Información; Système d'information*

In-Kind Contribution: A non-financial contribution or form compensation such as materials, goods, or services. *Contribuciones en Especie; Contribution en nature*

Inputs: The resources used in a program. *Insumos; Intrants*

Inreach: In family planning, this involves using resources within a health facility to improve the understanding and knowledge of the facility's family services (as compared with **Outreach**). Inreach addresses missed opportunities to provide information about the facility's family planning services to staff, clients, and potential clients in all departments of the facility. Inreach activities include improving linkages and referrals between departments, posting signs about services throughout the facility, and orienting staff from other departments to the family planning services. *Conocimiento Interno («Inreach»); Diffusion interne*

Insertion Visit: Generally used to describe a visit made by a client for the insertion of an IUD or contraceptive implant. Different types of visits are often designated by a program or clinic so that specific costs may be assigned or fees charged for each type of visit. *Visita de Inserción; Visite pour insertion*

Institutionalization: The internalization by an organization or program of an activity, system, or practice, to the extent that the activity, system, or practice will continue to operate in spite of personnel turnover, and independently of external inputs or involvement. *Institucionalización; Institutionnalisation*

Integration/Integrated Services: This refers to a program that combines family planning services with maternal and child health, nutrition, immunization, and other reproductive health services, such as control and treatment of sexually transmitted diseases. *Integración/Servicios Integrados; Intégration/Services intégrés*

Intermediate Outputs: Medium-term results that are critical to the achievement of long-term results. *For example, the number of workshops or courses held is a medium-term result that is critical to achieving the long-term result of having qualified providers. Resultados Intermedios; Résultats intermédiaires*

Intermediate Warehouse: A supplies depot located in a specific region of a country. It distributes commodities only for that area. *Bodega (almacén) Intermedia; Magasin intermédiaire*

Internal Audit: An activity carried out by employees to check an organization's internal controls and accounting system. *Auditoría Interna; Audit interne*

Internal Coordination: The logical organization of and communication about activities within an organization, such that all staff members are aware of the roles and responsibilities of each department and the interaction between departments. *Coordinación Interna; Coordination interne*

Internal Environment: Leadership, policies, systems, technology, financial capability, etc., that influence the effectiveness of an organization or program. Other factors in the internal environment include: management structure, management systems, staff capabilities, etc. *Contexto Interno; Environnement interne*

Internal Organization: The internal structure and arrangement of an organization or program as it pertains to the allocation of and relationship between different functional areas such as planning, budgeting, financial management, supervision, and others. The internal organization of a program is particularly important as programs become more decentralized and/or integrate several programs into a single program. *Organización Interna; Organisation interne*

Inventory: The amount of stock (contraceptives, commodities, and other clinic supplies) that is on hand (for use by a program or clinic) at a given point in time. *Inventario; Stocks*

Inventory Control Card: See **Stock Card**.

J ob Description: A document that at a minimum states the job title and provides a description of the tasks and responsibilities of the position, the direct supervisory relationships with other staff, and the skills and qualifications required for the position. *Descripción del Cargo; Description de poste*

Lead Time: The amount of time (usually expressed in months or weeks) that it takes for a shipment to arrive once an order has been placed. *Tiempo de Espera; Délai de livraison*

Lead Time Quantity: Based on past records, the amount of contraceptive stock that will be dispensed during the time between placing an order and receiving new stock. *Cantidad para Cubrir el Tiempo de Espera; Quantité couvrant le délai de livraison*

Liabilities: The obligations or debts owed to suppliers, employees, banks, or the government. *Pasivos; Passif*

Line Graph: A graph that represents data or sets of data that have been collected over a period of time. The data are plotted on a graph corresponding to standard intervals of time and a line is drawn connecting the data points. The line in the graph allows managers to see trends in the data (an increase, decrease, or no change) over a period of time. Line graphs are often used to analyze trends in new acceptors, continuing clients, dropouts, new acceptors using a particular method, and others. Line graphs (updated regularly) help managers to follow a trend over a period of time and take actions to manage the trend. *Gráfica Lineal; Graphique linéaire*

Line Item: The category in a Budget, Chart of Accounts, or Financial Statement which represents an account used to record transactions for a particular type of income, expense, asset, or liability. *Partida o Rubro; Rubrique*

Logistics Management: See **Contraceptive Supply Management**.

Long-Acting Methods (or Long-Term Methods): Contraceptive methods that remain effective for a relatively long period of time. Experts may differ in the methods they include under this term. Some experts include only IUDs, implants, and injectables, some also include oral contraceptive pills, and some include voluntary sterilization. *Métodos de Larga Duración; Méthodes de longue durée*

Lot Number: Refers to each different production batch (lot) of contraceptives at the time of manufacture. *Número de Lote; Numéro de lot*

Maintenance Cost: Generally refers to the cost of maintaining a facility and may include repairs, cleaning, rent, taxes, insurance, etc. *Costo de Mantenimiento; Coût d'entretien*

Managed Care: An arrangement between a purchaser and a provider of health and family planning services for an agreed set of services in return for a predetermined price (generally a fixed monthly rate per member). *Paquete de Servicios; Systéme contrôlé de prestations sanitaires*

Management Accounting: Collecting information from the financial accounting system and other financial data (such as budgets) and combining this information with statistical data (such as service outputs) to produce information which is useful for making managerial decisions. *Contabilidad Administrativa; Comptabilité de gestion*

Management Components: The basic elements used to analyze the way an organization functions. The four basic management components are mission, strategy, structure, and systems. (See also **Mission Statement, Strategy, Organizational Structure**, and **Management Functions/Systems.**) *Componentes Administrativos; Composantes de gestion*

Management Functions/Systems: The basic management functions of program planning, budgeting, determining staff roles and responsibilities, training, supervising staff, managing resources (including money, contraceptive and commodities supplies, and other program equipment or services), monitoring program activities, evaluating program achievements, and managing the provision of client services. *Funciones/Sistemas Administrativos; Fonctions/Systèmes de gestion*

Management Information System (MIS): A system designed by an organization to collect and report information on a program, and which allows managers to plan, monitor, and evaluate the operations and the performance of the whole program. *Sistema de Información Gerencial (SIG); Système d'information de gestion (SIG)*

Managing Board: A formal group of advisors who provide general strategic and financial oversight to an organization and are responsible for maintaining and promoting the stability and sustainability of the organization. *Junta Administrativa; Comité de gestion*

Mapping: A process by which information or data are laid out on a diagram or representation of a community, village, or other defined territory for the purposes of tracking changes in the data. *Mapeo; Etablissement de cartes*

Market Analysis: An examination of the environment in which an organization or program provides or sells goods or services. A market analysis typically includes conducting a survey of a program's current clients (their needs, satisfaction with services, socio-economic status, etc.), a survey of the community (to learn more about potential clients and the existing demand for services), and a survey of the other family planning service providers in the area (the types of services they provide, the cost and quality of services, etc.). This information provides a program or organization with critical information about underserved populations in their area, the level of access to services, feedback on clients' satisfaction with services, the ability of clients to pay or the amount they can pay for services, and other information about the role the program should play in relation to other service providers in order to maintain a competitive edge. Having the ability to address these factors serves to strengthen program sustainability. *Análisis del Mercado; Analyse du marché*

Marketing: The activities related to designing and pricing goods and services so that they are bought or used by the public, informing the public of the available services and their prices, and promoting the value of those goods and services for the purpose of generating demand. *Mercadeo; Marketing*

Matrix (also known as a Comparison Table): A chart used for analyzing two or more sets or types of information (such as the number of users of each contraceptive method by type of client, such as new acceptor or revisit). A comparison table can also be used for comparing organizational processes or activities against a set of criteria that reflect organizational priorities, resources, and constraints to help managers prioritize areas for improvement. *Matriz; Matrice*

Mature Stage: The fourth and last stage of organizational development, during which an organization develops its ability to effectively manage the organization and adjust its mission, strategy, structure, and systems in response to internal and external challenges in order to increase sustainability. (See **Stages of Organizational Development**.) *Etapa de Madurez; Phase de maturité*

Maximum Quantity: The maximum quantity is the largest amount of stock (of each contraceptive item) that a facility should ever have in inventory. The quantity should be set high enough to maintain adequate stock between orders and low enough to prevent overstocking and wastage due to expiration. It is calculated separately for each contraceptive item and consists of the minimum quantity of stock plus the amount that is used between regular orders. (A formula for calculating maximum and minimum stock levels and quantities can be found on pages 10 and 11 of Volume I, Number 4 of *The Family Planning Manager*, "Improving Contraceptive Supply Management.") *Cantidad Máxima; Quantité maximum*

Max/Min (Maximum-Minimum) Stock Level: Assigned minimum and maximum stock levels designed to ensure that a program doesn't run out of contraceptive supplies and also doesn't become overstocked. Minimum and maximum levels are expressed in terms of a certain number of months' worth of supply. *Sistema Max/Min; Système Max/Min (Maximum-Minimum)*

Medical Record: See **Client Record**.

Membership Fees: Fixed fees charged to clients or members of an organization, usually on a yearly basis, entitling them to a range of services. *Cuotas de Afiliación; Cotisations*

Merit Awards: Promotions or financial rewards given to employees in recognition of outstanding performance. *Premio al Mérito; Récompenses au mérite*

Method Mix: A summary, usually represented in percentages, showing the proportion of all users (of a general or specific population) that are using each contraceptive method. *Mezcla de Métodos; Gamme des méthodes*

Methodology: The means and logical procedure by which a program plan or approach is implemented, such as on-the-job-training versus formal training. *Metodología; Méthodologie*

Micro-Manage: The practice of providing unnecessary and excessive oversight in the management of staff and staff activities. *Micro-Administrar; Micro-gestion*

Minimum Quantity: The minimum quantity is the least amount of stock (of each contraceptive item) that a facility should ever have in inventory. The minimum quantity should be set high enough to prevent shortages and stock-outs, even if deliveries are late or demand unexpectedly increases. The minimum quantity is the safety stock quantity plus the amount of stock used between placing and receiving an order. (A formula for calculating maximum and minimum stock levels and quantities can be found on pages 10 and 11 of Volume I, Number 4 of *The Family Planning Manager*, "Improving Contraceptive Supply Management.") *Cantidad Mínima; Quantité minimum*

Missed Opportunity: An occasion that offered a chance for a beneficial activity to occur (service provision, employee feedback, etc.) but was overlooked. *Oportunidad Perdida; Occasion manquée*

Missing Client: See **No-Show Client**.

Mission Statement (also known as Organizational Mission): A brief general statement describing the type of organization, its main purpose, and its values. The mission of an organization provides the rationale for defining goals and objectives. *Declaración de Misión; Enoncé de mission*

Monitoring: The process of periodically checking the status of a program, by observing whether activities are being conducted as planned. *Monitoreo; Suivi*

Monthly Summary of Family Planning Activities: The form used to record the monthly totals for all the data collected on the Daily Family Planning Activity Records. Generally, the clinic manager keeps one copy and another copy is sent to the program supervisor who aggregates the monthly data for all the clinics in the region or district. *Resumen Mensual de Actividades de Planificación Familiar; Récapitulatif mensuel des activités de planification familiale*

Months of Supply (also known as Months' Worth of Supply): This term is used to express the amount of a supply on hand (of a specific contraceptive or commodity) in terms of the number of months that quantity would last if it is dispensed at current (average) rates. It is the quantity on hand (of the specific contraceptive or commodity) divided by the average monthly consumption (AMC) of that item. *Meses de Suministros; Mois d'approvisionnement*

Mutually Accountable: A situation in which multiple parties or individuals are jointly responsible for the outcome(s) of an activity or activities. *Responsabilidad Conjunta; Mutuellement responsable*

New Acceptor (also known as New User): Someone who accepts a contraceptive method for the first time. Programs differ in their definition of new acceptors/new users. Some include only those persons who are using contraception for the first time and have never used any form of contraception before. Some also include those persons who are using a particular contraceptive method for the first time (even though they have used a different method before). Still others may include those persons who are accepting a method from (an agent of) that particular program for the first time (even though they may have used a method provided by another program before). Whatever definitions your program uses, it is critical that the definitions be clear and understood by all staff, so that service data in all the service facilities will be collected and reported on in the same way. *Aceptante Nuevo; Nouvel accepteur*

New Client (also known as First Visit or First Consultation of a Client): Someone who receives services from (an agent of) a family planning program who has not received services from that program before. Programs differ in their definitions of a new clients. Some programs include persons who receive any type of service (including counseling) who have not received services from that program before. Other programs include only persons who are accepting a family planning method for the first time and have never used contraceptives before from any program. Still other programs distinguish new clients (of a program) from new acceptors/users (of a method). Whatever definitions your program uses, it is critical that the definitions be clear and understood by all staff, so that service data in all the service facilities will be collected and reported on in the same way. *Cliente Nuevo; Nouveau client*

No-Show Client (also known as a Missing Client): A client who does not come for a scheduled visit or has not returned to the clinic for services for a long period of time. *Cliente que No Asiste; Client non-assidu*

No-Show Rate: Often expressed as a percentage, the no-show rate can be calculated most easily in a clinic that uses an appointment system, in which it is known when and how many clients are due to return to the clinic for services. The no-show rate is calculated by taking the total number of clients who came to the clinic for services (during a specific period of time) divided by the number of clients who were due to come to the clinic for services during the same period of time. Multiplying the result by 100 gives the percent of no shows for the designated period of time. Such an analysis can also be done for a specific contraceptive method or age group of clients. (For more information on measuring no-show rates, please refer to Volume II, Number 3 of *The Family Planning Manager*, "Reducing Discontinuation in Family Planning Programs".) *Tasa de Inasistencia; Taux de clientes non-assidus*

Objectives: The anticipated results or outcomes of a program, representing changes in the knowledge, attitudes, and behavior of the program's clients, described in measurable terms and indicating a specific period of time during which these results will be achieved. Objectives should be Specific, Measurable, Appropriate, Realistic, and Time bound (SMART). *Objetivos Específicos; Objectifs*

Observation Guides: A form designed to help the trainer or supervisor to assess, through observation, the student's grasp of the subjects being taught. *Guías de Observación; Grilles d'observation*

Observation-Study Visits: An organized series of visits to other program sites or organizations for the purpose of studying and learning about the other program and sharing successful experiences for replication or adaptation. *Visitas de Observación-Estudio; Visites d'observation et d'étude*

Operating Center: Any logical division of the operations of a program, such as a department, a clinic, or one region's CBD program. Many organizations find it useful to produce financial information for each operating center. *Centro Operativo; Centre d'opérations*

Operating Costs (also known as Recurrent Costs): Regular expenses of running programs and providing services which are incurred year after year (as opposed to **Capital Costs**). *Costos de Operación; Coûts d'exploitation*

Operational Information: Information that is needed to plan program activities such as the use of time, people, and money, and which is used to assess how well a family planning program is functioning. *Información Operacional; Information opérationnelle*

Operational Plan: Different from a strategic plan (which sets forth the general strategies a program will use or initiatives it will undertake to achieve its objectives), an operational plan sets forth the specific projects or activities (consistent with the strategic plan) that will be conducted, and the timetable and resources needed for completing those projects or activities. (See also **Action Plan**.) *Plan Operativo; Plan opérationnel*

Order Interval: An established and regular number of months between placing orders for contraceptive supplies. The order interval should be set individually for each method of contraception to correspond to the desired maximum and minimum inventory levels. *Intervalo entre Pedidos; Intervalle entre les commandes*

Organization Type: The structural or legal definition an organization, such as private commercial organization, private non-profit, public agency, non-governmental organization, or affiliate or subsidiary of a larger organization. *Tipo de Organización; Type d'organisation*

Organizational Chart (also known as an Organogram): A chart showing the working relationships of all staff positions within an organization or program and the formal supervisory structure and reporting relationships between different functions and positions of the management and staff. *Diagrama Organizacional; Organigramme*

Organizational Mission: See **Mission Statement.**

Organizational Stability: The ability of an organization to effectively use management controls and systems to prevent any major disruptions in services in spite of unexpected changes in the external environment or turnover of personnel, especially senior personnel. *Estabilidad Organizacional; Stabilité de l'organisation*

Organizational Structure: The internal lines of authority and communication within an organization which define how programs and departments are managed, which types of activities are carried out by which programs or departments, and the functional and supervisory relationships between the staff and the manager of those departments. (See also **Organizational Chart.**) *Estructura Organizacional; Structure organisationnelle*

Organogram: See **Organizational Chart.**

Outlet: The final distribution point where clients receive their contraceptives (clinic, pharmacy, CBD workers, etc.). *Local o Punto de Distribución; Point de distribution (final)*

Output Information: Information concerning the products or accomplishments (in numerical terms) of the activities of an individual or program over a specific period of time. *Informe de Resultados; Information sur les résultats*

Outreach: Activities related to providing information and services to the community outside of the clinic facility, usually by working with community groups or volunteers. *Extensión («Outreach»); Activités d'extension*

Overhead Costs: See **Indirect Costs.**

Paper Trail: Records of the movement of resources (human, financial, and material), kept to enable such movement to be traced and resources to be accounted for. *Comprobantes; Trace écrite*

Pareto Analysis: Based on the principle set forth by an Italian economist Vilfredo Pareto, which states that only a few factors are responsible for producing most of the results (positive or negative), a Pareto Analysis helps to identify the "vital few" factors that need to be improved in order to achieve the desired results. Performing this analysis helps managers to concentrate their efforts on a few activities and thereby use their scarce resources efficiently and effectively to achieve results. (For instructions on how to perform a Pareto Analysis, please refer to Volume II, Number 1 of *The Family Planning Manager*, "Using CQI to Strengthen Family Planning Programs" and the supplement, *Manager's Toolbox for CQI*.) *Análisis de Pareto; Analyse de Pareto*

Participative Style: A style of management in which the supervisor or manager actively works with his or her staff and listens to their ideas, acknowledges their points of view and accomplishments, encourages joint discussions of issues, and finds solutions together. *Estilo Participativo; Style de participation*

Patient Flow Analysis: See Client Flow Analysis.

Payables: See Accounts Payable.

Performance Appraisal: An established procedure for evaluating employee performance, conducted at predetermined intervals, usually annually or semi-annually. *Reconocimiento del Desempeño; Evaluation de la performance*

Performance Information: Information that is needed to plan program objectives and to evaluate the impact of a program's activities on the target population. *Información de Desempeño; Information sur la performance*

Performance Targets and Objectives: The end results that are expected to be achieved by an organization or an individual employee by the end of a specific time period. Performance targets generally relate to a shorter time period (several months) and pertain to very specific tasks. Performance objectives relate to longer time periods (one year) and determine the type and scope of activities that an organization, program, or staff member will undertake for the purpose of achieving the desired results. *Objetivos/Metas de Desempeño; Cibles et objectifs de performance*

Periodic Review System (also known as Fixed Order Interval System): A system of inventory control and resupply where stock levels are reviewed at predetermined time intervals and orders are placed based on current stock levels, safety stock level, and an established maximum. Through this method, the reorder is made on a scheduled basis, however, the quantity of the order may vary each time. *Sistema Periódico de Inventario; Système de revue périodique*

Perquisites: A reward in cash or in kind, which is in addition to or in place of one's salary, such as health benefits, club membership, free meals, or parking. *Gratificación; Gratification*

Personnel Category: The different types of personnel. In a family planning program personnel categories include doctor, nurse, pharmacist, pharmacy assistant, counselor, outreach worker, registration clerk, etc. Personnel categories are often defined for the purpose of establishing consistent salary levels and are useful when determining personnel costs associated with the types of services provided. *Categoría de Personal; Catégorie de personnel*

Personnel Committee: Usually a sub-committee of a larger group such as a board of directors, which focuses on personnel issues, concerns, and trends, and advises the larger group, board, or organization of necessary changes. *Comité del Personal; Comité du personnel*

Personnel Cost (or Total Personnel Cost): The cost of paying personnel (including allowances) for their time in performing a specific service, combination of services, or set of services over a specific period of time. *Costo del Personal (o Costo Total del Personal); Coûts du personnel (ou Coûts totaux du personnel).*

Personnel Cost Per Visit-Type: The cost of a single type of visit, such as a visit to insert an IUD, taking into account only the cost of the various personnel involved in providing that service. *Costo del Personal por Tipo de Visita; Coût du personnel par type de visite*

Personnel Management: Responsibilities related to hiring and firing staff, supervising, promoting, organizing, motivating staff, and developing their professional capabilities. Personnel management requires strong interpersonal communication skills and skills in group facilitation, conflict resolution, and problem solving. *Administración del Personal; Gestion du personnel*

Personnel Manual: A document that details the personnel policies and administrative procedures of an organization, including a description of the organizational structure and duties of key staff positions. *Manual del Personal; Manuel du personnel*

Petty Cash: A form of imprest fund, whereby a small amount of cash is set aside for small immediate cash outlays and is replenished periodically as it is used. *Caja Chica; Petite caisse*

Phased Training: Training conducted in stages, alternating with periods of on-the-job work experience. *Adiestramiento en Fases; Formation par étapes*

Pie Chart: A graph that represents summary data or percentages as wedges in a circle, or pie shape, so that the relationship between the data can be seen and analyzed more easily. Pie charts can be used to analyze the method mix of any type of client or for all clients in a program or clinic. Pie charts allow managers to compare proportions and represent summary data for a specific period of time, such as one month, quarter, or year. *Gráfica de Sectores; Graphique «camembert»*

Planning: A continuing process of analyzing program data, making decisions, and formulating plans for action in the future, aimed at achieving program goals. *Planeación; Planification*

Plateau Effect or "Plateauing": A situation in which a program's performance—number of people served and actively practicing family planning—has leveled off. In many cases, a program that has plateaued has already achieved a contraceptive prevalence rate (CPR) of 40 to 50 percent, has the capability to serve more clients, and must consider new ways to attract and retain clients, reduce barriers to services, reorganize programs and systems that provide services, and make other types of strategic decisions that will increase program performance. *«Estancamiento»; Effet de plateau*

Pooling: Combining resources, expertise, equipment, etc., for use toward a common purpose. This helps to save scarce resources and reduces the possibility of duplication of or gaps in services. *Combinación; Regroupment*

Population-Based Forecasts: Forecasts of contraceptive supply requirements based on the proportion of the target population that the program intends to serve and the anticipated level of demand for each contraceptive method. *Proyecciones Basadas en Información Censual o en Encuestas Demográficas; Prévisions basées sur la population*

Population-Based Survey: A survey in which information is obtained directly from a representative sample of the population or population group of interest to the program, such as women of reproductive age. Information is typically obtained through interviews, rather than from service records or other indirect sources. (See also **Cluster Survey**.) *Encuesta Basada en la Población; Enquête auprès de la population*

Population Density: The total number of people living in a defined area such as a community, district, capital city, country, region, or square kilometer or square mile. *Densidad Poblacional; Densité de population*

Population Distribution: The arrangement of population geographically as it is spread over a defined area such as community, district, capital city, country, region, etc. Knowing the distribution of population is important to managers as they plan new programs and the locations of service facilities. *Distribución de la Población; Distribution de la population*

Post-test: Given to clients, employees, trainees, or any other specific group of people who are being evaluated after a program has been completed or during the implementation, for the purpose of measuring the progress toward planned objectives. *Examen Post-Prueba; Post-test*

Potential Client: Any person of reproductive age who is sexually active, not currently using the services of a clinic or community-based family planning program, and does not intend to have children at the current time. Potential clients also include couples who have problems with infertility, but want to have children. Programs should seek to attract such persons to the program and provide them with appropriate services. *Cliente Potencial; Client potentiel*

Potential User (also known as Potential Acceptor): For women, a potential acceptor is any woman of reproductive age who is at risk of pregnancy, not currently using contraception, and not intending to become pregnant at this time. For men, a potential acceptor is any sexually active man not currently using contraception. *Usuario Potencial; Utilisateur potentiel*

Pre-test: Given to clients, employees, trainees, or any other specific group who are being evaluated, for the purpose of determining a baseline against which future results will be measured. *Examen Pre-Prueba; Pré-test*

Privatization: Privatization refers to the transfer of specific management functions, such as contraceptive procurement, logistics, and training, to *private non-profit or commercial organizations* outside the government structure. Although often used to describe a form of decentralization, some experts believe that privatization is not a means of decentralization because, in privatizing, a government relinquishes responsibility, rather than transfers power to lower levels. *Privatización; Privatisation*

Problem Solving: A critical management skill that involves objectively identifying the causes of a problem and proposing potential, often creative, solutions to the problem, which will be agreeable to multiple parties or individuals. *Resolución de Problemas; Résolution de problèmes*

Procedure Visit: Generally used to describe a visit made by a client for a specific medical procedure, such as voluntary sterilization or the insertion or removal of an IUD or contraceptive implants. Different types of visits are often designated by a program or clinic so that specific costs may be assigned or fees charged for each type of visit. *Visita de Procedimiento; Visite pour intervention médicale*

Process Analysis: Any type of analysis in which a process, processes, or a sequence of activities is studied. Examples of process analyses are: flowcharting, decision-tree analysis, and client flow analysis. *Análisis del Proceso; Analyse de processus*

Process Information: Different from output information which identifies products, outcomes, or accomplishments (in numerical terms), process information is qualitative, providing information about the ways that people and materials are used to produce specific outputs. *For example, by using process information, managers can determine the cause of a contraceptive stockout (a negative output) by analyzing each (process) step in the logistics system. Información sobre el Proceso; Information sur les processus*

Professional Development (also known as Staff Development): The process of increasing the professional capabilities of staff by providing (or providing access to) training and educational opportunities. This can include on-the-job training, outside training, or observation of the work of others. Professional development is widely recognized as a way to maintain staff morale, build the institutional capacity of a program, and attract and maintain high quality staff. *Desarrollo Profesional; Développement professionnel*

Professional Fees: Costs generally incurred through contractual agreements with *individuals* for specialized services such as lectures, training, and evaluation, as opposed to costs incurred through long-term contractual agreements with outside *institutions* for services such as vehicle maintenance, janitorial services, advertising, or promotion services, which are referred to as purchased services. (See **Purchased Services**.) *Honorarios Profesionales; Honoraires*

Profit and Loss Statement: See **Income Statement**.

Program Components: Functional units of an organization that provide services aimed at accomplishing organizational goals, such as a CBD component, a clinic component, or an IEC component. *Componentes del Programa; Volets du programme*

Programmatic Reporting: An established system or process for reporting detailed information on the activities undertaken during a specific period of time. Programmatic reports are usually in narrative form and generally only report non-financial information about activities and progress made toward achieving objectives. *Informes Programáticos; Rapport programmatique*

Project Activity Timeline: See **Chronogram**.

Public Affairs: Activities that promote an organization's program, services, and image to the public. **Relaciones Públicas; Affaires publiques**

Pull System: A supply system which requires that outlets request the amounts of commodities they need from higher-level storage facilities. *Sistema de Requisición; Système de commande (réquisition)*

Purchased Services: Long-term contractual services or agreements with outside *institutions* for services such as vehicle maintenance, janitorial services, advertising or promotion services. Although similar, contractual agreements with *individuals* are often for a specialized service such as lectures, training, and evaluation, in which case the service is referred to as a fee-based service. (See **Professional Fees**.) *Servicios Adquiridos; Services achetés (ou sous-traitance)*

Push System: A supply system which allocates supplies down through the intermediate or central warehouses to the outlet level; outlets receive contraceptives without ordering them. *Sistema de Asignación; Système d'allocation*

Quality Management: Quality management involves monitoring products or services to ensure that suppliers and providers are following accepted standards to meet desired outcomes and, if problems are observed, are taking the actions necessary to improve the products or services. *Administración de la Calidad; Gestion de la qualité*

Quality Management System: In family planning, a system that brings together in a harmonizing and reinforcing manner the various activities that help to assure and continuously improve the quality of family planning services throughout a service-delivery network. In an effective quality management system, supervisors at all levels must have updated knowledge and skills in both service delivery and management areas. *Sistema de Administración de la Calidad; Système de gestion de la qualité*

Quarterly Reporting Form: A form used for reporting quarterly summary information such as the number and types of clients served (new acceptors and revisit clients), the quantities of contraceptives (each type and brand) on hand at the beginning of the quarter, the quantities received and dispensed over a three-month period, the quantities requested for resupply for the next quarter, any adjustments or losses, and ending balances. *Formulario de Informe Trimestral; Fiche de rapport trimestriel*

Random Variations: Non-systematic inconsistencies or irregularities in data. When analyzing data, small (non-systematic) irregularities are often insignificant and can be disregarded. *Variaciones al Azar; Variations aléatoires*

Rapid Assessment: A quick, economical, sample-based study conducted to determine the extent or causes of a problem or to determine specific client or program needs that were identified through service statistics or other large studies. *Evaluación Rápida; Evaluation rapide*

Rate: A measure of an event (numerator) within a specific population (denominator) covering a specific period of time. *For example, the infant mortality rate is the number of infants that die in the first year of life (numerator) among all live births (denominator) in a specific one-year period. Infant mortality rates are usually expressed as the number of deaths per 1000 live births. Tasa; Taux*

Ratio: A proportion obtained by dividing one quantity by another quantity. *For example, eighteen family planning nurses (numerator) divided by six clinics (denominator) is a ratio of three nurses to one clinic. Razón; Ratio*

Receivables: See **Accounts Receivable.**

Recurrent Costs: See **Operating Costs.**

Referral System: An established system that defines when a client should be referred to another facility for services (often for treating medical complications or providing clinical methods or surgical procedures), how the client will get to the clinic (for instance, whether an outreach worker will accompany the client to the clinic), who the client should contact at the referral site, and what documentation should be presented by or given to the client at the referral site. Effective referral systems help to expand access to services and long-term clinical methods and serve to enhance the quality of services provided by a smaller satellite clinic. *Sistema de Referencia; Système de référence*

Refresher Training: Periodic training given to staff for the purpose of reinforcing skills or introducing new concepts or techniques. *Capacitación de Apoyo; Recyclage*

Registration Fees: A fixed fee collected from clients at each visit regardless of the types of services provided. *Tarifas de Ingreso; Droits d'inscription (ou d'admission)*

Remuneration: Payment for goods provided, services rendered, or losses incurred. *Remuneración; Rémunération*

Reporting Channels: An established system within a supervisory structure for reporting information and data. Appropriate reporting channels are critical, particularly as the provision of different types of services becomes more integrated and/or program management becomes more decentralized. *Canales para la Rendición de Informes; Voies de communication formelle*

Reproductive Health: A state of physical, mental, and social well-being and not merely the absence of disease and infirmity, in all matters relating to the reproductive system and to its functions and processes. Reproductive health therefore implies that people are able to have a satisfying and safe sex life and that they have the capability to reproduce and the freedom to decide if, when, and how often to do so.

Implicit in this last condition is the right of men and women to be informed of and to have access to safe, effective, affordable, and acceptable methods of family planning of their choice, as well as other methods of their choice for regulation of fertility which are not against the law, and the right of access to appropriate health-care services that will enable women to go safely through pregnancy and childbirth and provide couples with the best chance of having a healthy infant.[1] (See **Reproductive Health Care/Services**.) *Salud Reproductiva; Santé réproductive*

Reproductive Health Care/Services: The variety of methods, techniques, and services that contribute to maintaining or improving a person's reproductive health and well-being by preventing and solving reproductive health problems.[2] (See **Reproductive Health**.) *Servicios de Salud Reproductiva; Prestations/services de santé réproductive*

Requisition and Issue Voucher: The form used by the clinic manager to request new supplies, by the warehouse manager to fill the order and record the quantities sent, and again by the clinic manager to check that the clinic received the correct quantities and types of supplies ordered. More than simply an order form, this form summarizes the average monthly consumption of each contraceptive ordered, the clinic's desired maximum quantity, and the quantity on hand at the time of the order, and therefore serves to justify the quantity ordered. *Formulario de Pedido y de Despacho; Bon de commande et de sortie*

Resource Management: The work of managing and controlling the limited resources needed to run a program such as people, money, and equipment. (Some people also consider time a resource.) *Administración de Recursos; Gestion des ressources*

Resources: The means available for use in conducting the planned activities, such as people, objects, and money. *Recursos; Ressources*

Responsibility Accounting: The recording and reporting of information in accordance with predetermined responsibility centers. *Contabilidad en Base a Responsabilidades; Comptabilité par centres de responsabilité*

---

[1]   *United Nations International Conference on Population and Development Programme of Action*, Cairo, September 23, 1994, paragraph 7.1.

[2]   Adapted from *United Nations International Conference on Population and Development Programme of Action*, Cairo, September 23, 1994, paragraph 7.1.

Responsibility Center (also known as Cost Center): A functional area which is the responsibility of a specific manager, such as a laboratory. *Centro de Responsabilidad; Centre de responsabilité*

Results Indicator: A measure showing the immediate effect of the program activities on the target population in relation to the objectives of the program. *Indicador de Resultados; Indicateur de résultats*

Revenue and Expense Report: See **Income Statement**.

Revenue Report: A daily, monthly, or quarterly report of monies or the equivalent received from sales, services, or fees. In accrual systems, revenues are recorded when they are earned, not when the actual cash or goods are received. *Informe de Ingresos; Etat des recettes*

Revenues: Monies or the equivalent received from sales, services, fees, donations, and grants. In the case of grants, only the portion that has been spent is actually revenue; the balance may have to be returned to the donor. In accrual systems, revenues are recorded when they are earned, not when the actual cash or goods are received. *Ingresos, Entradas, Recibos; Revenus*

Revisit (also known as Follow-up Visit): A visit made by a client to a clinic often for the purposes of checking up on the client's success or comfort with a contraceptive method or to address medical complications or side-effects. The term is also used to describe a visit for the resupply of a contraceptive. *Visita Subsecuente; Revisite*

S afety Stock: The amount of stock (number of months' supply) below the minimum level which serves as a cushion or buffer against major fluctuations in contraceptive demands or unexpected shipment delays. *Existencias de Seguridad; Stock de sécurité*

Satellite Services: Services that are provided to a community or several communities at a specific time (usually once a month) and at a designated location. Satellite services often provide integrated health, maternal and child health, and family planning services. (See also **Five-Table System**.) *Servicios Satélites; Points de services périphériques*

Selective Supervision: The procedure for supervising specific items on a less frequent and rotating basis, due to time constraints. *Supervisión Selectiva; Supervision sélective*

Self-Evaluation Guidelines (also known as Self-Assessment Tool or Checklist): Guidelines or a series of checklists that pose specific questions for evaluating the abilities of staff or the performance or functioning of a program. *Normas de Auto-Evaluación; Directives pour l'auto-évaluation*

Self-Sufficiency: The level of organizational development that is reached when the organization is able to function independently of outside (donor) assistance. Self-sufficient organizations are capable of mobilizing a wide range of resources to avoid dependence on a single financial resource and have the management and leadership capability to adapt their programs to a changing environment. (See also **Sustainability**.) *Autosuficiencia; Autosuffisance*

Service-Based Forecasts: Forecasts based on an analysis of the existing program's service statistics and the projected number of clients that a program expects to serve. *Proyecciones Basadas en el Servicio; Prévisions basées sur les prestations de services*

Service Capacity: The maximum volume of services that can be provided with a given set of resources. *For example, the maximum number of vasectomies that a doctor can carry out in a working day. Capacidad de Servicio; Capacité de service*

Service Delivery Approach: Designed to reach and attract different client groups, service delivery approaches include community-based services, clinic-based services, employer-based services, hospital-based services, in-home or depot services, and community gatherings for information, education, communication (IEC) about family planning. *Enfoque de la Prestación de Servicios; Approche de prestation de services*

Service Fees: Fees charged to a client for each service provided, such as counseling, examination, laboratory testing, and contraceptive supplies. Some programs set a standard charge for an initial visit and a revisit. An initial visit might include the cost of an examination, counseling, and a contraceptive method, whereas the revisit might cover the cost of a resupply of contraceptives and consultation. *Tarifas por Servicios; Paiements des prestations*

Service Marketplace: The target area or region that a program intends to reach in delivering its services to a population. *Mercado de Servicios; Zone desservie*

Service Quality: Service quality refers to a number of inter-related factors including the way in which individuals are treated by providers, the scope of services and contraceptives available to clients, the quality of the information provided to the clients and quality of the counseling skills, the promotion of individual choice, the technical competence of providers, and the accessibility and continuity of services. *Calidad de los Servicios; Qualité des services*

Service Stops: Different stages or locations within a clinic where a client receives specific types of services. Service stops often include: registering with the registration clerk, being weighed, having blood pressure taken, seeing a counselor, being examined by a nurse or doctor, and checking out at the registration desk. *Estaciones de Servicios; Postes de travail*

Session Plan: See **Supervisor's Visit Plan**.

Shelf Life: The length of time a contraceptive can be stored under normal circumstances without losing its efficacy. Poor storage conditions (such as extremes in temperature) can reduce the shelf life of a product. *Vida Util; Durée de vie*

Short Shipments: When suppliers send incomplete shipments of contraceptives. *Embarques Incompletos; Livraisons incomplètes*

Short-Term Methods: Contraceptive methods that remain effective for a relatively short period of time. Experts differ in the methods they include under this term. Some experts include only spermicides, diaphragms, and condoms; others also include oral contraceptive pills. *Métodos de Corto Plazo; Méthodes à court terme*

Site Training: An integrated approach to training that views the service-delivery site as a system and treats staff as members of the team that makes the system work. The goal of site training is to improve systems at a local site through effective teamwork and by ensuring that all members of the team have the knowledge and skills they need to fulfill their respective roles on the team. *Capacitación en Servicio; Formation sur le site*

Situation Analysis: A systematic process for analyzing the internal environment and capabilities of an organization and the external political, social, economic, and programmatic environment in which a program works. Such an analysis is performed for the purposes of comparing a present situation against an ideal situation in order to determine a course of action for improving program management, performance, and sustainability. *Análisis Situacional; Analyse de situation*

Sliding Fee Scale: A system of charging clients for services based on household income and family size, allowing clients to pay what they can afford. *Escala Variable de Tarifas; Echelle discriminatoire de tarifs*

Social Marketing: A strategy modeled after commercial product marketing in which contraceptives and other products related to sexual and reproductive health are promoted, distributed, and sold at relatively low prices through existing commercial outlets. Social marketing advertises reproductive health and family planning to different segments of the population by using such commercial outlets as radio, newspaper advertisements, and television to provide family planning information, education, and communication. *Mercadeo Social; Marketing social*

Split Shipments: Usually requested by the recipient, when a large shipment is divided into smaller shipments and sent at regular intervals to accommodate the recipient's storage space constraints. *Embarques Divididos; Livraisons partielles*

Staff Development: See **Professional Development**.

Staff Motivation: The personnel activities of an organization or supervisor that are designed to reaffirm the importance of the staff's jobs to the achievements of the program and to improve the skills, motivation, and qualifications of employees. Such actions or activities include providing training, giving positive and constructive feedback on a regular basis, showing appreciation for their work, and engaging them in problem solving. *Motivación del Personal; Motivation du personnel*

Staff Responsibilities: The specific responsibilities or set of responsibilities of different staff positions for which staff can be held accountable. Such responsibilities can usually be quantified, such as providing counseling to an average number of clients over a specific period of time, or providing medical services to a district clinic three days a week. *Responsabilidades del Personal; Responsabilités du personnel*

Staff Roles: The broad responsibilities attached to different staff positions. *For example, the roles of managers include leadership, understanding, problem solving, advice, and encouragement. Funciones del Personal; Rôle du personnel*

Stages of Organizational Development: The four stages that characterize the development of an organization: Emergence, Growth, Consolidation, and Mature. These stages are based on the principle that organizations develop in a systematic way over time and portray distinct characteristics during each stage in relation to mission, strategy, structure, and systems. (See **Emergent Stage, Growth Stage, Consolidation Stage,** and **Mature Stage.**) *Etapas del Desarrollo de una Organización; Phases de développement d'une organisation*

Start-Up Organization: Usually a small organization in the early years of its development. Many start-up organizations are characterized by highly creative leadership, highly innovative initiatives, and a small, highly committed and motivated staff. *Organización Incipiente (o de Arranque); Organisation qui démarre*

State-of-the-Art: The current level of refinement of a particular developing technology. *De Punta; Niveau de pointe*

Status of Supplies Chart: A worksheet for calculating the average monthly consumption (AMC) and the maximum and minimum stock quantities. The status of supplies chart allows managers to record on a single chart information about the desired minimum and maximum stock quantities for all types of contraceptives based on recent consumption patterns. *Tabla para Control de Suministros; Tableau de la situation des stocks*

Stock Card (also known as Inventory Control Card or Bin Card): The form used to record all stock transactions (contraceptives received or dispensed) and the quantities of contraceptive currently in stock and on order. A separate stock card should be maintained for each type and brand of contraceptive. *Tarjeta de Control de Inventario; Fiche de stock*

Stock on Hand (also known as Balance on Hand): The quantity of each contraceptive or commodity in stock at any given time. *Existencias Disponibles; Stock disponible*

Stock on Order: The quantity of stock of each contraceptive that has been ordered but has not yet been received (by the clinic or facility). *Existencias en Pedido; Stock en commande*

Stockout: A situation in which a program or clinic runs out of supplies of one or more contraceptive methods (or other drug or equipment supplies) and does not have any supplies on hand to serve the client. *Desabastecimiento; Rupture de stocks*

Stock Position: The number of months of supply that you have available at any given time for a single type and brand of contraceptive or commodity. The stock position is calculated by dividing the quantity of stock on hand by the average monthly consumption of that contraceptive or item. *Situación de Existencias; Situation des stocks*

Strategic Management: A way of managing the direction of a program by identifying the specific services that the organization is best suited to deliver and the population groups the organization can most effectively serve, and by making a realistic assessment of available resources for carrying out the work. Strategic management requires managers to think strategically, ask questions such as "Is the program doing the right things?" and consider and anticipate trends in the external environment that will affect the achievement of organizational goals. *Administración Estratégica; Gestion stratégique*

Strategic Plan: The document that is the result of long-range (strategic) planning. It usually covers a period of three to five years, sets forth the mission and goals of the program, prioritizes strategies, and formulates the financial basis for achieving the goals. *Plan Estratégico; Plan stratégique*

Strategic Planning: Long-range planning, covering a period of three to five years, that includes setting goals, strategies, and objectives for your program. *Planeación Estratégica; Planification stratégique*

Strategic Thinking: A critical management skill that requires having the ability to assess a program in relation to its mission, its future goals, and the external environment in which it works. Strategic thinking requires managers to examine whether their programs are "doing the right things" in order to achieve their mission. *Pensamiento Estratégico; Pensée stratégique*

Strategy: The approach or approaches that serve to fulfill the mission and that will be used to achieve organizational or programmatic goals. *Estrategia; Stratégie*

Subsidizing Program Costs: See **Cross-Subsidization**.

Subsystem: A system within the larger system that separates functional divisions of an organization, such as commodities, training, or service delivery, etc. *Subsistema; Sous-système*

Supervisor's Visit Plan (also known as a Session Plan): A statement or checklist used by supervisors that outlines the items, skills, and statistics to be monitored during each supervisory session. This plan should also include program support activities, such as collecting reporting forms and replenishing supplies, and any post-session activities to be completed by the supervisor. *Plan de Visita del Supervisor; Plan de visite du superviseur*

Supervisory Protocol: An established system for supervising staff (clinical and non-clinical). A supervisory protocol should clearly describe supervisory procedures and schedules, organizational philosophy on supervision, tools for effective supervision (such as job descriptions and performance objectives), criteria for promotion, and techniques for motivating and supporting staff. *Protocolo de Supervisión; Protocole de supervision*

Supervisory Schedule: A written plan of supervisory sessions showing the name of the employee involved and the date, time, and content of upcoming supervisory sessions. A supervisory schedule is used for planning purposes and for communicating to employees such upcoming supervisory activities. *Cronograma de Supervisión; Calendrier de supervision*

Supervisory Session: A meeting with one or more staff members in order to review the work that has been accomplished and to make plans for future work and subsequent supervisory sessions. *Sesión de Supervisión; Session de supervision*

Supervisory Structure: The formal structure of reporting relationships between different functions and positions of the management and staff. *Estructura de Supervisión; Structure de supervision*

Supervisory System: The methods and procedures used to monitor the volume and quality of work performed by subordinate staff, as well as to provide necessary support to staff. The system includes site visits, employee performance appraisals, individual and group staff meetings, reviewing reporting forms, etc. *Sistema de Supervisión; Système de supervision*

Survey of Family Planning Providers: A study of other family planning providers, usually those that work in the same area as the program conducting the study. The information is used to compare the types and quality of services offered by the other providers and to determine areas for coordination, referral, or new service opportunities. *Encuesta a los Proveedores de Servicios de Planificación Familiar; Enquête auprès des prestataires de planification familiale*

Sustainability: The ability of a program to provide quality services to its clients, expand its scope of services and client base, increase or maintain demand for services, and generate income from the program and through local funding mechanisms, while decreasing its dependence on funds derived from external donors. (See also **Self-Sufficiency**.) *Sustentabilidad; Viabilité*

SWOT Analysis (Strengths, Weaknesses, Opportunities, and Threats): The process of analyzing an organization's or program's internal strengths and weaknesses, as well as the opportunities and threats that exist outside the organization or program. *Análisis FODA; Analyse FFOM*

T ally **Sheet**: A chart designed to easily collect and organize data. Tally sheets are used to list the types of data that will be collected and to record the number of occurrences or observations that are counted in each category. *Hoja de Registro; Feuille de pointage (Liste des informations et données)*

Target Group: The specific population group or groups intended as beneficiaries of a program. This will be either all or a subset of potential users such as adolescents, pregnant women, rural residents, or the residents of a particular geographic area. *Grupo Objetivo; Groupe cible*

Targets: Objectives that have been broken down into smaller units and restated in numerical terms. They pertain to a specific program component, such as a clinical IEC component, and encompass a specific period of time such as a quarter, month, or week. *Metas; Cibles*

Task Analysis: An examination of all the duties and activities that are carried out by an individual employee or position, for the purpose of determining the required skills, knowledge, attitudes, resources, and risks involved with each task. *Análisis de Tareas; Analyse des tâches*

Task Definition: The duties and activities that are specified as the responsibility of a particular employee or staff position. *Definición de Tareas; Définition des tâches*

Tasks: Activities broken down into specific assignments or duties. *Tareas; Tâches*

Team Approach: A philosophy and a technique that relies on developing and working with a group of people with different skills and perspectives to identify and discuss issues, define causes of problems (or successes), and find and implement solutions in order to achieve a common goal. *Enfoque de Equipo; Approche d'équipe*

Team Supervision Process: Any established process for supervising staff using a participative, team approach that involves supervisors and staff in the entire process. *Proceso de Supervisión en Equipo; Processus de supervision en équipe*

Termination Policy: The standard policy, usually stated in a personnel manual, describing the grounds for employee dismissal and the rights of an employee upon dismissal. *Normas de Despidos; Procédure de rupture de contrat*

Third-Party Payments: A system whereby a third party (such as an employer, an insurance company, or health plan) pays for services provided to the client. There may also be co-payments, whereby the client pays part of the fees. *Sistema de Pagos de Terceros (Co-Pagos); Paiements par un tiers (ou Co-paiements)*

"To Do" Lists: Informal lists of activities and tasks to be carried out over a short period of time, usually less than one month. "To do" lists are revised regularly to incorporate new activities that replace those that have been completed. *Lista de «Asuntos Pendientes»; Listes des choses «à faire»*

Total Visit Cost: The cost of providing services for different types of visits (for example, first pill visit, IUD insertion visit, counseling visit), including direct personnel costs and contraceptive supplies, and a proportion of overhead costs. Used for comparing cost effectiveness and efficiency of services and in setting fees. *Costo Total por Visita; Coût total par visite*

Trend Analysis: The representation of data to show an increasing, decreasing, or unchanging pattern of data over a period of time. A trend analysis is often performed by creating a line graph from a set of data. *Análisis de Tendencias; Analyse de tendances*

Two-Tier Information System: An information system that is designed to collect output information on a routine basis, and asks managers to also collect process information to help them determine where a problem may have occurred so that it can be corrected. *Sistema Bifurcado de Información; Système d'information à deux niveaux*

Underserved Populations: Groups of people that are not normally served or not well-served by established service delivery programs. In family planning, some examples of underserved populations are adolescents, men, low-parity women, the urban poor, unmarried people, and people who live in remote rural areas. *Sectores Desatendidos de la Población o Carentes de Servicios; Populations mal desservies (sous-servies)*

Unit Cost (of Contraceptive Products): The total cost of a single contraceptive product unit, such as a cycle of pills, a set of surgical gloves, a Norplant® kit, a single condom, etc., including transport costs, customs, taxes, and other costs. *Costo Unitario (de los Productos Anticonceptivos); Coût unitaire (des produits contraceptifs)*

Unmet Demand or Unmet Need: This term is used to describe the number of people or the percentage of the population who desire to use contraceptives to space or limit births but for a variety of reasons, including lack of access to information or services, are not currently using contraceptives. *Demanda no Cubierta o Necesidad no Cubierta; Demande non satisfaite ou besoin non satisfait*

User Continuity Program: A systematic approach implemented to increase the rate of continuing users in a service delivery system. To institute a user continuity program, acceptable rates or numbers of continuing users must be determined for each service center, and activities for client follow-up must be carried out on a regular basis. *Programa para Aumentar la Tasa de Continuidad de Usuarios Activos; Programme pour accroître le nombre d'utilisateurs actifs*

User Fees: See Client Fees.

Variable Costs or Expenses: Expenses that vary according to the level of service provided or number of people served. Contraceptive expenses, for example, vary depending on the number of users of each method. *Costos o Gastos Variables; Coûts (ou dépenses) variables*

Variable Order Interval System: See Continuous (Perpetual) Review System.

Vehicle Usage Report: A log that records vehicular use. It includes the date, destination, purpose of the trip, beginning and ending odometer reading, petrol purchases, and repairs. It is used to calculate the cost per mile or kilometer and to control and monitor costs. *Informe por Uso de Vehículos; Carnet de bord*

Vertical Services/Approach: An approach in which services, such as family planning, maternal and child health, nutrition, immunization, and other reproductive health services are provided through separate facilities with separate staff managed at the central level by separate divisions or ministries that operate independently from one another. *Servicios Verticales o Enfoque Vertical; Approche de services verticaux*

Visit-Type: A individual type of visit made by a client to a clinic such as a first or initial visit, insertion visit, removal visit, resupply visit, complications visit, education or counseling visit, etc. Visit-types are usually defined for the purposes of determining the average cost of providing each type of service. *Tipo de Visita; Type de visite*

Volunteer Services: An approach used to support a local public- or private-sector program in which members of the community assist government workers, or fieldworkers employed by non-governmental organizations (NGOs), to carry out functions related to motivation, contraceptive resupply, and follow up. Workers may receive a small honorarium, reimbursement for travel expenses, or other tangible rewards but are not paid a regular wage. *Servicios Voluntarios; Services bénévoles (de volontaires)*

W aivers/Waiver System: A system used to determine under what conditions a client will not be charged for services or when a portion of the client fee will be drawn from a reserve fund to pay part of the fee for the client. A waiver system uses a standard set of criteria to determine which clients are eligible for such financial support. *Exoneraciones/ Sistema de Exoneraciones y Excepciones; Exonérations/Système de dérogation*

Work Plan: A document developed by the manager and the staff, covering a specified period of time, that lists all planned activities, the date by which they will be accomplished, the resources that they will require, and the people responsible for carrying them out. *Plan de Trabajo; Plan de travail*

Work Process: The process or sequence of activities that is carried out in order to complete a piece of work. *For example, the work process for registering a client in a clinic might consist of greeting the client, taking his or her name, checking to see if the client is a new or returning client, opening a new client record and having the client fill out the necessary* *forms, or pulling the existing client record, collecting any registration fees (if appropriate), asking the client to be seated until she or he can be seen by a service provider, and notifying the service provider that the client is ready to be seen.* **Proceso de Trabajo; Processus de travail**

Working Capital: The amount of short-term funds available for operations, or the excess of current assets over current liabilities. *Capital de Trabajo; Fonds de roulement*

List of Terms and Foreign-Language Equivalents

English with Spanish- and French-language equivalents:

English	Spanish	French
Acceptance Rate	Tasa de Aceptación	Taux d'acceptation
Accounting System	Sistema Contable	Système de comptabilité
Accounts Payable	Cuentas por Pagar	Comptes à payer
Accounts Receivable	Cuentas por Cobrar	Comptes à recevoir
Accrual Accounting	Contabilidad sobre Bases Devengadas	Comptabilité d'exercice
Action Plan	Plan de Acción	Plan d'action
Active Users	Usuarios Activos o Regulares	Utilisateurs actifs
Activities	Actividades	Activités
Activity Planning	Planeación de Actividades	Planification des activités
Advisory Board	Junta de Asesores	Conseil consultatif
Allocation of Costs	Asignación de Costos	Répartition des coûts
Appointment Card	Tarjeta de Citas	Fiche de rendez-vous
Asset	Activo	Actif
Average Lead Time	Tiempo de Espera Promedio	Délai moyen de livraison
Average Monthly Consumption (AMC)	Consumo Mensual Promedio (CMP)	Consommation mensuelle moyenne (CMM)
Bad Debt	Deuda Incobrable	Créance irrécouvrable

Balance on Hand	Saldo Disponible	Stock résiduel
Balance Sheet	Balance General	Bilan
Bank Reconciliation	Concilación Bancaria	Reconcilation (ou rapprochement bancaire)
Bar Chart	Gráfica de Barras	Graphique à colonnes
Barriers to Services	Barreras a los Servicios	Obstacles aux services
Baseline Survey	Encuesta de Base	Enquête de base
Benchmarking	Técnica de Análisis de Casos Modelo («Benchmarking»)	Technique du modèle parfait
Benchmarks	Requisitos Previos («Benchmarks»)	Jalons de performance progressifs
Board of Directors	Junta Directiva	Conseil d'administration
Brainstorming	Lluvia de Ideas	Lancement d'idées («Brainstorming»)
Break-Even Point	Punto de Equilibrio	Seuil de rentabilité
Budget Performance Report	Informe de Ejecución del Presupuesto	Rapport de performance budgétaire
Business Plan	Plan de Negocios	Plan d'entreprise
Capital Costs	Costos de Inversión (Gastos de Capital)	Coûts d'investissement
Cash Accounting	Contabilidad de Caja	Comptabilité de caisse

Cash Flow Projection Worksheet	Planilla de Proyecciones del Flujo de Fondos	Formulaire de projection de l'état de la trésorerie
Cash Flow Statement	Estado de Flujo de Fondos	Etat de la trésorerie
Cause-and-Effect Diagram	Diagrama de Causa y Efecto	Diagramme de cause à effet
Central Warehouse	Bodega (almacén) Central	Magasin central
Chart of Accounts	Catálogo de Cuentas	Tableau des comptes
Chronogram	Cronograma	Chronogramme
Client Characteristics	Características del Cliente	Caractéristiques des clients
Client/Clinic Data	Datos sobre Clientes/ Clínica	Données sur les clients ou sur les formations sanitaires
Client Fees	Tarifas para los Clientes	Paiements effectués par les clients
Client Flow Analysis	Análisis del Flujo de Clientes	Analyse du flux des clients
Client Flow Chart	Tabla del Flujo de Clientes	Tableau du flux des clients
Client Flow Form	Formulario de Flujo de Clientes	Formulaire de flux des clients
Client Motivation	Motivación del Cliente	Motivation des clients
Client Profile	Perfil del Cliente	Profil des clients
Client Record	Expediente del Cliente	Dossier du client

Client Referral Card	Tarjeta de Referencia del Cliente	Carte de référence du client
Client Satisfaction	Satisfacción del Cliente	Satisfaction des clients
Client Survey	Encuesta a Clientes	Enquête auprès des clients
Client Waiting Time	Tiempo de Espera de Clientes	Temps d'attente des clients
Clinic Management	Administración de la Clínica	Gestion de la formation sanitaire
Clinic Performance	Rendimiento de la Clínica	Performance de la formation sanitaire
Clinic Protocol	Norma (o Guía) Clínica	Protocole sanitaire
Cluster Survey	Encuesta de Grupos	Enquête par grappes
Cold Chain Maintenance	Mantenimiento de la Cadena de Frío	Entretien de la chaîne du froid
Community-Based Services (CBS)	Servicios Comunitarios (SC)	Services à base communautaire (SBC)
Community Participation	Participación Comunitaria	Participation communautaire
Community Survey	Encuesta de la Comunidad	Enquête communautaire
Comparison Table	Tabla Comparativa	Tableau de comparaison
Competency-Based Training	Capacitación Funcional (basada en la competencia)	Formation basée sur les compétences

Consolidated Budget	Presupuesto Consolidado	Budget consolidé
Consolidation Stage	Etapa de Consolidación	Phase de consolidation
Contact Time	Tiempo de Contacto	Temps de contact
Continuation Rate	Tasa de Continuación	Taux de continuation
Continuing Users	Usuarios Continuos o Subsecuentes	Utilisateurs assidus
Continuous Quality Improvement (CQI)	Proceso de Mejoramiento Continuo de la Calidad (PMC)	Amélioration continue de la qualité (ACQ)
Continuous (Perpetual) Review System	Sistema Continuo (Perpetuo) de Inventario	Système de revue continuelle ou perpétuelle
Contraceptive Data Analysis Chart	Tabla de Análisis de Datos sobre Anticonceptivos	Tableau d'analyse des données sur les contraceptifs
Contraceptive Prevalence	Prevalencia de Uso de Anticonceptivos	Prévalence contraceptive
Contraceptive Product Cost	Costo del Anticonceptivo	Coûts des produits contraceptifs
Contraceptive Supply Management	Administración de Suministros Anticonceptivos	Gestion des stocks de contraceptifs
Control Systems	Sistemas de Fiscalización	Systèmes de contrôle
Coordination	Coordinación	Coordination
Co-Payment Scheme	Esquema de Pagos Compartidos	Système de co-paiement

COPE (Client-Oriented, Provider Efficient)	"COPE" (Dirigido al Cliente, Eficiente para el Proveedor)	COPE (Client orienté, prestation efficace)
Cost Accounting	Contabilidad de Costos	Comptabilité analytique
Cost Analysis	Análisis de Costos	Analyse des coûts
Cost Center	Centro de Costo	Centre de coût
Cost-Effectiveness	Costo-Efectividad	Coût-efficacité
Cost per Couple-Year of Protection	Costo por Año de Protección Pareja	Coût par couple-année de protection
Cost per Year of Use	Costo por Año de Uso	Coût par année d'utilisation
Cost-Sharing	Colaboración entre Programas para la Reducción de Costos	Partage des coûts
Cost Variance	Variación de Costos	Variance des coûts
Couple-Years of Protection (CYP)	Años Protección Pareja (APP)	Couple-années de protection (CAP)
CQI Core Group	Núcleo del PMC (o Grupo Interno para el PMC)	Groupe-noyau pour l'ACQ
Cross-Functional Team	Equipo Interfuncional	Equipe à fonctions multiples
Cross-Subsidization/ Cross-Subsidies	Subsidios Cruzados	Subvention croisée
Cross-Tabulation	Tabulación Cruzada	Tableau croisée
Cross-Training	Capacitación Interfuncional	Formation polyvalente

Current Assets (or Short-Term Assets)	Activo Circulante (Activos a corto plazo)	Actifs courants ou à court terme
Daily Activity Register	Registro Diario de Actividades	Registre journalier des activités
Daily Feedback Forms	Formularios Diarios de Retroalimentación	Formulaires pour la rétro-information journalière
Data Analysis	Análisis de Datos	Analyse des données
Decentralization	Descentralización	Décentralisation
Decision Tree	Arbol de Decisiones	Arbre de décisions
Deconcentration	Desconcentración	Déconcentration
Delegation	Delegación	Délégation
Depot Services	Servicios de Almacén (o de Distribución Local)	Services au dépôt communautaire
Depreciation	Depreciación	Amortissement
Devolution	Devolución	Dévolution
Direct Costs	Costos Directos	Coûts directs
Discontinuation Rate	Tasa de Abandono	Taux de discontinuation
Discontinuer	«Abandono»	Discontinuateur
Distribution-Based Forecasts	Proyecciones Basadas en la Distribución	Prévisions basées sur la distribution
"Doing the Right Things"	«Hacer las Cosas Correctas»	«Faire les choses nécessaires»

"Doing Things in the Right Way"	«Hacer las Cosas en Forma Correcta»	«Faire les choses correctement»
Dropout	Desertor	Abandon
Effectiveness	Efectividad	Efficacité
Efficiency	Eficiencia	Efficience
ELCO Map	Mapa PAEL	Carte ELCO
Emergency Order	Pedido de Emergencia	Commande d'urgence
Emergent Stage	Etapa de Surgimiento (o Etapa Emergente)	Phase d'émergence
Endowment	Dotación	Dotation
Equity	Capital Contable o Patrimonio	Capitaux propres
Evaluation	Evaluación	Evaluation
Exit Interview	Entrevista de Salida	Entretien à la sortie
Expenditures	Erogaciones	Dépenses
Expenses	Gastos	Frais
Experiential Learning	Aprendizaje de Experiencias	Apprentissage par l'expérience
Expiration Date	Fecha de Expiración	Date de péremption
External Audit	Auditoría Externa	Audit externe
External Coordination	Coordinación externa	Coordination externe
External Environment	Contexto Externo	Environnement externe
Facilitative Supervision	Supervisión Facilitadora	Supervision à but de facilitation

Facilitator	Facilitador	Animateur
Family Planning Activities Worksheet	Planilla de Actividades de Planificación Familiar	Fiche de calcul des activités de planification familiale
Family Planning Commodities	Suministros de Planificación Familiar	Produits pour la planification familiale
Feedback	Retroalimentación	Rétro-information
Fee-For-Service Program	Programa de Cobro de Tarifas por Servicios	Programme de paiement des prestations
Financial Audit	Auditoría Financiera	Audit financier
Financial Management	Administración Financiera	Gestion financière
Financial Position	Posición Financiera	Situation financière
Financial Reporting	Informes Financieros	Rapport financier
Financial Statement	Estados Financieros	Etat financier
First Consultation of a Client	Primera Consulta de un Cliente	Première consultation d'un client
First-to-Expire, First-Out (FEFO)	Primero en Expirar, Primero en Salir (PEPS)	Premier à périmer, premier sorti (PPPS)
First Visit	Primera Visita	Première visite
Five-Table System	Sistema de Cinco Mesas	Système des cinq tables
Fixed Assets (or Long-Term Assets)	Activos fijos o bien duraderos	Immobilisations
Fixed Costs or Expenses	Costos o Gastos Fijos	Coûts (ou frais) fixes

Fixed Order Interval System	Sistema de Pedidos de Intervalos Fijos	Système de commande à intervalles fixes
Flowchart	Diagrama de Flujo	Diagramme de processus
Focus Group	Grupo Focal	Groupe de discussion focalisée
Follow-up Visit	Visita de Control o Consecutiva	Visite de suivi
Formal Training	Capacitación Formal	Formation formelle
Frequency Table	Tabla de Frecuencias	Tableau de fréquence
Functional Allocation	Distribución Funcional	Répartition des fonctions
Functional Responsibilities	Responsabilidades Funcionales	Responsabilités de fonction
Fund Accounting	Contabilidad de Fondos	Comptabilité par fonds
Fund Balance	Balance de Fondos o Reserva	Bilan des fonds (ou Réserves)
Fund Raising	Recaudación de Fondos	Mobilisation de fonds
"Funnel" Approach	Integración Tipo «Embudo»	Approche de «l'entonnoir»
Gantt Chart	Gráfica de Gantt	Tableau de Gantt
General Administration	Administración General	Administration générale
Goals	Objetivos Generales	Buts
Grade	Grado o Nivel	Grade

Grants	Donaciones	Subventions
Graph	Gráfica	Graphique
Grievance Policy	Normas para Manejo de Quejas y Reclamos	Procédure de soumission de doléances
Growth Stage	Etapa de Crecimiento	Phase de croissance
Histogram	Histograma	Histogramme
Historical Data	Datos Históricos	Données rétrospectives
"Hourglass" Approach	Integración Tipo «Reloj de Arena»	Approche du «sablier»
Household Survey	Encuesta de Hogares	Enquête auprès des ménages
Identification Codes	Códigos de Identificación	Codes d'identification
Impact	Impacto	Impact
Imprest Fund	Fondo de Caja Chica	Caisse d'avance
Incentive Grants	Donaciones para Incentivar	Subventions qui contiennent des primes
Incentive System	Sistema de Incentivos	Système de primes d'encouragement
Income and Expense Report	Estado de Ingresos y Egresos	Etat des recettes et des dépenses
Income Statement	Estado de Pérdidas y Ganancias	Etat des revenus et des dépenses
Indicator	Indicador	Indicateur

Indirect Costs	Costos Indirectos	Coûts indirects
Informal Training	Capacitación Informal	Formation informelle
Information Flow Table	Gráfica de Flujo de Información	Tableau de circulation de l'information
Information System	Sistema de Información	Système d'information
In-Kind Contribution	Contribuciones en Especie	Contribution en nature
Inputs	Insumos	Intrants
Inreach	Conocimiento Interno («Inreach»)	Diffusion interne
Insertion Visit	Visita de Inserción	Visite pour insertion
Institutionalization	Institucionalización	Institutionnalisation
Integration/Integrated Services	Integración/Servicios Integrados	Intégration/Services intégrés
Intermediate Outputs	Resultados Intermedios	Résultats intermédiaires
Intermediate Warehouse	Bodega (almacén) Intermedia	Magasin intermédiaire
Internal Audit	Auditoría Interna	Audit interne
Internal Coordination	Coordinación Interna	Coordination interne
Internal Environment	Contexto Interno	Environnement interne
Internal Organization	Organización Interna	Organisation interne
Inventory	Inventario	Stocks

Inventory Control Card	Tarjeta de Control de Inventario	Fiche de contrôle des stocks
Job Description	Descripción del Cargo	Description de poste
Lead Time	Tiempo de Espera	Délai de livraison
Lead Time Quantity	Cantidad para Cubrir el Tiempo de Espera	Quantité couvrant le délai de livraison
Liabilities	Pasivos	Passif
Line Graph	Gráfica Lineal	Graphique linéaire
Line Item	Partida o Rubro	Rubrique
Logistics Management	Administración Logística	Gestion de la logistique
Long-Acting Methods	Métodos de Larga Duración	Méthodes de longue durée
Lot Number	Número de Lote	Numéro de lot
Maintenance Cost	Costo de Mantenimiento	Coût d'entretien
Managed Care	Paquete de Servicios	Systéme contrôlé de prestations sanitaires
Management Accounting	Contabilidad Administrativa	Comptabilité de gestion
Management Components	Componentes Administrativos	Composantes de gestion
Management Functions/Systems	Funciones/Sistemas Administrativos	Fonctions/Systèmes de gestion
Management Information System (MIS)	Sistema de Información Gerencial (SIG)	Système d'information de gestion (SIG)

Managing Board	Junta Administrativa	Comité de gestion
Mapping	Mapeo	Etablissement de cartes
Market Analysis	Análisis del Mercado	Analyse du marché
Marketing	Mercadeo	Marketing
Matrix	Matriz	Matrice
Mature Stage	Etapa de Madurez	Phase de maturité
Maximum Quantity	Cantidad Máxima	Quantité maximum
Max/Min (Maximum-Minimum) Stock Level	Sistema Max/Min	Système Max/Min (maximum-minimum)
Medical Record	Expediente o Historia Clínica	Dossier médical
Membership Fees	Cuotas de Afiliación	Cotisations
Merit Awards	Premio al Mérito	Récompenses au mérite
Method Mix	Mezcla de Métodos	Gamme des méthodes
Methodology	Metodología	Méthodologie
Micro-Manage	Micro-administrar	Micro-gestion
Minimum Quantity	Cantidad Mínima	Quantité minimum
Missed Opportunity	Oportunidad Perdida	Occasion manquée
Mission Statement	Declaración de Misión	Enoncé de mission
Monitoring	Monitoreo	Suivi

Monthly Summary of Family Planning Activities	Resumen Mensual de Actividades de Planificación Familiar	Récapitulatif mensuel des activités de planification familiale
Months of Supply	Meses de Suministros	Mois d'approvisionnement
Mutually Accountable	Responsabilidad Conjunta	Mutuellement responsable
New Acceptor	Aceptante Nuevo	Nouvel accepteur
New Client	Cliente Nuevo	Nouveau client
New User	Usuario Nuevo	Nouvel utilisateur
No-Show Client	Cliente que No Asiste	Client non-assidu
No-Show Rate	Tasa de Inasistencia	Taux de clients non-assidus
Objectives	Objetivos Específicos	Objectifs
Observation Guides	Guías de Observación	Grilles d'observation
Observation-Study Visits	Visitas de Observación-Estudio	Visites d'observation et d'étude
Operating Center	Centro Operativo	Centre d'opérations
Operating Costs	Costos de Operación	Coûts d'exploitation
Operational Information	Información Operacional	Information opérationnelle
Operational Plan	Plan Operativo	Plan opérationnel
Order Interval	Intervalo entre Pedidos	Intervalle entre les commandes
Organization Type	Tipo de Organización	Type d'organisation

Organizational Chart	Diagrama Organizacional	Organigramme
Organizational Mission	Misión de la Organización	Mission de l'organisation
Organizational Stability	Estabilidad Organizacional	Stabilité de l'organisation
Organizational Structure	Estructura Organizacional	Structure organisationnelle
Organogram	Organigrama	Organigramme
Outlet	Local o Punto de Distribución	Point de distribution (final)
Output Information	Informe de Resultados	Information sur les résultats
Outreach	Extensión («Outreach»)	Activités d'extension
Overhead Costs	Costos Generales	Frais généraux
Paper Trail	Comprobantes	Trace écrite
Pareto Analysis	Análisis de Pareto	Analyse de Pareto
Participative Style	Estilo Participativo	Style de participation
Patient Flow Analysis	Análisis del Flujo de Pacientes	Analyse du flux des patients
Payables	Cuentas por Pagar	Dettes
Performance Appraisal	Reconocimiento del Desempeño	Evaluation de la performance
Performance Information	Información de Desempeño	Information sur la performance
Performance Targets and Objectives	Objetivos/Metas de Desempeño	Cibles et objectifs de performance

Periodic Review System	Sistema Periódico de Inventario	Système de revue périodique
Perquisites	Gratificación	Gratification
Personnel Category	Categoría de Personal	Catégorie de personnel
Personnel Committee	Comité del Personal	Comité du personnel
Personnel Cost (or Total Personnel Cost)	Costo del Personal (o Costo Total del Personal)	Coûts du personnel (ou Coûts totaux du personnel)
Personnel Cost Per Visit-Type	Costo del Personal por Tipo de Visita	Coût du personnel par type de visite
Personnel Management	Administración del Personal	Gestion du personnel
Personnel Manual	Manual del Personal	Manuel du personnel
Petty Cash	Caja Chica	Petite caisse
Phased Training	Adiestramiento en Fases	Formation par étapes
Pie Chart	Gráfica de Sectores	Graphique «camembert»
Planning	Planeación	Planification
Plateau Effect or "Plateauing"	«Estancamiento»	Effet de plateau
Pooling	Combinación	Regroupment
Population-Based Forecasts	Proyecciones Basadas en Información Censual o en Encuestas Demográficas	Prévisions basées sur la population

Population-Based Survey	Encuesta Basada en la Población	Enquête auprès de la population
Population Density	Densidad Poblacional	Densité de population
Population Distribution	Distribución de la Población	Distribution de la population
Post-test	Examen Post-Prueba	Post-test
Potential Acceptor	Aceptante Potencial	Accepteur potentiel
Potential Client	Cliente Potencial	Client potentiel
Potential User	Usuario Potencial	Utilisateur potentiel
Pre-test	Examen Pre-Prueba	Pré-test
Privatization	Privatización	Privatisation
Problem Solving	Resolución de Problemas	Résolution de problèmes
Procedure Visit	Visita de Procedimiento	Visite pour intervention médicale
Process Analysis	Análisis del Proceso	Analyse de processus
Process Information	Información sobre el Proceso	Information sur les processus
Professional Development	Desarrollo Profesional	Développement professionnel
Professional Fees	Honorarios Profesionales	Honoraires
Program Components	Componentes del Programa	Volets du programme
Programmatic Reporting	Informes Programáticos	Rapport programmatique

Project Activity Timeline	Cronograma de Actividades del Projecto	Calendrier des activités du projet
Public Affairs	Relaciones Públicas	Affaires publiques
Pull System	Sistema de Requisición	Système de commande (réquisition)
Purchased Services	Servicios Adquiridos	Services achetés (ou sous-traitance)
Push System	Sistema de Asignación	Système d'allocation
Quality Management	Administración de la Calidad	Gestion de la qualité
Quality Management System	Sistema de Administración de la Calidad	Système de gestion de la qualité
Quarterly Reporting Form	Formulario de Informe Trimestral	Fiche de rapport trimestriel
Random Variations	Variaciones al Azar	Variations aléatoires
Rapid Assessment	Evaluación Rápida	Evaluation rapide
Rate	Tasa	Taux
Ratio	Razón	Ratio
Receivables	Cuentas por Cobrar	Créances
Recurrent Costs	Costos Recurrentes	Dépenses de fonctionnement ou Coûts récurrents
Referral System	Sistema de Referencia	Système de référence

Refresher Training	Capacitación de Apoyo	Recyclage
Registration Fees	Tarifas de Ingreso	Droits d'inscription (ou d'admission)
Remuneration	Remuneración	Rémunération
Reporting Channels	Canales para la Rendición de Informes	Voies de communication formelle
Reproductive Health	Salud Reproductiva	Santé réproductive
Reproductive Health Care/Services	Servicios de Salud Reproductiva	Prestations/services de santé réproductive
Requisition and Issue Voucher	Formulario de Pedido y de Despacho	Bon de commande et de sortie
Resource Management	Administración de Recursos	Gestion des ressources
Resources	Recursos	Ressources
Responsibility Accounting	Contabilidad en Base a Responsabilidades	Comptabilité par centres de responsabilité
Responsibility Center	Centro de Responsabilidad	Centre de responsabilité
Results Indicator	Indicador de Resultados	Indicateur de résultats
Revenue and Expense Report	Estado de Ingresos y Egresos	Etat des recettes et des dépenses
Revenue Report	Informe de Ingresos	Etat des recettes
Revenues	Ingresos, Entradas, Recibos	Revenus

Revisit	Visita Subsecuente	Revisite
Safety Stock	Existencias de Seguridad	Stock de sécurité
Satellite Services	Servicios Satélites	Points de services périphériques
Selective Supervision	Supervisión Selectiva	Supervision sélective
Self-Assessment Tool or Checklist	Lista de Verificación para la Autoevaluación	Outil ou Liste aide-mémoire pour l'auto-évaluation
Self-Evaluation Guidelines	Normas de Auto-Evaluación	Directives pour l'auto-évaluation
Self-Sufficiency	Autosuficiencia	Autosuffisance
Service-Based Forecasts	Proyecciones Basadas en el Servicio	Prévisions basées sur les prestations de services
Service Capacity	Capacidad de Servicio	Capacité de service
Service Delivery Approach	Enfoque de la Prestación de Servicios	Approche de prestation de services
Service Fees	Tarifas por Servicios	Paiements des prestations
Service Marketplace	Mercado de Servicios	Zone desservie
Service Quality	Calidad de los Servicios	Qualité des services
Service Stops	Estaciones de Servicios	Postes de travail
Session Plan	Plan de Sesión	Plan des tournées de supervision

Shelf Life	Vida Util	Durée de vie
Short Shipments	Embarques Incompletos	Livraisons incomplètes
Short-Term Methods	Métodos de Corto Plazo	Méthodes à court terme
Site Training	Capacitación en Servicio	Formation sur le site
Situation Analysis	Análisis Situacional	Analyse de situation
Sliding Fee Scale	Escala Variable de Tarifas	Echelle discriminatoire de tarifs
Social Marketing	Mercadeo Social	Marketing social
Split Shipments	Embarques Divididos	Livraisons partielles
Staff Development	Desarrollo del Personal	Perfectionnement du personnel
Staff Motivation	Motivación del Personal	Motivation du personnel
Staff Responsibilities	Responsabilidades del Personal	Responsabilités du personnel
Staff Roles	Funciones del Personal	Rôle du personnel
Stages of Organizational Development	Etapas del Desarrollo de una Organización	Phases de développement d'une organisation
Start-Up Organization	Organización Incipiente (o de Arranque)	Organisation qui démarre
State-of-the-Art	De Punta	Niveau de pointe

Status of Supplies Chart	Tabla para Control de Suministros	Tableau de la situation des stocks
Stock Card	Tarjeta de Estiba	Fiche de stock
Stock on Hand	Existencias Disponibles	Stock disponible
Stock on Order	Existencias en Pedido	Stock en commande
Stockout	Desabastecimiento	Rupture de stocks
Stock Position	Situación de Existencias	Situation des stocks
Strategic Management	Administración Estratégica	Gestion stratégique
Strategic Plan	Plan Estratégico	Plan stratégique
Strategic Planning	Planeación Estratégica	Planification stratégique
Strategic Thinking	Pensamiento Estratégico	Pensée stratégique
Strategy	Estrategia	Stratégie
Subsystem	Subsistema	Sous-système
Supervisor's Visit Plan	Plan de Visita del Supervisor	Plan de visite du superviseur
Supervisory Protocol	Protocolo de Supervisión	Protocole de supervision
Supervisory Schedule	Cronograma de Supervisión	Calendrier de supervision
Supervisory Session	Sesión de Supervisión	Session de supervision

Supervisory Structure	Estructura de Supervisión	Structure de supervision
Supervisory System	Sistema de Supervisión	Système de supervision
Survey of Family Planning Providers	Encuesta a los Proveedores de Servicios de Planificación Familiar	Enquête auprès des prestataires de planification familiale
Sustainability	Sustentabilidad	Viabilité
SWOT Analysis (Strengths, Weaknesses, Opportunities, and Threats)	Análisis FODA (Fortalezas, Oportunidades, Debilidades y Amanazas)	Analyse FFOM (Forces, Faiblesses, Opportunités et Menaces)
Tally Sheet	Hoja de Registro	Feuille de pointage (Liste des informations et données)
Target Group	Grupo Objetivo	Groupe cible
Targets	Metas	Cibles
Task Analysis	Análisis de Tareas	Analyse des tâches
Task Definition	Definición de Tareas	Définition des tâches
Tasks	Tareas	Tâches
Team Approach	Enfoque de Equipo	Approche d'équipe
Team Supervision Process	Proceso de Supervisión en Equipo	Processus de supervision en équipe
Termination Policy	Normas de Despidos	Procédure de rupture de contrat

Third-Party Payments	Sistema de Pagos de Terceros (Co-Pagos)	Paiements par un tiers (ou Co-paiments)
"To Do" Lists	Lista de «Asuntos Pendientes»	Listes des choses «à faire»
Total Visit Cost	Costo Total por Visita	Coût total par visite
Trend Analysis	Análisis de Tendencias	Analyse de tendances
Two-Tier Information System	Sistema Bifurcado de Información	Système d'information à deux niveaux
Underserved Populations	Sectores Desatendidos de la Población o Carentes de Servicios	Populations mal desservies (sous-servies)
Unit Cost (of Contraceptive Products)	Costo Unitario (de los Productos Anticonceptivos)	Coût unitaire (des produits contraceptifs)
Unmet Demand or Unmet Need	Demanda no Cubierta o Necesidad no Cubierta	Demande non satisfaite ou besoin non satisfait
User Continuity Program	Programa para Aumentar la Tasa de Continuidad de Usuarios Activos	Programme pour accroître le nombre d'utilisateurs actifs
Variable Costs or Expenses	Costos o Gastos Variables	Coûts (ou dépenses) variables
Variable Order Interval System	Sistema de Pedidos de Intervalos Variables	Système de commande à intervalles variables
Vehicle Usage Report	Informe por Uso de Vehículos	Carnet de bord

Vertical Services/ Approach	Servicios Verticales o Enfoque Vertical	Approche de services verticaux
Visit-Type	Tipo de Visita	Type de visite
Volunteer Services	Servicios Voluntarios	Services bénévoles (de volontaires)
Waiver System	Sistema de Exoneraciones y Excepciones	Système de dérogation
Waivers	Exoneraciones	Exonérations
Work Plan	Plan de Trabajo	Plan de travail
Work Process	Proceso de Trabajo	Processus de travail
Working Capital	Capital de Trabajo	Fonds de roulement

Bibliography of Family Planning Glossaries

Following is a bibliography of other population and family planning glossaries currently in print and available from organizations working in the field of population. This list was provided in part by the JHPIEGO Corporation and the USAID Reproductive Health Materials Working Group.

Published Glossaries

AVSC International. *AVSC's Glossary of Terminology*. AVSC International, New York, NY, 1995. Published in English.

Edmans, E. et al. *Glossary of Family Planning Terms*. INTRAH, School of Medicine, University of North Carolina, Chapel Hill, NC, 1987. Published in English and French.

Haupt, A. and T. T. Kane. *Population Handbook: International Edition*. The Population Reference Bureau, International Programs, Washington, DC, 1991. Published in English, French, Spanish, and Arabic.

Newman, C. and J. Birkmayer. *Glossary of Training Evaluation Terms*. INTRAH, School of Medicine, University of North Carolina, Chapel Hill, NC, 1992. Published in English and French.

Population Resource Center. *Population Glossary*. Population Resource Center, Washington, DC, 1994. Available in English.

Rodriguez-Garcia, R. et al. *Glossary of Natural Family Planning Terms*. Institute for Reproductive Health, Georgetown University, Washington, DC, 1988. Published in English, French, Spanish, and Portuguese.

Vandewalle, E. *Multilingual Demographic Dictionary*. Ordina Editions, Liège, Belgium, 1982. Published in English, French, and Spanish.

Veney, J. and P. Gorbach. *Definitions for Program Evaluation Terms*. The EVALUATION Project, Carolina Population Center, University of North Carolina, Chapel Hill, NC, 1993. Published in English.

Wolff, J. and J. Miller, eds. "Building a Common Vocabulary: A Glossary of Terms" *The Family Planning Manager*. Family Planning Management Development, Management Sciences for Health, Boston, MA. Vol. IV, No. 3, 1995. Published in English, French, and Spanish.

Glossaries Within Publications

Angle, M. and C. Murphy. *Guidelines for Clinical Procedures in Family Planning: A Reference for Trainers*. INTRAH, University of North Carolina, Chapel Hill, NC, 1993. Published in English and French.

Garcia-Nunez, J. *Improving Family Planning Evaluation*. Kumarian Press, West Hartford, CT, 1992. Published in English.

Hatcher, R. et al. *Contraceptive Technology*. Irvington Publishers, North Stratford, NH, 1994. Published in English.

Johns Hopkins University, Center for Communication Programs. *Service Providers Guide to Family Planning*. Johns Hopkins University, Center for Communication Programs, Population Communications Services, Baltimore, MD, 1990. Published in English.

Kent, M. *World Population: Fundamentals of Growth*. Population Reference Bureau, Washington, DC, 1995. Published in English.

Wolff, J., L. Suttenfield, and S. Binzen, eds. *The Family Planning Manager's Handbook: Basic Skills and Tools for Managing Family Planning Programs*. Kumarian Press, West Hartford, CT, 1991. Published in English, French, and Spanish. Available from Kumarian Press in West Hartford, CT, and Management Sciences for Health in Boston, MA.

Introducción

El proyecto Family Planning Management Development (FPMD) trabaja en conjuncto con los administradores de programas de planificación familiar y de salud a nivel público y privado de los países en desarrollo con el fin de mejorar su capacidad gerencial y contribuir a la sustentabilidad y efectividad de sus programas.

En 1991, el proyecto publicó el *Manual del Administrador de Planificación Familiar*, el primer manual escrito específicamente para los Administradores de programas de planificación familiar. A partir de 1992 el proyecto comenzó a publicar una revista bimensual de educación gerencial continua titulada *Actualidad Gerencial en Planificación Familiar*, que trata sobre estrategias gerenciales específicas para mejorar los servicios de salud y planificación familiar. Dichas publicaciones fueron traducidas posteriormente al español y al francés. En el transcurso de los últimos años, muchos administradores han efectuado comentarios favorables con respecto a la utilidad del glosario que contenía el *Manual*, y más recientemente con respecto a un glosario publicado en una edición de *Actualidad Gerencial*. El presente *Glosario de Bolsillo* combina los glosarios de estas dos publicaciones en un solo libro y relaciona cada término con los términos equivalentes en español y francés.

A medida que un número cada vez mayor de administradores participan en esta colaboración de sud a sud y que los nuevos programas se desarrollan en base a aquellos que han logrado el éxito deseado tanto dentro de los países como entre éstos, el conocimiento de las prácticas gerenciales básicas y el uso de un vocabulario común se torna cada vez más importante. El propósito del presente glosario es mejorar la comprensión de los términos y prácticas gerenciales utilizados en los programas de planificación familiar y promover un vocabulario de trabajo común para todos los administradores a nivel mundial.

Cada sección del *Glosario de Bolsillo* está organizada de la misma manera, comenzando con el glosario completo de términos y definiciones, listados alfabéticamente en el idioma correspondiente e incluyendo los equivalentes apropiados para cada término en los otros dos idiomas. Después del glosario de términos se incluye sólo una lista de todos los términos y sus equivalentes en los otros idiomas y finalmente una bibliografía de los glosarios de planificación familiar.

Español

Esperamos que este *Glosario de Bolsillo* sea de utilidad para los diferentes tipos de administradores que trabajan en programas de salud y planificación familiar a nivel mundial y que les sea de utilidad para mejorar el nivel de comprensión y el empleo de prácticas gerenciales sólidas que, a la postre, contribuirán el éxito de sus programas en a la prestación de servicios de salud reproductiva de alta calidad.

Glosario de Términos

«**A** bandono» (también conocido como Desertor): La persona que utilizaba un método anticonceptivo pero que, debido a diversas razones, no lo utiliza actualmente ni ningún otro método anticonceptivo. La persona que es considerada un «abandono» por una clínica o programa es aquella que ya no acude a dicha clínica en busca de servicios. A pesar de que esto podría implicar que la persona ya no está utilizando la anticoncepción, en algunos casos el cliente podría estar recibiendo servicios en otro centro. A fin de hacer un seguimiento del número de personas que abandonan, es importante que cada programa defina (para cada tipo de usuario de un método en particular) cuánto tiempo se puede ausentar el cliente de la clínica después de una cita programada (o después de la fecha fijada para su reabastecimiento de anticonceptivos) antes de ser considerada en «abandono». *Por ejemplo, una usuaria de la píldora podría considerarse en «abandono» si han pasado tres meses de la fecha en que debía recoger sus nuevos ciclos de píldoras. Sin embargo una usuaria de DIU no se puede considerar un «abandono» aún si no acude a la clínica durante todo un año, a no ser que hubiese tenido una cita o se la hubiese llamado para que acuda a una visita de control.* **Discontinuer; Discontinuateur**

Aceptante Nuevo (también conocido como Usuario Nuevo): Persona que acepta por primera vez usar un método anticonceptivo. Los programas cuentan con definiciones diferentes de los aceptantes/usuarios nuevos. Algunos incluyen solamente a aquellas personas que están usando un método anticonceptivo por primera vez, que no hayan utilizado nunca antes ningún método anticonceptivo. Otros incluyen también a las personas que utilizan un método anticonceptivo en particular por primera vez (aunque ya hubiesen anteriormente usado un método anticonceptivo diferente). Otros podrían incluir además a aquellas personas que aceptan por primera vez un método de (un agente de) ese programa en particular (aunque ya hubiesen usado anteriormente un método anticonceptivo ofrecido por un programa diferente). Cualquiera que sea la definición que utiliza el programa, es de importancia crítica que las definiciones sean claras y que todo el personal las entienda, para que los datos sobre servicios en todos los centros sean recopilados y reportados de la misma manera. *New Acceptor; Nouvel accepteur*

Aceptante Potencial: Ver **Usuario Potencial.**

Actividades: Acciones que realiza el personal del programa para alcanzar las metas del mismo. *Activities; Activités*

Español

Activo: Cualquier objeto de valor que ayude a la organización a proporcionar un servicio a sus clientes, por ejemplo: efectivo, terrenos, edificios, equipo, inventarios (para suministros, como resultado de una operación de venta), mobiliario y cuentas por cobrar. *Asset; Actifs*

Activo Circulante (Activos a Corto Plazo): Activo que se usa comúnmente dentro de un mismo año, tal como la disponibilidad de dinero y suministros de oficina y médicos. *Current or Short-Term Assets; Actifs courants ou à courte terme*

Activos Fijos o Bien Duraderos: Bienes tangibles que tienen una vida útil de más de un año, tales como terrenos, edificios, mobiliario y equipo pesado. *Fixed or Long-Term Assets; Immobilisations*

Adiestramiento en Fases: Adiestramiento que se realiza por etapas, alternando con períodos de experiencias en el trabajo. *Phased Training; Formation par étapes*

Administración de la Calidad: Corresponde al control de los productos o servicios para asegurar que los proveedores cumplan con las normas aceptadas para lograr los resultados deseados y, si se observan problemas, adoptar las acciones necesarias para mejorar los productos o servicios. *Quality Management; Gestion de la qualité*

Administración de la Clínica: Todos los aspectos relativos a la administración efectiva de una clínica, incluyendo las actividades de planeación, la organización del espacio y del proceso de trabajo en la clínica para prestar servicios a los clientes, el manejo de recursos financieros y programáticos (incluyendo los suministros de la clínica y los anticonceptivos), el manejo de información, el monitoreo del progreso logrado hacia los objetivos y la supervisión del personal clínico y no clínico. *Clinic Management; Gestion de la formation sanitaire*

Administración de Recursos: Trabajo relativo al manejo y control de los recursos necesarios para operar un programa, tales como personas, dinero y equipo. (Algunas personas consideran también que el tiempo es un recurso.) *Resource Management; Gestion des ressources*

Administración de Suministros Anticonceptivos (también conocido como Administración Logística): La administración de todos los aspectos del ciclo de abastecimiento: selección de productos, proyección, adquisición, almacenamiento y manejo de inventario, distribución y uso, para que un producto anticonceptivo que no ha expirado aún, sea puesto a disposición de los clientes en cantidades suficientes, cuando lo necesiten. *Contraceptive Supply Management; Gestion des stocks de contraceptifs*

Administración del Personal: Responsabilidades relacionadas con la contratación y despido del personal, la supervisión, promoción, organización, motivación y desarrollo de las habilidades profesionales del mismo. La administración del personal requiere de habilidades de comunicación interpersonal muy sólidas y de la capacidad para facilitar el trabajo en equipo y resolver conflictos y problemas. *Personnel Management; Gestion du personnel*

Administración Estratégica: Forma de dirigir un programa mediante la identificación de los servicios específicos que la organización está en mejores condiciones de prestar y los grupos poblacionales a los que puede ofrecer dichos servicios en forma más efectiva, en base a una evaluación realista de los recursos disponibles para llevar a cabo el trabajo. La administración estratégica requiere que los administradores piensen en forma estratégica, formulen preguntas tales como «¿Está el programa haciendo las cosas correctas?» y consideren y anticipen las tendencias del medio externo que afectarán el logro de las metas de la organización. *Strategic Management; Gestion stratégique*

Administración Financiera: Proceso para la ejecución y manejo de los sistemas de control financiero, la recopilación de datos financieros, el análisis de informes financieros y la toma de decisiones financieras consistentes en base a dichos análisis. La administración financiera requiere de conocimientos sobre el examen e interpretación de tres documentos clave: la planilla de proyección del flujo de fondos, el balance general y el estado de pérdidas y ganancias. *Financial Management; Gestion financière*

Administración General: Actividades, o en el caso de un presupuesto, los gastos asociados al desarrollo normal de los negocios, tales como correo, portes, fotocopias, teléfono, servicios de agua potable y electricidad, gastos bancarios, registro de vehículos y otros costos administrativos usuales (se excluyen los costos del personal). *General Administration; Administration générale*

Administración Logística: Ver **Administración de Suministros Anticonceptivos**.

Análisis de Costos: Estudio de los costos (personal, productos, equipo, etc.) asociados a la ejecución de un proyecto, programa, servicio u otras actividades. *Cost Analysis; Analyse des coûts*

Análisis de Datos: El proceso de examinar datos y determinar patrones o tendencias. Este procedimiento da nueva información a los administradores sobre sus programas y servicios y les ayuda a tomar mejores decisiones a nivel administrativo. *Data Analysis; Analyse des données*

Análisis de Pareto: Basado en el principio planteado por el economista italiano Vilfredo Pareto, que establece que solamente un número limitado de factores es responsable de la mayor parte de los resultados (sean estos negativos o positivos), un Análisis de Pareto ayuda a identificar el mínimo número de «factores vitales» que deben mejorarse para lograr los resultados deseados. Al efectuar este análisis, los administradores pueden concentrar sus esfuerzos en un número reducido de actividades y de esta manera utilizar sus escasos recursos en forma eficiente y efectiva para lograr los resultados esperados. (Las instrucciones para realizar un Análisis de Pareto se encuentran en el Volumen II, Número 1 de *Actualidad Gerencial*, «La Utilización del PMC para Reforzar la Planificación Familiar» y su suplemento, *Instrumentos Gerenciales para el PMC*.) *Pareto Analysis; Analyse de Pareto*

Análisis de Tareas: Examen de todas las obligaciones y actividades que lleva a cabo un empleado en particular con el propósito de determinar las habilidades requeridas, las actitudes, los recursos y los riesgos que implica cada tarea. *Task Analysis; Analyse des tâches*

Análisis de Tendencias: Representación de datos para mostrar un patrón creciente, decreciente o estable a través de un período. Un análisis de tendencias se realiza frecuentemente con una gráfica lineal utilizando un conjunto de datos. *Trend Analysis; Analyse de tendances*

Análisis del Flujo de Clientes (también conocido como Análisis del Flujo de Pacientes): Proceso para determinar la eficiencia de la prestación de servicios en un centro de salud. Se basa en las observaciones del movimiento de clientes en el centro de salud y se realiza en el seguimiento del tiempo que espera un cliente antes de ser atendido por una persona y el tiempo que tarda con cada una de dichas personas en la clínica. *Client Flow Analysis; Analyse du flux des clients*

Análisis del Mercado: Examen del medio en el cual una organización o programa presta o vende bienes y servicios. Un análisis de mercado generalmente incluye una encuesta de los clientes actuales (sus necesidades, el grado de satisfacción con los servicios obtenidos, la situación socioeconómica, etc.), una encuesta de la comunidad (a fin de conocer mejor a los clientes potenciales y la demanda actual de servicios) y una encuesta de otros proveedores de servicios de planificación familiar del área (los tipos de servicios que prestan, el costo y la calidad de los mismos, etc.) Este estudio da a la organización o programa información crítica sobre las poblaciones desatendidas o carentes de servicios, la capacidad de pago de los clientes o el valor que pueden pagar por los servicios y otra información sobre el papel que debería desempeñar el programa frente a otras agencias de servicios para mantenerse competitivo. La habilidad para encarar estos factores sirve para fortalecer el autofinanciamiento del programa. *Market Analysis; Analyse du marché*

Análisis del Proceso: Tipo de análisis en el cuál se estudia uno o varios procesos o una secuencia de actividades. Algunos ejemplos de análisis de procesos son: el diagrama de flujo, el análisis del árbol de decisiones y el análisis del flujo de clientes. *Process Analysis; Analyse de processus*

Análisis FODA (Fortalezas, Oportunidades, Debilidades y Amenazas): El proceso de analizar los puntos fuertes y débiles de una organización así como las oportunidades y amenazas existentes fuera de la organización o programa. *SWOT Analysis; Analyse FFOM*

Análisis Situacional: Proceso sistemático para analizar tanto el medio interno y la capacidad de una organización, como el contexto externo, político, social, económico y programático dentro del cuál se cumple un programa. Dicho análisis se realiza con el propósito de comparar una situación actual contra una situación ideal para determinar un curso de acción para mejorar la administración del programa, el rendimiento y la sustentabilidad del mismo. *Situation Analysis; Analyse de situation*

Años Protección Pareja (APP): Indicador que representa el número total de años de protección anticonceptiva que produce un método. El APP para cada método se calcula dividiendo el número de unidades distribuidas entre el factor que representa las unidades necesarias (de dicho método) para proteger de un embarazo a una pareja durante un año. *Couple-Years of Protection (CYP); Couple-années de protection (CAP)*

Aprendizaje de Experiencias: Método de enseñanza que utiliza la participación activa y el uso aplicado de nuevas técnicas mediante la simulación y la experiencia en el trabajo, como complemento de la charla o clase. *Experiential Learning; Aprentissage par l'expérience*

Arbol de Decisiones: Serie de preguntas que se utiliza como herramienta para analizar si la capacitación es necesaria para resolver un problema de desempeño. *Decision Tree; Arbre de décisions*

Asignación de Costos: En un sistema de contabilidad, es la asignación de costos a los diferentes programas, centros de operación, o tipos de servicios. *Por ejemplo, el sistema contable podría asignar 50 por ciento del salario del Coordinador de Capacitación a Gastos Generales y 10 por ciento a cada uno de los cinco diferentes programas. Allocation of Costs; Répartition des coûts*

Auditoría Externa: Actividad llevada a cabo por una persona o grupo independiente a fin de verificar la exactitud de los estados financieros de una organización. *External Audit; Audit externe*

Auditoría Financiera: Revisión periódica formal de las cuentas y registros financieros de una organización o programa, generalmente hecha con el objeto de verificar si los fondos fueron utilizados para los propósitos planteados y de acuerdo con las prácticas estándar de administración financiera. *Financial Audit; Audit financier*

Auditoría Interna: Actividad llevada a cabo por los empleados a fin de verificar los controles internos y el sistema contable de una organización. *Internal Audit; Audit interne*

Autofinanciamiento: Habilidad que tiene un programa para generar ingresos mediante mecanismos locales de financiamiento, cuando disminuye su dependencia de los fondos de donantes externos. (Ver también **Autosuficiencia** y **Sustentabilidad**.)

Autosuficiencia: Nivel de desarrollo de una organización que se alcanza cuando la organización puede funcionar en forma independientemente sin asistencia externa (donantes). Las organizaciones autosuficientes son capaces de movilizar una amplia gama de recursos que evitan la dependencia de un solo recurso financiero y poseen la capacidad administrativa y de liderazgo para adaptar sus programas a un medio cambiante. (Ver también **Autofinanciamiento** y **Sustentabilidad**.) *Self-Sufficiency; Autosuffisance*

B alance de Fondos o Reserva (también conocido como **Capital Contable** o **Patrimonio**): En una organización sin fines de lucro, el saldo de fondos constituye el valor neto de dicha organización, que se calcula restando el valor de los gastos del total de los ingresos. *Fund Balance; Bilan des fonds (ou Réserves)*

Balance General: Informe financiero que resume el valor de los activos, pasivos y reservas de las organizaciones en un determinado momento. *Balance Sheet; Bilan*

Barreras a los Servicios: Leyes o políticas nacionales o gubernamentales, prácticas o procedimientos profesionales, requisitos administrativos u otros reglamentos oficiales y no oficiales que impiden que la gente reciba los servicios por factores debidos a su edad, género, estado civil, paridad, situación financiera, lugar de residencia, etc. *Barriers to Services; Obstacles aux services*

Bodega (almacén) Central: Unidad de almacenamiento que maneja y guarda todos los suministros y material anticonceptivo recibidos de fuera del país, o de compras locales de gran volumen. *Central Warehouse; Magasin central*

Bodega (almacén) Intermedia: Depósito de productos localizado en una región específica de un país. Distribuye recursos sólo para esa área. *Intermediate Warehouse; Magasin intermédiaire*

C **aja Chica:** Tipo de fondo fijo, donde una cantidad pequeña de efectivo esta apartado para gastos inmediatos y cuya reposición se lleva a cabo en forma periódica, conforme se vaya utilizando. *Petty Cash; Petite caisse*

Calidad de los Servicios: La calidad se refiere a un número de factores interrelacionados que incluyen cómo las personas que prestan los servicios tratan a los clientes, el alcance de los servicios y de los métodos anticonceptivos disponibles para los clientes, la calidad de información ofrecida y la calidad de la consejería, la promoción de la selección del método en forma individual, la competencia técnica de quienes ofrecen los servicios y la accesibilidad y continuidad de los servicios. *Service Quality; Qualité des services*

Canales para la Rendición de Informes: Sistema establecido en una estructura de supervisión para reportar información y datos. Los canales apropiados para la rendición de informes son críticos, particularmente cuando la prestación de los diferentes tipos de servicios se torna más integrada y/o la gerencia se hace más descentralizada. *Reporting Channels; Voies de communication formelle*

Cantidad Máxima: El número máximo de existencias (de cada producto anticonceptivo) que un centro debería tener en su inventario. Dicha cantidad debe ser lo suficientemente alta para mantener un nivel de productos adecuado entre pedidos y lo suficientemente baja para prevenir niveles de productos demasiado altos y evitar el desperdicio por expiración de los mismos. La cantidad máxima se calcula en forma separada para cada artículo y toma en cuenta la cantidad mínima de existencias más una cantidad que se utiliza en el intervalo entre pedidos regulares. (Puede verse la fórmula para el cálculo de los niveles de existencias mínimo y máximo en las páginas 10 y 11 del Volumen I, Número 4 de *Actualidad Gerencial*, «Cómo Mejorar la Administración de los Suministros de Anticonceptivos».) *Maximum Quantity; Quantité maximum*

Cantidad Mínima: Es la menor cantidad de existencias (de cada anticonceptivo) que un centro debería tener siempre en el inventario. Esta cantidad mínima debe ser lo suficientemente alta para evitar que se agote el inventario, aún cuando los embarques se atrasen o la demanda aumente inesperadamente. La cantidad mínima está dada por las existencias de seguridad más la cantidad de productos utilizada entre la colocación de un pedido y el recibo del mismo. (La fórmula para calcular los niveles de existencias mínimo y máximo se encuentran en las páginas 10 y 11 del Volumen I, Número 4 de *Actualidad Gerencial*, «Cómo Mejorar la Administración de los Suministros de Anticonceptivos».) *Minimum Quantity; Quantité minimum*

Cantidad para Cubrir el Tiempo de Espera: La cantidad de anticonceptivos distribuidos en el lapso transcurrido entre la colocación de un pedido y la recepción de las nuevas existencias, según registros previos. *Lead Time Quantity; Quantité couvrant le délai de livraison*

Capacidad del Servicio: El volumen máximo de servicios que se puede prestar con un conjunto dado de recursos. *Por ejemplo, el número máximo de vasectomías que un médico puede realizar en un día de trabajo. Service Capacity; Capacité de service*

Capacitación de Apoyo: Actualización periódica que se da al personal con el propósito de fortalecer las habilidades o introducir nuevos conceptos o técnicas en su área de competencia. *Refresher Training; Recyclage*

Capacitación en Servicio: Enfoque integrado de la capacitación que considera al centro de prestación de servicios como un sistema y considera al personal como integrante del equipo que hace que el sistema funcione. El mejoramiento de los sistemas en el lugar de trabajo a través del trabajo de equipo efectivo y la certeza que todos los miembros del equipo posean los conocimientos y habilidades que necesitan para cumplir con sus funciones dentro del equipo es la meta de la capacitación en servicio. *Site Training; Formation sur le site*

Capacitación Formal: Curso de instrucción que tiene objetivos específicos de aprendizaje y que se realiza fuera del trabajo regular. *Formal Training; Formation formelle*

Capacitación Funcional (basada en la competencia): Capacitación que se dedica exclusivamente a enseñar las habilidades, conocimientos y actitudes que se relacionan con trabajos específicos. El contenido de esta capacitación muchas veces se define con la colaboración de los mismos participantes. *Competency-Based Training; Formation basée sur les compétences*

Capacitación Informal: Capacitación que ocurre dentro del trabajo y se lleva a cabo generalmente mediante instrucciones o guía personal del supervisor u otro empleado, o mediante la observación del trabajo que realizan otros trabajadores. *Informal Training; Formation informelle*

Capacitación Interfuncional: La capacitación del personal para realizar las funciones de otros miembros del personal, para que cuando algunos de los integrantes del personal se encuentren demasiado ocupados o enfermos, los demás puedan desempeñar tales funciones. *Cross-Training; Formation polyvalente*

Capital Contable o Patrimonio (también conocido como Balance de Fondos o Reserva): «Valor neto» de una organización que se obtiene restando el total de los pasivos del total de los activos. *Equity; Capitaux propres*

Capital de Trabajo: La cantidad de fondos de corto plazo disponibles para las operaciones, equivalente al excedente de los activos a corto plazo y los pasivos exigibles a corto plazo. *Working Capital; Fonds de roulement*

Características del Cliente: Información sobre las características y necesidades del cliente que se utiliza para analizar la clientela de un programa para darle atención de alta calidad basada en las necesidades de la misma. Las características de los clientes incluyen: edad, estado civil, número de embarazos, presencia de enfermedades de transmisión sexual (ETS), nivel educativo, preferencia por el espaciamiento de los nacimientos o por la suspensión definitiva de la fecundidad, etc. *Client Characteristics; Caractéristiques des clients*

Catálogo de Cuentas: Documento dentro de un sistema de contabilidad que enumera los programas, los centros operativos y las categorías en las cuales los ingresos y egresos serán registrados, asignando un número para cada rubro o línea. *Chart of Accounts; Tableau des comptes*

Categoría de Personal: Los diferentes tipos de personal. En un programa de planificación familiar las categorías de personal incluyen médicos, enfermeras, farmacéuticos, ayudantes de farmacia, asesores, extensionistas, recepcionistas, etc. Las categorías de personal se definen frecuentemente para establecer niveles salariales constantes que son útiles para determinar el costo del personal asociado a los diferentes tipos de servicios. *Personnel Category; Catégorie de personnel*

Centro de Responsabilidad (también conocido como Centro de Costo): Un área funcional de responsabilidad de un administrador específico, tal como un laboratorio. *Responsibility Center; Centre de responsabilité*

Centro Operativo: Una división lógica de las operaciones de un programa, tal como un departamento, una clínica o un programa regional de Servicios Comunitarios. Muchas organizaciones encuentran de gran utilidad el producir información financiera por centro operativo. *Operating Center; Centre d'opérations*

Cliente Nuevo (también conocido como Primera Visita o Primera Consulta de un Cliente): Persona que recibe servicios por primera vez de (un agente de) un programa de planificación familiar y que no ha recibido servicios de ese programa con anterioridad. Los programas cuentan con definiciones diferentes de los clientes nuevos. Algunos incluyen a las personas que reciben cualquier tipo de servicio (incluso consejería) y que no han recibido servicios de ese programa con anterioridad. Otros incluyen solamente a las personas que aceptan por primera vez un método de planificación familiar y que nunca han usado un método anticonceptivo de ningún otro programa. Otros programas distinguen entre los clientes nuevos (de un programa) y los aceptantes/usuarios nuevos (de un método). Cualquiera que sea la definición que utiliza el programa, es de importancia crítica que las definiciones sean claras y que todo el personal las entienda, para que los datos sobre servicios en todos los centros sean obtenidos y reportados de la misma manera. *New Client; Nouveau client*

Cliente Potencial: Cualquier persona en edad reproductiva que sea sexualmente activa, que no esté utilizando actualmente los servicios de una clínica o programa comunitario de planificación familiar y que no tenga la intención de engendrar hijos por el momento. Son clientes potenciales también las parejas que tienen problemas de infertilidad, pero que desean tener familia. Los programas deberían tratar de atraer a dichas personas y prestarles los servicios apropiados. *Potential Client; Client potentiel*

Cliente que No Asiste: Cliente que no asiste a una cita programada o que no regresa a la clínica para recibir otros servicios durante un período largo de tiempo. *No-Show Client; Cliente non-assidu*

Códigos de Identificación: Serie de números o letras utilizadas en un sistema de información gerencial para ayudar a diferenciar la localización específica de los servicios (o el tipo de clínica), los tipos de visitas (primeras visitas, visitas subsecuentes, visitas de procedimiento), los tipos de servicios o anticonceptivos ofrecidos (IEC, inserción de DIU, reabastecimiento de píldoras) y otras categorías de datos. Para que sean de utilidad, todas las personas que utilizan el sistema de información gerencial deben utilizar los mismos códigos de identificación en forma consistente. *Identification Codes; Codes d'identification*

Colaboración entre Programas para la Reducción de Costos: Sistema en el cual se reducen los costos operativos mediante la coordinación entre organizaciones en actividades como compras conjuntas al por mayor, uso compartido de clínicas, bodegas, vehículos, etc. *Cost-Sharing; Partage des coûts*

Combinación: Agrupación de esfuerzos, experiencia, equipo, etc. a utilizarse para un fin común. Esto ayuda a ahorrar los escasos recursos y reduce la posibilidad de duplicar servicios o causar interrupciones en los mismos. *Pooling; Regroupement*

Comité del Personal: Generalmente un sub-comité de un grupo más grande tal como una junta directiva, que trata asuntos relativos al personal, sus preocupaciones y tendencias y asesora en general a los empleados, a la junta directiva o a la organización sobre los cambios necesarios que deben efectuarse. *Personnel Committee; Comité du personnel*

Componentes Administrativos: Elementos básicos utilizados para analizar la forma cómo una organización funciona. Los cuatro componentes básicos de la administración son: la misión, la estrategia, la estructura y los sistemas. (Ver también **Declaración de Misión, Estrategia, Estructura Organizaciónal** y **Funciones/Sistemas Administrativos**.) *Management Components; Composantes de gestion*

Componentes del Programa: Unidades funcionales de una organización que suministran servicios destinados a lograr los objetivos, tales como el plan de Servicios Comunitarios, plan de las clínicas y plan de IEC. *Program Components; Volets du programme*

Comprobantes: Registros que documentan los movimientos de recursos (humanos, financieros, materiales) que permiten identificar a qué cuentas deben asignarse y poder rastrear tales movimientos. *Paper Trail; Trace écrite*

Conciliación Bancaria: Ajuste al saldo de la cuenta bancaria para reflejar los depósitos y los cheques que han sido girados, pero aún no cobrados. *Bank Reconciliation; Reconciliation (ou rapprochemente bancaire)*

Conocimiento Interno («Inreach»): En planificación familiar, esto se refiere a la utilización de los recursos de un centro de salud para mejorar los conocimientos y familiarizarse con los servicios de planificación familiar que ofrece dicho centro (en comparación con **Extensión** o «Outreach»). El concepto incluye las oportunidades perdidas para dar información sobre los servicios de planificación familiar al personal, a los clientes y a los clientes potenciales en todos los departamentos del centro de salud. Las actividades están orientadas al mejoramiento de los vínculos y las referencias entre los diferentes departamentos, la colocación de noticias informando sobre los servicios ofrecidos y la orientación del personal de otros departamentos sobre los servicios de planificación familiar. *Inreach; Diffusion interne*

Consumo Mensual Promedio (CMP): Número promedio de unidades de un tipo o marca específico de un anticonceptivo que se distribuye en el lapso de un mes. El promedio se basa generalmente en las cantidades que han sido distribuidas durante un período de seis meses. *Average Monthly Consumption (AMC); Consommation mensuelle moyenne (CMM)*

Contabilidad Administrativa: Recopilación de información del sistema de contabilidad financiera y otros datos financieros (como presupuestos) y la combinación de dicha información con los datos estadísticos (como los resultados de los servicios) para producir información que sea de utilidad para la toma de decisiones de tipo administrativo. *Management Accounting; Comptabilité de gestion*

Contabilidad de Caja: Sistema contable o presupuestal que solamente registra los ingresos cuando se reciben y los gastos cuando se efectúan (opuesto a **Contabilidad sobre Bases Devengadas**). *Cash Accounting; Comptabilité de caisse*

Contabilidad de Costos: Proceso contable que distribuye costos a centros de responsabilidad determinados, tales como programas o departamentos de servicios. *Cost Accounting; Comptabilité analytique*

Contabilidad de Fondos: Sistema de contabilidad que clasifica y registra los egresos e ingresos dentro diferentes cuentas de los donantes. *Fund Accounting; Comptabilité par fonds*

Contabilidad en Base a Responsabilidades: Registro y reportaje de información en base a centros de responsabilidad predeterminados. *Responsibility Accounting; Comptabilité par centres de responsabilité*

Contabilidad sobre Bases Devengadas: Sistema de contabilidad acumulada que registra los ingresos cuando se producen, los egresos cuando se generan y la depreciación del activo fijo, tal como edificios o equipo pesado (contrario a la **Contabilidad de Caja**). *Accrual Accounting; Comptabilité d'exercice*

Contexto Externo: Condiciones prevalentes en el país o región que afectan el desarrollo y ejecución del programa de planificación familiar, tales como los aspectos demográficos, culturales, políticos, económicos, de salud, las características del mercado y las fuentes de financiamiento y de bienes de consumo. *External Environment; Environnement externe*

Contexto Interno: El liderazgo, las políticas, sistemas, tecnología, capacidad financiera, etc. que influyen sobre la efectividad de una organización o programa. Otros factores del contexto interno son: la estructura administrativa, los sistemas administrativos, la capacidad del personal, etc. *Internal Environment; Environnement interne*

Contribuciones en Especie: Aportes no financieros o formas de compensación, tales como materiales, bienes o servicios. *In-Kind Contribution; Contribution en nature*

Coordinación: La colaboración de los diferentes individuos, departamentos y organizaciones para lograr una meta común. *Coordination; Coordination*

Coordinación Externa: Proceso de identificar los objetivos comunes y las funciones de diferentes organizaciones, y de colaborar entre éstas para desarrollar actividades y así alcanzar tales objetivos. Frecuentemente la distribución de estas actividades y responsabilidades entre las organizaciones, se determina de acuerdo con las fortalezas específicas de cada una de ellas. *External Coordination; Coordination externe*

Coordinación Interna: Organización lógica de la comunicación en una organización y a su vez, la comunicación de actividades dentro de la misma, para que todo el personal conozca los roles y responsabilidades de cada departamento, así como la interacción entre ellos. *Internal Coordination; Coordination interne*

«COPE» (en español Dirigido al Cliente, Eficiente para el Proveedor): Técnica de tecnología sencilla para mejorar los servicios ofrecidos a los clientes. La «COPE» permite que los equipos locales de personas que prestan servicios evalúen su propio trabajo con el fin de identificar y encontrar soluciones a los problemas que se presentan en sus centros. *COPE (Client-Oriented, Provider Efficient); COPE (Client orienté, prestation efficace)*

Costo de Mantenimiento: Este término generalmente se refiere al costo de mantenimiento de un centro y puede incluir las reparaciones, la limpieza, el alquiler, los impuestos, los seguros, etc. *Maintenance Cost; Coût d'entretien*

Costo del Anticonceptivo: El costo del anticonceptivo es uno de los componentes del costo de los servicios cuando éstos se determinan en un programa. Cuando se reciben anticonceptivos en donación, debe estimarse su costo y el que tienen los gastos de transporte internacional, local, almacenaje, aduana e impuestos. *Contraceptive Product Cost; Coûts des produits contraceptifs*

Costo del Personal (o Costo Total del Personal): El presupuesto para pagos al personal (incluyendo primas) por el tiempo empleado en la prestación de un servicio específico, una combinación de varios servicios o un conjunto de servicios durante un período específico. *Personnel Cost (or Total Personnel Cost); Coûts du personnel (ou Coûts totaux du personnel)*

Costo del Personal por Tipo de Visita: El costo de un tipo de visita, como una visita para la inserción de un DIU, que toma en cuenta solamente el costo del personal incluido en la prestación de dicho servicio. *Personnel Cost Per Visit-Type; Coût du personnel par type de visite*

Costo-Efectividad: Método para medir la eficiencia relativa de un programa mediante la comparación del costo con el impacto, utilizando un indicador como la tasa de prevalencia [de uso de] anticonceptivos. Uno de los propósitos de un estudio costo-efectividad consiste en identificar las estrategias del programa y las modalidades operativas para lograr el mayor impacto con el menor costo. *Cost-Effectiveness; Coût-efficacité*

Costo por Año de Uso (también conocido como Costo por Año de Protección Pareja): Costo promedio de proveer un anticonceptivo a un cliente durante un año. Se calcula utilizando el costo total por visita (personal y suministros), el número de visitas subsecuentes por año y el tiempo promedio de uso de dicho anticonceptivo. El costo por año de uso es una medida de resultados—esto es el costo total de la protección de una pareja en un año (APP). *Cost Per Year of Use; Coût par année d'utilisation*

Costo Total por Visita: Costo de los servicios para diferentes tipos de visitas (por ejemplo la primera visita para la píldora, una consulta para la inserción de un DIU, una sesión de consejería), que incluye los costos directos del personal, el de los anticonceptivos y una proporción de los gastos o costos generales. El cálculo se utiliza para comparar el costo-efectividad, la eficiencia de los servicios y para fijar tarifas. *Total Visit Cost; Coût total par visite*

Costo Unitario (de los Productos Anticonceptivos): Costo por unidad de un anticonceptivo, como un ciclo de píldoras, un par de guantes quirúrgicos, un kit de Norplant®, un condón, etc. que incluye costos de transporte, aduana, impuestos y otros. *Unit Cost (of Contraceptive Products); Coût unitaire (des produits contraceptifs)*

Costos de Inversión (Gastos de Capital): Gastos que se generan por la adquisición, construcción y renovación de los activos fijos tales como terrenos, edificios y equipo pesado (contrario a **Costos de Operación**). *Capital Costs; Coûts d'investissement*

Costos de Operación (también conocidos como Costos Recurrentes): Gastos regulares para financiar los programas y la prestación de servicios año a año (contrario a **Costos de Inversión**). *Operating Costs; Coûts d'exploitation*

Costos Directos: Costos que están directamente asociados, o son atribuibles, a una actividad o departamento específico (tales como las tarifas de capacitación o las matrículas de inscripción para un programa de capacitación, seminario o conferencia; los costos de los anticonceptivos; los sueldos y salarios del personal; los costos de los servicios adquiridos, etc.) Dichos costos presupuestados deberían ser claramente identificables en un plan de actividades. *Direct Costs; Coûts directs*

Costos Indirectos (también conocidos como Costos Generales): Son los costos operativos de una organización que son compartidos por más de una actividad o departamento (por ejemplo, los costos de mantenimiento de un edificio y los de agua potable y electricidad). *Indirect Costs; Coûts indirects*

Costos o Gastos Fijos: Gastos que no varían de acuerdo a la cantidad de personas a las cuales se da servicio, o el número de servicios proporcionados, tales como gastos de la oficina matriz, seguros, rentas o interés de una hipoteca. *Fixed Costs or Expenses; Côuts (ou frais) fixes*

Costos o Gastos Variables: Gastos que varían de acuerdo con el nivel de servicio proporcionado o del número de personas atendidas. Los costos por anticonceptivos, por ejemplo, varían dependiendo del número de usuarios de cada método. *Variable Costs or Expenses; Côuts (ou dépenses) variables*

Costos Recurrentes: Ver **Costos de Operación**.

Cronograma (también conocido como Gráfica de Gantt): Resumen de un plan de trabajo, en forma gráfica, que muestra las actividades más importantes de un proyecto en secuencia cronológica. El cronograma muestra el mes o trimestre en que se llevará a cabo cada actividad y la persona o personas responsables de realizarlas. Este instrumento ayuda a los administradores a monitorear las actividades y los resultados a corto plazo, facilitando el desarrollo del proyecto y la administración de los recursos del mismo. *Chronogram; Chronogramme*

Cronograma de Supervisión: Plan escrito de sesiones de supervisión que muestra el nombre del empleado a visitarse y la fecha, hora y contenido de las sesiones de supervisión programadas. Un cronograma de supervisión se utiliza para planear y para comunicar a los empleados las futuras actividades de supervisión. *Supervisory Schedule; Calendrier de supervision*

Cuentas por Cobrar: Dinero que se le adeuda a la organización correspondiente a facturas que haya emitido. *Accounts Receivable; Comptes à recevoir (ou créances)*

Cuentas por Pagar: Dinero que debe la organización de acuerdo a cuentas o recibos enviados por el acreedor. *Accounts Payable; Comptes à payer (ou dettes)*

Cuotas de Afiliación: Cuotas fijas cobradas a los clientes o miembros de una organización, generalmente por un año, las cuales dan derecho a recibir una gama de servicios. *Membership Fees; Cotisations*

D atos Históricos: Datos recopilados de informes anteriores, tales como los informes de distribución de anticonceptivos, los registros diarios de actividades, las tarjetas de inventario, etc. *Historical Data; Données rétrospectives*

Datos sobre Clientes/Clínica: Información resumida sobre los clientes a los cuales presta servicios una clínica o un programa comunitario. Los datos sobre clientes/clínica incluyen típicamente: tipos de métodos anticonceptivos utilizados por los clientes de un programa (mezcla de métodos), número de usuarios regulares que reciben servicios de una clínica o programa en un mes o año, número de nuevos aceptantes de un método anticonceptivo en una clínica o programa, número de personas que abandonan un método o clientes que han abandonado un programa. Igualmente es información resumida sobre la edad promedio, estado civil y número de hijos de los clientes. *Client/Clinic Data; Données sur les clients ou sur les formations sanitaires*

De Punta: Nivel actual de perfeccionamiento de una tecnología desarrollada en particular. *State-of-the-Art; Niveau de point*

Declaración de Misión (también conocida como Misión de la Organización): Breve declaración general que describe el tipo de organización, su propósito principal y sus valores. La misión de una organización es una exposición razonada para la definición de las metas y objetivos. *Mission Statement; Enoncé de mission*

Definición de Tareas: Obligaciones y actividades específicas de un empleado en particular. *Task Definition; Définition des tâches*

Delegación: La delegación dentro del programa de descentralización significa que el nivel central transfiere la responsabilidad de funciones administrativas específicas, tales como el desarrollo de la capacitación gerencial, a *organizaciones o agencias que se encuentran fuera de la estructura burocrática regular,* para que dichas funciones estén controladas sólo indirectamente por el gobierno central. *Delegation; Délégation*

Demanda no Cubierta o Necesidad no Cubierta: Este término se utiliza para describir al número de personas o al porcentaje de la población que desea utilizar anticonceptivos a fin de espaciar o limitar los nacimientos, pero que debido a una serie de razones, incluyendo la falta de acceso a la información o a los servicios, no utiliza anticonceptivos actualmente. *Unmet Demand or Unmet Need; Demande non satisfaite ou besoin non satisfait*

Densidad Poblacional: Número total de habitantes que viven en un área determinada tal como una comunidad, distrito, ciudad capital, país, región, por kilómetro cuadrado o por milla cuadrada. *Population Density; Densité de population*

Depreciación: Práctica contable que distribuye el costo de un activo fijo a lo largo de su vida útil estimada. La depreciación puede efectuarse como una transacción contable o puede ser «financiada» mediante el depósito sistemático de efectivo en un fondo especial para la reposición de actives. *Por ejemplo, un vehículo con valor de $20,000 con un tiempo de vida estimado de diez años, generará una depreciación anual de $2,000. Depreciation; Amortissement*

Desabastecimiento: Situación en la que un programa o clínica agota los suministros de uno o más métodos anticonceptivos (u otros medicamentos o equipo) y carece de los productos suficientes para cubrir la demanda de los clientes. *Stockout; Rupture de stocks*

Desarrollo Profesional (también conocido como Desarrollo del Personal): Proceso de mejoramiento de la capacidad profesional del personal mediante capacitación y el acceso a oportunidades educativas. El desarrollo profesional puede incluir la capacitación en el servicio, la capacitación externa u observación del trabajo de otros. Es ampliamente reconocido que el desarrollo profesional mantiene alta la moral del personal, mejora la capacidad institucional de un programa y atrae y mantiene un personal de alta calidad. *Professional Development; Développement professionnel*

Descentralización: Proceso de transferencia de la responsabilidad, autoridad y control de las funciones administrativas específicas o generales a niveles inferiores de una organización, sistema o programa. (Ver **Desconcentración, Delegación, Devolución** y **Privatización**.) *Decentralization; Décentralisation*

Desconcentración: La deconcentración en un programa de descentralización significa que algunas funciones administrativas, tales como la elaboración de presupuestos para el programa, se transfieren del nivel central a *las unidades de campo de nivel inferior dentro de la misma agencia u organización,* pero el nivel central sigue controlando el programa en general. *Deconcentration; Déconcentration*

Descripción del Cargo: Documento que detalla el nombre del cargo y hace una descripción de las tareas y responsabilidades del mismo, la relación directa de supervisión con otro personal, y las habilidades y calificaciones requeridas para dicho cargo. *Job Description; Description de poste*

Desertor: Ver «**Abandono**».

Deuda Incobrable: Cuentas por cobrar que se consideran incobrables. *Bad Debt; Créance irrécouvrable*

Devolución: La devolución dentro del programa de descentralización se refiere a la transferencia de poder a las *unidades gubernamentales sub-nacionales* recientemente creadas o fortalecidas, cuyas actividades están fuera del control directo del gobierno central. Dentro de este enfoque, la responsabilidad, autoridad y control de un programa se transfieren generalmente a un gobierno departamental, provincial o municipal. *Devolution; Dévolution*

Diagrama de Causa y Efecto: Instrumento utilizado frecuentemente en un programa de mejoramiento continuo de la calidad para agrupar las ideas de la gente en forma ordenada sobre las causas de un problema particular. También se conoce como diagrama en «esqueleto de pescado» debido a la forma que adopta cuando ilustra las causas primarias y secundarias de un problema. *Cause-and-Effect Diagram; Diagramme de cause à effet*

Diagrama de Flujo: Esquema utilizado para analizar un proceso o actividad que muestra la secuencia de las actividades, los pasos y las decisiones que tienen lugar dentro de un proceso determinado, tal como el registro de un cliente en una clínica. Al definir el punto de arranque y el punto final del proceso y analizar cada paso del mismo, los administradores pueden identificar las áreas problemáticas y las mejoras potenciales que pueden efectuarse para lograr los resultados deseados. *Flowchart; Diagramme de processus*

Diagrama Organizacional (también conocido como Organigrama): Esquema que muestra las relaciones laborales de todo el personal de una organización o programa y la estructura formal de supervisión así como las relaciones de subordinación entre las diferentes funciones, cargos administrativos y del personal. *Organizational Chart; Organigramme*

Distribución de la Población: La distribución geográfica de la población en un área determinada tal como una comunidad, distrito, ciudad capital, país, región, etc. Es importante que los administradores conozcan la distribución de la población para planear nuevos programas y determinar la ubicación de nuevos centros de prestación de servicios. *Population Distribution; Distribution de la population*

Distribución Funcional: Actividad que presenta en forma gráfica, los nombres de las organizaciones participantes y sus principales responsabilidades en varias áreas funcionales, para propósitos de identificación de deficiencias y duplicación de servicios. *Functional Allocation; Répartition des fonctions*

Donaciones: Fondos o donativos entregados a una organización o programa para llevar a cabo programas o servicios específicos. Generalmente los gobiernos y los donantes locales e internacionales hacen estos donaciones. *Grants; Subventions*

Donaciones para Incentivar: Fondos utilizados para premiar el desempeño del programa, el logro de los objetivos, o para motivar a los programas a lanzar nuevas iniciativas. Los donaciones para incentivar se utilizan para motivar a los programas y a los empleados a que continúen persiguiendo sus objetivos y mantengan o mejoren la calidad del programa. *Incentive Grants; Subventions qui contiennent des primes*

Dotación: Donación de valor financiero considerable que puede ser vendida o invertida para generar ingresos adicionales por concepto de intereses, alquileres o dividendos y que puede ser utilizada en el futuro para cubrir las necesidades institucionales para los propósitos especificados por el donante. *Endowment; Dotation*

E **fectividad**: Medida en la que un programa efectúa los cambios deseados o logra sus objetivos a través de la prestación de servicios. *Effectiveness; Efficacité*

Eficiencia: Medida en la que un programa utiliza apropiadamente los recursos y cumple las actividades en forma oportuna. *Efficiency; Efficience*

Embarques Divididos: Ocurren cuando un embarque grande se separa en embarques más pequeños y se envía en intervalos regulares para no recargar las deficiencias de almacenamiento del destinatario, generalmente son pedidos por el destinatario. *Split Shipments; Livraisions partielles*

Embarques Incompletos: Ocurren cuando los proveedores envían sólo una parte de los embarques de anticonceptivos solicitados. *Short Shipments; Livraisions incomplètes*

Encuesta a Clientes: Encuesta realizada frecuentemente mediante entrevistas para determinar cuáles son las necesidades de los clientes, si se están cubriendo sus necesidades, cuál es su opinión sobre la calidad de la atención, sus posibilidades económicas para pagar por los servicios y otras características de una población determinada de clientes. *Client Survey; Enquête auprès des clients*

Encuesta a los Proveedores de Servicios de Planificación Familiar: Estudio de otras agencias u organismos de servicios de planificación familiar, que generalmente trabajan en la misma área que el programa que efectúa el estudio. La información se utiliza para comparar los tipos y la calidad de los servicios ofrecidos por otras agencias y para determinar las áreas de coordinación, referencia o nuevas oportunidades de servicios. *Survey of Family Planning Providers; Enquête auprès des prestataires de planification familiale*

Encuesta Basada en la Población: Estudio en el cual la información se obtiene directamente de una muestra representativa de la población o de un grupo poblacional de interés para el programa, como las mujeres en edad reproductiva. La información se obtiene generalmente a través de entrevistas, en vez de recurrir a los registros u otras fuentes indirectas. (Ver también **Encuesta de Grupos**.) *Population-Based Survey; Enquête auprès de la population*

Encuesta de Base: Encuesta que se realiza al inicio de un proyecto para establecer los datos claves con los cuales se compararán los resultados obtenidos en el futuro. *Baseline Survey; Enquête de base*

Encuesta de Grupos: Técnica de investigación que permite que los administradores y evaluadores estudien pequeños conglomerados poblacionales y utilicen los resultados para representar una porción mayor de la población general, obteniéndose así una retroalimentación más rápida del impacto de las actividades del programa. En estas encuestas de grupos pueden utilizarse técnicas de muestreo por estratos, mediante las cuáles se divide a la población en categorías diferentes de interés para el programa (tales como edad, paridad, lugar de residencia y nivel de educación) con el fin de mejorar la exactitud de los resultados. *Cluster Survey; Enquête par grappes*

Encuesta de Hogares: Estudio que obtiene información sobre la ocupación de los integrantes de una pareja, el método anticonceptivo que utilizan y/o han utilizado en el pasado, si la mujer está embarazada o amamantando, los nacimientos recientes, el número total de nacimientos y muertes e información sobre la salud reproductiva de la pareja y la historia de planificación familiar que interesa al programa. Las encuestas de hogares se utilizan para conocer el nivel o el indicador con el cuál se comparan los futuros resultados. *Household Survey; Enquête auprès des ménages*

Encuesta de la Comunidad: Estudio de una comunidad en la cual existe o se planea un programa de planificación familiar. En una encuesta comunitaria, los entrevistadores/ investigadores frecuentemente recopilan información sobre los conocimientos, actitudes y prácticas actuales de los anticonceptivos. Puede recopilarse información adicional sobre la percepción de los servicios de un programa (ya sea que las personas encuestadas utilicen o no dichos servicios), la fuente de servicios, ingresos y otros indicadores socioeconómicos que ayudarán a los administradores a planear o mejorar el programa. *Community Survey; Enquête communautaire*

Enfoque de Equipo: Filosofía y técnica que se apoyan en el desarrollo y el trabajo de un grupo de personas que cuenta con habilidades y perspectivas diferentes para identificar y discutir los temas, definir las causas de los problemas (o los éxitos logrados), encontrar soluciones y realizarlas para lograr una meta común. *Team Approach; Approche d'équipe*

Enfoque de la Prestación de Servicios: Sistema para cubrir y atraer a diferentes grupos de clientes. Los enfoques de prestación de servicios incluyen: servicios comunitarios, servicios clínicos, servicios ofrecidos por la empresa, servicios hospitalarios, servicios domiciliarios y las reuniones comunitarias para ofrecer información, educación, comunicación (IEC) sobre planificación familiar. *Service Delivery Approach; Approche de prestation de services*

Entrevista de Salida: Contacto que se lleva a cabo con los usuarios cuando salen de la clínica de planificación familiar para registrar su opinión sobre los servicios que recibieron. La entrevista puede consistir en una conversación informal o en la aplicación de un cuestionario más formal que explore un aspecto particular de los servicios. *Exit Interview; Entretien à la sortie*

Equipo Interfuncional: Grupo de individuos de diferentes programas, tales como enfermería, servicios de laboratorio, administración y extensión, etc. que trabajan juntos para lograr una meta común. *Cross-Functional Team; Equipe à fonctions multiples*

Erogaciones: Pagos efectuados en efectivo o en cheque. *Expenditures; Dépenses*

Escala Variable de Tarifas: Sistema para cobrar a los clientes tarifas por servicios en base a los ingresos del hogar y al tamaño de la familia, con lo cual se facilita que los clientes paguen de acuerdo a sus posibilidades. *Sliding Fee Scale; Echelle discriminatoire de tarifs*

Esquema de Pagos Compartidos: Sistema de pago de servicios, en donde el usuario paga una parte de la tarifa la cual es complementada por un tercero, puede ser un empleado, una compañía de seguros, o un plan de salud de pre-pago anticipado. *Co-Payment Scheme; Système de co-paiement*

Estabilidad Organizacional: Habilidad de una organización para utilizar en forma efectiva los controles y sistemas administrativos para evitar interrupciones en los servicios pese a los cambios inesperados que pueden surgir en el medio externo o a cambios de personal, especialmente el de mayor jerarquía. *Organizational Stability; Stabilité de l'organisation*

Estaciones de Servicios: Las diferentes etapas o sitios de una clínica en los cuales un cliente recibe tipos específicos de servicios. Las estaciones de servicios incluyen frecuentemente: la inscripción con la recepcionista, la determinación de su peso, la medición de la presión arterial, una sesión con un consejero, el examen realizado por una enfermera o médico y el registro de una próxima cita con la recepcionista. *Service Stops; Postes de travail*

Estado de Flujo de Fondos: Ver **Planilla de Proyecciones del Flujo de Fondos**.

Estado de Pérdidas y Ganancias (también conocido como Estado de Ingresos y Egresos): Informe periódico que resume los ingresos y egresos, y que muestra un superávit (ganancia) o déficit (pérdida) durante el período que cubre el informe. *Income Statement; Etat des revenus et des dépenses*

Estados Financieros: Informes que cubren un período (mes o año) y que resumen los ingresos y gastos del período (Estado de Ingresos y Egresos) y los activos y pasivos (Balance General) al finalizar el mismo. *Financial Statement; Etat financier*

«**Estancamiento**»: Situación en la cual el rendimiento de un programa— el número de personas que recibe servicios y practica activamente la planificación familiar—se ha nivelado. En muchos casos, un programa que se ha nivelado ha logrado alcanzar una tasa de prevalencia anticonceptiva (TPA) del 40 al 50 por ciento, tiene la capacidad para servir a más clientes y debe considerar nuevas maneras para atraer y retener clientes, reducir las barreras a los servicios, reorganizar programas y sistemas para la prestación de servicios y adoptar otros tipos de decisiones estratégicas que mejorarán el desempeño del programa. *Plateau Effect or "Plateauing"; Effet de plateau*

Estilo Participativo: Estilo de administración en el cuál el supervisor o administrador trabaja activamente con el personal a su cargo, escucha sus ideas, reconoce sus puntos de vista y logros, promueve las discusiones conjuntas de diversos temas y fomenta la búsqueda de soluciones en forma conjunta. *Participative Style; Style de participation*

Estrategia: Enfoque o enfoques que sirven para cumplir la misión y que serán utilizados para lograr las metas de la organización o del programa. *Strategy; Stratégie*

Estructura de Supervisión: Estructura formal que describe las relaciones de subordinación existentes entre los diferentes cargos y funciones del personal administrativo y del otro personal en una organización. *Supervisory Structure; Structure de supervision*

Estructura Organizacional: Estructura interna de autoridad y comunicación de una organización que define la forma como deben manejarse los programas y departamentos, qué tipos de actividades se llevan a cabo por ciertos departamentos o programas y las relaciones funcionales y de supervisión entre el personal y el administrador de dichos departamentos. (Ver también **Diagrama Organizacional.**) *Organizational Structure; Structure organisationnelle*

Etapa de Consolidación: La tercera etapa del desarrollo de una organización durante la cual ésta se concentra en el desarrollo y mejoramiento de sus sistemas para optimizar la efectividad administrativa, y su capacidad interna para movilizar y controlar recursos para el autofinanciamiento de la organización y del programa. (Ver **Etapas del Desarrollo de una Organización.**) *Consolidation Stage; Phase de consolidation*

Etapa de Crecimiento: Es la segunda etapa del desarrollo de una organización. En esta etapa, las organizaciones formulan una misión clara, definen las estrategias para lograr dicha misión, plantean metas y objetivos específicos y elaboran y utilizan planes operativos para lograr dichos objetivos. Durante esta etapa, a medida que las actividades y servicios se amplían rápidamente, la dependencia de la organización en los recursos externos para apoyar dichos programas y servicios también se aumenta. (Ver **Etapas del Desarrollo de una Organización.**) *Growth Stage; Phase de croissance*

Etapa de Madurez: La cuarta y última fase del desarrollo de una organización durante la cual ésta desarrolla su capacidad para administrarse efectivamente y adaptar su misión, estrategia, estructura y sistemas en respuesta a los retos internos y externos, a fin de mejorar el autofinanciamiento. (Ver **Etapas del Desarrollo de una Organización.**) *Mature Stage; Phase de maturité*

Etapa de Surgimiento (o Etapa Emergente): La primera etapa en el desarrollo de una organización en la cual la iniciación de servicios es la meta principal. Esta etapa se caracteriza por una definición incompleta o poco clara de la misión de la organización, una estructura organizativa simple, sistemas y programas básicos y una alta dependencia financiera externa. (Ver **Etapas del Desarrollo de una Organización.**) *Emergent Stage; Phase d'émergence*

Etapas del Desarrollo de una Organización: Las cuatro etapas que caracterizan el desarrollo de una organización: Surgimiento, Crecimiento, Consolidación y Madurez. Estas etapas se basan en principios que establecen que las organizaciones se desarrollan en forma sistemática a través del tiempo y adquieren distintas características durante cada etapa en lo referente a la misión, estrategia, estructura y sistemas. (Ver **Etapa de Surgimiento, Etapa de Crecimiento, Etapa de Consolidación** y **Etapa de Madurez.**) *Stages of Organizational Development; Phases de développement d'une organisation*

Evaluación: Estudio de un programa en el cuál pueden utilizarse diversos procesos para recopilar y analizar información a fin de determinar si el programa está cumpliendo las actividades que planteó y la medida en la que ha logrado los objetivos planteados (por medio de estas actividades). Los resultados de una evaluación pueden ser utilizados para conocer en qué areas es más efectivo el programa y qué modificaciones deben realizarse para mejorarlo. *Evaluation; Evaluation*

Evaluación Rápida: Estudio de corta duración y económico, basado en una muestra y realizado con el fin de determinar el alcance o las causas de un problema o para determinar las necesidades específicas de un cliente o programa que fueron identificadas mediante estadísticas de servicios y otros estudios de mayor envergadura. *Rapid Assessment; Evaluation rapide*

Examen Post-Prueba: Se aplica a todos los clientes, empleados, participantes o cualquier otro grupo específico de personas, después de terminar un programa o durante la ejecución del mismo, con el propósito de medir el progreso hacia los objetivos planeados. *Post-test; Post-test*

Examen Pre-Prueba: Se aplica a los clientes, empleados, participantes o cualquier otro grupo específico de personas que vaya a ser evaluado, ello se hace con el propósito de determinar una base sobre la cual se medirán los futuros resultados. *Pre-test; Pré-test*

Existencias de Seguridad: Cantidad de producto (número de meses de abastecimiento) por debajo del nivel mínimo que sirve como colchón o amortiguador cuando se presentan fluctuaciones en la demanda de métodos anticonceptivos o se retrasan los embarques de nuevos suministros. *Safety Stock; Stock de sécurité*

Existencias Disponibles (también conocidas como Saldo Disponible): Cantidad de cada anticonceptivo o producto en el inventario en un momento determinado. *Stock on Hand; Stock disponible*

Existencias en Pedido: Cantidad de existencias de cada tipo de anticonceptivo que fueron solicitadas pero que no han sido aún recibidas (en la clínica o centro). *Stock on Order; Stock en commande*

Exoneraciones/Sistema de Exoneraciones y Excepciones: Sistema utilizado para determinar bajo qué condiciones dejará de cobrarse el costo de los servicios a un cliente en particular, o cuándo éste pagará una parte de la tarifa para complementar al cliente con fondos de una reserva constituida para dicho fin. Un sistema de exoneraciones usa un conjunto de criterios estándar para determinar cuales clientes son elegibles para recibir dicho apoyo financiero. *Waivers/Waiver System; Exonérations/Système de dérogation*

Expediente del Cliente (también conocido como Expediente Médico o Historia Clínica): Ficha o formulario que se llena para cada cliente y que contiene información sobre los antecedentes médicos y de planificación familiar, su estado de salud y los exámenes médicos. Dicha ficha debe incluir (como mínimo) el nombre, dirección, sexo, edad, paridad, historia de salud reproductiva y método anticonceptivo utilizado. La ficha se guarda en la clínica y es actualizado por el personal cada vez que un cliente regresa para solicitar otros servicios. *Client Record; Dossier du client*

Expediente Médico o Historia Clínica: Ver **Expediente del Cliente**.

Extensión («Outreach»): Actividades relacionadas con la información y servicios a la comunidad por fuera de las instalaciones de la clínica o centro, generalmente a través del trabajo realizado con los grupos comunitarios o con voluntarios. *Outreach; Activités d'extension*

Facilitador: Persona que asiste, alienta y apoya a un grupo de gente en forma participativa para realizar un trabajo conjunto, tomar decisiones y resolver conflictos para lograr una meta común. *Facilitator; Animateur*

Fecha de Expiración: La fecha determinada por el fabricante, luego de la cuál el anticonceptivo o cualquier otro producto no debe ser distribuido o utilizado por los clientes. *Expiration Date; Date de péremption*

Fondo de Caja Chica: Flujo de fondos separado para cubrir gastos inmediatos en efectivo, que se restituye periódicamente de acuerdo con el monto gastado. *Imprest Fund; Caisse d'avance*

Formulario de Flujo de Clientes: Formulario utilizado para registrar la información necesaria para realizar un análisis del flujo de clientes. En el formulario se registra el número del cliente, el método de planificación familiar, el tipo de visita, la hora de llegada a la clínica y el tiempo y la duración de cada contacto con el personal de la misma. *Client Flow Form; Formulaire de flux des clients*

Formulario de Informe Trimestral: Formulario utilizado para la rendición de informes trimestrales resumidos tales como el número y tipo de clientes a los que se prestó servicios (nuevos aceptantes y clientes subsecuentes), las cantidades de anticonceptivos (de cada tipo y marca) disponibles al principio del trimestre, las cantidades recibidas y distribuidas durante un período de tres meses, las cantidades de productos solicitadas para el próximo trimestre, cualquier ajuste o pérdidas y los balances finales. *Quarterly Reporting Form; Fiche de rapport trimestriel*

Formulario de Pedido y de Despacho: Formulario utilizado por el administrador de la clínica para solicitar nuevos suministros, por el administrador de la bodega para llenar el pedido y registrar las cantidades despachadas y nuevamente por el administrador para verificar si la clínica ha recibido las cantidades y los tipos correctos de suministros solicitados. *Requisition and Issue Voucher; Bon de commande et de sortie*

Formularios Diarios de Retroalimentación: Cuestionarios de evaluación diseñados para dar a los docentes y administradores una valiosa retroalimentación sobre la satisfacción de los participantes durante la capacitación; se utilizan diariamente. *Daily Feedback Forms; Formulaires pour la rétro-information journalière*

Funciones/Sistemas Administrativos: Las funciones administrativas básicas de planeación, elaboración de presupuestos, determinación de las funciones y responsabilidades del personal, capacitación, supervisión del personal, administración de recursos (incluyendo dinero, anticonceptivos y otros suministros, equipos o servicios del programa), monitoreo de las actividades del programa, evaluación de los logros del programa y administración de los servicios que se ofrecen a los clientes. *Management Functions/Systems; Fonctions/ Systèmes de gestion*

Funciones del Personal: Las responsabilidades generales que tiene cada uno de los cargos del personal. *Por ejemplo, las funciones de los administradores incluyen el liderazgo, la comprensión, la ayuda para resolución de problemas, la asistencia técnica y el estímulo a los demás miembros del personal. Staff Roles; Rôle du personnel*

G astos: Todos los costos en que se incurre en la operación de un programa. En el sistema de contabilidad sobre bases devengadas, un gasto se registra en el sistema contable en el momento de incurrirse, antes de efectuar el pago en efectivo. *Expenses; Dépenses*

Grado o Nivel: En la descripción de un cargo, es el nivel estándar o rango en el que se basa la escala salarial. Es determinado, en parte, por las habilidades y los requisitos necesarios para efectuar el trabajo. *Grade; Grade*

Gráfica: Se utiliza para analizar datos. La gráfica ilustra las relaciones o patrones existentes entre los números y los conjuntos de números, que serían difíciles de apreciar si sólo se consideran los datos sin procesar. (Ver **Gráfica Lineal, Gráfica de Barras** y **Gráfica de Sectores**.) *Graph; Graphique*

Gráfica de Barras: Gráfica que representa datos o conjuntos de datos en barras horizontales o verticales de tal forma que la relación entre los datos pueda verse e interpretarse con mayor facilidad. Pueden utilizarse gráficas de barras para analizar la mayor parte de los tipos de datos sobre servicios y mostrar las diferencias entre varias categorías de datos, tales como el número de usuarias de anticonceptivos, no usuarias y clientes que abandonan el método. *Bar Chart; Graphique à colonnes*

Gráfica de Flujo de Información: Gráfica que muestra los tipos de información (los indicadores) que serán recolectados, cómo serán recolectados y difundidos, quién los recolectará, a quién serán enviados, cómo serán utilizados y el nivel de detalle que se requiere. Esta gráfica tiene como propósito asegurar un flujo apropiado de la información en la secuencia correcta y comunicar al personal cómo funciona el sistema de información. *Information Flow Table; Tableau du circulation de l'information*

Gráfica de Gantt: Ver **Cronograma de Actividades del Proyecto**.

Gráfica de Sectores: Esquema que representa los datos resumidos o porcentajes a modo de tajadas de un círculo o torta, para que pueda verse y analizarse más fácilmente la relación entre los datos. Las gráficas de sectores pueden utilizarse para analizar la mezcla de métodos de cualquier tipo de cliente o de todos los clientes en un programa o clínica. Las gráficas de sectores permiten a los administradores comparar las proporciones y representar en forma resumida los datos correspondientes a un período específico, tales como un mes, un trimestre o un año. *Pie Chart; Graphique «camembert»*

Gráfica Lineal: Gráfica que representa los datos o el conjunto de datos que han sido recopilados durante un período. Los datos son registrados en una gráfica que corresponde a los intervalos de tiempo estándar unidos por una línea que conecta los puntos marcados. La línea de la gráfica permite a los administradores apreciar las tendencias de los datos (aumento, disminución o ausencia de cambios) a través de un período. Frecuentemente se utiliza para analizar las tendencias de los nuevos aceptantes, los usuarios continuos, los «abandonos», los nuevos aceptantes de un método en particular y otros. Las gráficas lineales (actualizadas regularmente) ayudan a los administradores a seguir una tendencia a través de un período y adoptar las medidas necesarias para manejar dicha tendencia. *Line Graph; Graphique linéaire*

Gratificación: Recompensa en efectivo o en especie, entregada en forma adicional o en lugar del salario de una persona, como un plan de salud, cuotas de afiliación, comida gratuita, o estacionamiento. *Perquisites; Gratification*

Grupo Focal: Discusión planeada y guiada con la participación de un grupo seleccionado de participantes para examinar un tema o varios temas específicos. Es un método cualitativo para obtener información. Los resultados de las discusiones del grupo focal se complementan generalmente o sirven para explicar mejor los datos cuantitativos obtenidos mediante encuestas u otros métodos cuantitativos. *Focus Group; Groupe de discussion focalisée*

Grupo Objetivo: Uno o varios grupos específicos de la población que se beneficiarán de un programa. El grupo objetivo estará compuesto por todos o por una parte de los usuarios potenciales, tales como los adolescentes, las mujeres embarazadas, los residentes rurales o los residentes de un área geográfica determinada. *Target Group; Groupe cible*

Guías de Observación: Forma diseñada para ayudar al capacitador o al supervisor a registrar, mediante la observación, la comprensión del estudiante de los temas enseñados. *Observation Guides; Grilles d'observation*

«**H** acer las Cosas Correctas»: Lema de una administración moderna que impulsa la solidez programática, estratégica y ética de un programa. Los administradores que se preocupan por «hacer las cosas correctas» tienen en mente la dirección estratégica de un programa u organización y consultan frecuentemente la misión, las metas y los objetivos que respaldan sus decisiones. *"Doing the Right Things"; «Faire les choses nécessaires»*

«**Hacer las Cosas en Forma Correcta**»: Lema de una administración moderna que promueve la forma más efectiva y eficiente de llevar a cabo las actividades. Los administradores se preocupan por «hacer las cosas en forma correcta» al realizar las operaciones cotidianas de un programa. *"Doing Things in the Right Way"; «Faire les choses correctement»*

Histograma: Tipo de gráfica de barras utilizado para ilustrar *datos de una categoría única y de valores continuos,* tales como la edad, que puede agruparse en 20–24, 25–29, 30–34, etc. Una gráfica de barras normal se utiliza para registrar los datos que representan *diferentes categorías,* tales como usuarios de anticonceptivos, no usuarios de anticonceptivos, residencia en áreas rurales o urbanas, etc. (Para mayor información sobre los histogramas y las gráficas de barras, favor consultar el Volumen II, Número 1 de *Actualidad Gerencial,* «La Utilización del PMC para Reforzar la Planificación Familiar» y el suplemento, *Instrumentos Gerenciales para el PMC.*) *Histogram; Histogramme*

Hoja de Registro: Tabla utilizada para recopilar y organizar datos. Las hojas de registro se utilizan para hacer un listado de los tipos de datos que serán obtenidos y para registrar el número de eventos u observaciones que se cuentan en cada categoría. *Tally Sheet; Feuille de pointage (Liste des informations et données)*

Honorarios Profesionales: Los costos derivados generalmente de contratos con *individuos* para la prestación de servicios especializados, tales como conferencias, capacitación y evaluación, a diferencia de los costos por contratos de largo plazo con *instituciones* ajenas al programa para la oferta de servicios como el mantenimiento de vehículos, los servicios de conserjería, propaganda o servicios de promoción los cuales se denominan servicios adquiridos. (Ver **Servicios Adquiridos.**) *Professional Fees; Honoraires*

I mpacto: Es la medida en la que el programa ha cambiado o mejorado los conocimientos, actitudes, comportamiento o salud de los participantes en un programa de planificación familiar y salud reproductiva. *Impact; Impact*

Indicador: Elemento que indica cierta condición, capacidad o medida numérica que, al registrarse, recopilarse y analizarse, facilita que los conceptos más complejos sean más susceptibles de medición y permite a los administradores y evaluadores comparar los resultados reales del programa con los resultados que se esperan. *Indicator; Indicateur*

Información de Desempeño: Información que se requiere para planear los objetivos de un programa y para evaluar el impacto de las actividades del mismo en la población objetivo. *Performance Information; Information sur la performance*

Información Operacional: Información que se requiere para planear las actividades del programa tales como el uso del tiempo, el personal y el dinero. También se utiliza para evaluar el funcionamiento de un programa de planificación familiar. *Operational Information; Information opérationelle*

Información sobre el Proceso: A diferencia de la información de resultados la cual identifica los productos, resultados o logros (en términos numéricos), la información sobre el proceso es cualitativa y provee información acerca de las formas como se utiliza a los individuos y materiales para producir resultados específicos. *Por ejemplo, al utilizar la información sobre el proceso, los administradores pueden determinar la causa de un desabastecimiento de anticonceptivos (un resultado negativo) mediante el análisis de cada (proceso) paso del sistema logístico. Process Information; Information sur les processus*

Informe de Ejecución del Presupuesto: Informe que compara los ingresos y gastos actuales con aquellos proyectados en el presupuesto. *Budget Performance Report; Rapport de performance budgétaire*

Informe de Ingresos: Informe diario, mensual o trimestral sobre el dinero o equivalente recibido por concepto de ventas, servicios o tarifas. En el sistema de costos sobre bases devengadas, los ingresos se registran cuando se alcanzan y no cuando se reciben el efectivo o los bienes. *Revenue Report; Etat des recettes*

Informe de Resultados: Información sobre los productos o logros (en términos numéricos) de las actividades de un individuo o programa a través de un período específico. *Output Information; Information sur les résultats*

Informe por Uso de Vehículos: Bitácora que registra el uso de los vehículos. En ella se incluye la fecha, el destino, el propósito del viaje, la lectura inicial y final del odómetro, el combustible consumido y las reparaciones. Se utiliza para calcular el costo por milla o kilómetro y para controlar y monitorear los gastos. *Vehicle Usage Report; Carnet de bord*

Informes Financieros: Sistema establecido para la rendición de informes periódicos sobre las transacciones y la situación financieras de una organización o programa. *Financial Reporting; Rapport financier*

Informes Programáticos: Sistema o proceso establecido para la rendición de información detallada sobre las actividades desarrolladas durante un período específico. Los informes programáticos son generalmente narrativos y sólo reportan información no financiera sobre las actividades y el progreso alcanzado para el logro de los objetivos. *Programmatic Reporting; Rapport programmatique*

Ingresos, Entradas, Recibos: En contabilidad de caja, este término se refiere al efectivo recibido. Es todo dinero o su equivalente recibido por la venta, servicios, honorarios y donaciones. En el caso de las donaciones, solamente la porción que ha sido erogada se considera un ingreso; el saldo debe ser devuelto al donante. En sistemas de acumulación, los ingresos son registrados cuando se devengan y no cuando se recibe el bien o el efectivo. *Revenues; Revenus*

Institucionalización: La adopción de una actividad, sistema o práctica por una organización o programa, en la medida que cualquiera de estas continuarán operando pese a los cambios de personal y en forma independiente de los insumos o aportes externos. *Institutionalization; Institutionnalisation*

Insumos: Recursos utilizados en un programa. *Inputs; Intrants*

Integración/Servicios Integrados: Se refiere a un programa que combina servicios de planificación familiar con servicios de salud materna e infantil, nutrición, vacunación y otros servicios de salud reproductiva, tales como el control y tratamiento de enfermedades de transmisión sexual. *Integration/Integrated Services; Intégration/ Services intégrés*

Integración Tipo «Embudo»: Se utiliza para describir un enfoque de prestación de servicios integrados. La integración tipo «embudo» se da casi siempre en una agencia u organización que separa sus diversos programas verticalmente a nivel nacional y distrital, pero integra los programas y servicios a nivel de la clínica/comunidad. (Ver también **Integración Tipo «Reloj de Arena».**) *"Funnel" Approach; Approche de «l'entonnoir»*

Integración Tipo «Reloj de Arena»: La integración tipo «reloj de arena» se utiliza para describir un enfoque de prestación de servicios integrados, e ilustra un programa combinado de naturaleza vertical y horizontal en el cuál el personal a nivel nacional se organiza en reparticiones separadas para planificación familiar, vacunación, control de enfermedades infecciosas, nutrición, salud materna, etc. Uno o más individuos coordinan los programas a nivel regional o distrital, y los proveedores de servicios son asignados a diversos programas separados. (Ver también **Integración Tipo «Embudo».**) *"Hourglass" Approach; Approche du «sablier»*

Intervalo entre Pedidos: Número determinado y pre-establecido de meses que transcurre entre pedidos de suministros anticonceptivos. El intervalo entre pedidos debería determinarse en forma individual para cada método anticonceptivo para que se ajuste a los niveles de existencias máximo y mínimo. *Order Interval; Intervalle entre les commandes*

Inventario: La cantidad de existencias (anticonceptivos, bienes y otros elementos de la clínica) que se encuentran disponibles (para utilizarse por una clínica o programa) en un momento determinado. *Inventory; Stocks*

J unta Administrativa: Grupo formal de asesores que brinda una perspectiva general de la organización desde el punto de vista estratégico y financiero y se responsabiliza de mantener y promover su estabilidad y su autofinanciamiento. *Managing Board; Comité de gestion*

Junta de Asesores: Grupo de profesionales externos con amplia experiencia que se responsabilizan en asesorar al personal gerencial de mayor jerarquía de una organización o programa. Una junta de asesores cuenta generalmente con una estructura más informal que la de una junta directiva, pero puede asumir responsabilidades similares, tales como ayudar al personal gerencial de mayor jerarquía a formular la misión y las normas de la organización, definir las directivas estratégicas y ofrecer una visión general del estado financiero de la organización o programa. *Advisory Board; Conseil consultatif*

Junta Directiva: Una junta directiva está generalmente compuesta por un grupo de profesionales con diferentes habilidades y experiencia que se responsabiliza de supervisar la estabilidad de la organización. A menudo las juntas son un requisito legal para una organización con o sin fines de lucro. Dado que los miembros de la junta directiva no son empleados de la organización y el trabajo que realizan es voluntario, las juntas directivas pueden guiar a la organización en forma efectiva y objetiva ya que no hay un incentivo financiero. Las áreas de responsabilidad incluyen: desarrollar un plan estratégico, apoyar el liderazgo y crecimiento de la organización, hacer supervisión financiera, mantener las relaciones entre la comunidad y el gobierno, asegurar la oferta de servicios de alta calidad y manejar las actividades propias de la junta directiva. *Board of Directors; Conseil d'administration*

Lista de «Asuntos Pendientes»: Lista informal de las actividades y tareas que deben realizarse en un período corto, generalmente menos de un mes. Debe revisarse continuamente para incorporar nuevas actividades y para verificar las que ya se realizaron. *"To Do" Lists; Listes de choses «à faire»*

Lista de Verificación para la Autoevaluación: Ver **Normas de Autoevaluación.**

Lluvia de Ideas: Actividad de grupo que permite que la gente genere ideas, formule preguntas y proponga soluciones en forma fluida. *Brainstorming; Lancement d'idées («Brainstorming»)*

Local o Punto de Distribución: Sitio final de entrega en el cual los usuarios reciben sus anticonceptivos (clínica, farmacia, trabajadores de Servicios Comunitarios, etc.). *Outlet; Point de distribution (final)*

Mantenimiento de la Cadena de Frío: Manejo de un sistema de congeladores, neveras, contenedores de hielo seco y otros recipientes utilizados para mantener la temperatura apropiada de las vacunas desde la fábrica hasta el sitio de administración. *Cold Chain Maintenance; Entretien de la chaîne du froid*

Manual del Personal: Documento que detalla las políticas de personal y los procedimientos administrativos de una organización, incluyendo una descripción de la estructura de la organización (organigrama) y las obligaciones del personal. *Personnel Manual; Manuel du personnel*

Mapa PAEL: Representación gráfica de la ubicación de las PArejas ELegibles en una comunidad o aldea (PAEL generalmente son parejas casadas en edad reproductiva, sin embargo la definición de pareja elegible varía según el país), que muestra dónde viven y el tipo de método anticonceptivo que están utilizando actualmente. Los trabajadores de campo utilizan generalmente este tipo de mapas para realizar un seguimiento de la situación reproductiva de cada pareja y cualquier cambio de método anticonceptivo que realice. *ELCO Map; Carte ELCO*

Mapeo: Proceso mediante el cuál se registra información o datos en un diagrama o plano de una comunidad, aldea u otro territorio definido con el propósito de monitorear cambios en los datos. *Mapping; Etablissement de cartes*

Matriz (también conocida como Tabla Comparativa): Tabla utilizada para analizar dos o más conjuntos o tipos de información (tales como el número de usuarios de cada método anticonceptivo por tipo de cliente, ya sean nuevos aceptantes o visitas subsecuentes). Puede utilizarse también una tabla para comparar los procesos o actividades con un conjunto de criterios que reflejen las prioridades de la organización, los recursos y las limitaciones a fin de ayudar a los administradores a fijar prioridades sobre las áreas que deben mejorarse. *Matrix; Matrice*

Mercadeo: Actividades relativas al diseño y determinación de precios de los bienes y servicios para que éstos sean adquiridos o utilizados, para informar al público sobre los servicios disponibles y los precios de los mismos y promover el valor de dichos bienes y servicios con el propósito de generar demanda. *Marketing; Marketing*

Mercado de Servicios: Area o región a las cuales un programa intenta llegar mediante la oferta de servicios a la población. *Service Marketplace; Zone desservie*

Mercadeo Social: Estrategia diseñada en base a la comercialización de productos en el mercado por la cual se promocionan, distribuyen y venden los anticonceptivos y otros productos relacionados con la salud sexual y reproductiva, a precios relativamente mas bajos que en lugares ya existentes. El mercadeo social promueve el uso de mensajes de salud reproductiva y planificación familiar a diferentes sectores de la población, utilizando medios comerciales, tales como la radio, los avisos de prensa y la televisión para ofrecer información, educación y comunicación en planificación familiar. *Social Marketing; Marketing social*

Meses de Suministros: Este término se utiliza para expresar la cantidad de suministros disponible (de un anticonceptivo o artículo específico) en relación con el número de meses que duraría esta cantidad si se distribuye a las tasas (promedio) actuales. Es la cantidad disponible (del anticonceptivo o artículo específico) dividida por la tasa mensual de consumo promedio de dicho producto. *Months of Supply; Mois d'approvisionnement*

Metas: Objetivos muy específicos a corto plazo y que pueden ser medidos en términos numéricos . Deben ser medibles, apropiadas, temporales, específicas y realistas y pertenecen a un conponente específico del programa. *Targets; Cibles*

Metodología: Medios y procedimientos lógicos mediante los cuales un programa o enfoque se pone en ejecución, tales como, la capacitación en servicio contra la capacitación formal. *Methodology; Méthodologie*

Métodos de Corto Plazo: Anticonceptivos que mantienen su eficacia durante un tiempo relativamente corto. Los expertos difieren sobre cuáles métodos deben incluirse bajo esta definición. Algunos expertos incluyen solamente a los espermicidas, diafragmas y condones, mientras que otros también incluyen los anticonceptivos orales. *Short-Term Methods; Méthodes à court terme*

Métodos de Larga Duración (o Métodos de Largo Plazo): Métodos anticonceptivos que siguen siendo efectivos durante un período relativamente largo. Los expertos pueden tener divergencias sobre los métodos así definidos. Algunos expertos incluyen solamente a los DIUs, implantes e inyectables, otros consideran los anticonceptivas orales y otros incluyen también la esterilización. *Long-Acting Methods; Méthodes de longue durée*

Mezcla de Métodos: Resumen, expresado generalmente como porcentajes, que muestra la proporción de todos los usuarios (de una población general o específica) que está utilizando determinado anticonceptivo. *Method Mix; Gamme des méthodes*

Micro-Administrar: La práctica de supervisar en forma innecesaria y excesiva al personal y las actividades que éste desempeña. *Micro-Manage; Micro-gestion*

Misión de la Organización: Ver **Declaración de Misión.**

Monitoreo: Proceso de verificación periódica de la situación de un programa, para determinar si las actividades se están cumpliendo en la forma planeada. *Monitoring; Suivi*

Motivación del Cliente: Información, educación, discusión o actividades promocionales que sirven para alentar a un cliente o a un cliente potencial a utilizar o continuar utilizando en forma regular anticonceptivos y servicios de salud reproductiva. *Client Motivation; Motivation des clients*

Motivación del Personal: Las actividades del personal o del supervisor de una organización que reafirman la importancia del trabajo realizado para lograr los objetivos del programa y mejorar las habilidades, la motivación y las calificaciones del personal. Las acciones o actividades de motivación incluyen la capacitación, la retroalimentación positiva y constructiva en forma regular, la apreciación por el trabajo que realiza el personal y su contribución a la resolución de problemas. *Staff Motivation; Motivation du personnel*

Norma (o Guía) Clínica: Lista de estándares médicos que debe seguir el personal. Esta contiene una descripción detallada de los procedimientos médicos y los patrones de calidad de los servicios que aseguran la protección y salud de los clientes de planificación familiar. *Clinic Protocol; Protocole sanitaire*

Normas de Auto-Evaluación (también conocidas como Lista de Verificación para la Auto-evaluación): Una serie de listas de verificación o pautas que formulan diferentes preguntas para evaluar las habilidades del personal o el rendimiento o funcionamiento de un programa. *Self-Evaluation Guidelines; Directives pour l'auto-évaluation*

Normas de Despidos: Norma estándar, generalmente establecida en el manual de personal, describe los términos de despido de un empleado y los derechos del mismo al ser despedido. *Termination policy; Procédure de rupture de contrat*

Normas para Manejo de Quejas y Reclamos: Política estándar, generalmente establecida en el manual de personal, describe los procedimientos mediante los cuales las quejas de los empleados se transmiten, procesan y resuelven. *Grievance Policy; Procédure de soumission de doléances*

Núcleo del PMC (o Grupo Interno para el PMC): El núcleo del PMC utilizado en un programa de mejoramiento continuo de la calidad, está conformado por un grupo de personas seleccionadas para dirigir el PMC. El grupo se responsabiliza de la planeación y ejecución del proceso, el arranque del mismo, la elaboración de materiales de capacitación, la organización y capacitación de todo el personal y el apoyo a todos los niveles de la organización. *CQI Core Group; Groupe-noyau pour l'ACQ*

Número de Lote: Código que se asigna a un producto farmacéutico para diferenciarlo cuando éste se fabrica en diferentes fechas. *Lot Number; Numéro de lot*

Objetivos/Metas de Desempeño: Resultados finales que una organización o empleado individual esperan lograr al final de un período específico. Las metas de desempeño se relacionan generalmente con un período más corto (varios meses) y se refieren a tareas muy específicas. Los objetivos de desempeño se refieren a períodos más largos (un año) y determinan el tipo y alcance de las actividades que una organización, programa o miembro del personal deberán llevar a cabo para lograr los resultados deseados. *Performance Targets and Objectives; Cibles et objectifs de performance*

Objetivos Específicos: Resultados esperados o expectativas de un programa; representan cambios en el conocimiento, actitudes o comportamientos de los clientes del programa; se describen en términos medibles e indican un período específico dentro del cuál se lograrán. Los objetivos deben ser MATER: Medibles, Apropiados, Temporales, Específicos, y Realistas. *Objectives; Objectifs*

Objetivos Generales: Los beneficios a largo plazo del programa para la población seleccionada, definidos en términos generales. *Goals; Buts*

Oportunidad Perdida: Ocasión que ofrecía una oportunidad de realizar una actividad beneficiosa (prestación de servicios, retroalimentación del personal, etc.) pero que fue desaprovechada. *Missed Opportunity; Occasion manquée*

Organigrama: Ver **Diagrama Organizacional.**

Organización Incipiente (o de Arranque): Generalmente una organización pequeña en su primera etapa de desarrollo. Muchas organizaciones incipientes se caracterizan por un liderazgo altamente creativo, iniciativas muy innovadores y un personal reducido pero altamente motivado. *Start-Up Organization; Organisation qui démarre*

Organización Interna: La estructura interna y el ordenamiento de una organización o programa en la asignación de las diferentes áreas funcionales y la relación entre éstas, incluidas la planeación, la elaboración de presupuestos, la administración financiera, la supervisión y otras. La organización interna de un programa es particularmente importante a medida que los programas se descentralizan y/o tienden a integrarse en uno solo. *Internal Organization; Organisation interne*

P aquete de Servicios: Convenio entre un comprador y un proveedor de servicios de salud y planificación familiar con respecto a un conjunto convenido de servicios a cambio de un precio predeterminado (generalmente una tasa mensual por cada miembro). *Managed Care; Système contrôlé de prestations sanitaires*

Participación Comunitaria: Como componente crítico de los programas de planificación familiar, la participación de la comunidad puede adoptar diversas formas; se da cuando los miembros de la comunidad y el gobierno del lugar desempeñan un papel importante en el manejo del programa local de planificación familiar. Igualmente, cuando aportan dinero o materiales, o tiempo de trabajo voluntario, creando así un sentimiento de pertenencia del programa y la aceptación de la responsabilidad en cuánto del logro de los objetivos planteados. *Community Participation; Participation communautaire*

Partida o Rubro: Categoría presupuestal, catálogo de cuentas o informes financieros que representa una cuenta, la cual es utilizada para registrar transacciones de un tipo particular de ingreso, egreso, activo o pasivo. *Line Item; Rubrique*

Pasivos: Obligaciones o deudas contraídas con los proveedores, empleados, bancos o el gobierno. *Liabilities; Passif*

Pedido de Emergencia: Pedido de anticonceptivos o suministros que se hace fuera del cronograma normal de pedidos, generalmente cuando las existencias han disminuido agudamente debido a un incremento imprevisto de la demanda. Los pedidos de emergencia se hacen generalmente por cantidades que aumenten el nivel de existencias y cubran la demanda hasta el próximo pedido, tomando en cuenta la cantidad que será distribuida mientras aquél se recibe. *Emergency Order; Commande d'urgence*

Pensamiento Estratégico: Habilidad administrativa crítica que requiere que la persona posea la habilidad para evaluar la Misión de un programa, sus metas futuras y el contexto externo en el que trabaja. El pensamiento estratégico hace necesario que los administradores examinen si sus programas están «haciendo las cosas correctas» para cumplir su misión. *Strategic Thinking; Pensée stratégique*

Perfil del Cliente: Representación numérica y/o porcentual de las características más importantes de los clientes de un programa. El perfil de un cliente permite que los administradores conozcan mejor los diversos tipos de clientes a los que presta servicios el programa (en algunos casos), las necesidades prioritarias de dichos clientes, para que el programa pueda prestarles mejores servicios y atraer nuevos clientes con necesidades similares. *Client Profile; Profil des clients*

Plan de Acción: Elaborado por un gerente y por el personal a su cargo, un plan de acción detalla las metas y objetivos del programa así como las actividades que se desarrollarán para lograrlos. El plan de acción cubre generalmente un período de un año, determina cuál es la persona o personas responsable(s) de la ejecución de cada actividad, muestra cuándo debe concluir cada una de éstas e indica cuáles son los recursos financieros necesarios. (Ver también **Plan Operativo**.) *Action Plan; Plan d'action*

Plan de Negocios: Desarrollado a menudo con el propósito de captar financiamiento para un programa o proyecto, un plan de negocios detalla las metas, actividades, fuentes de ingresos, otros recursos financieros y el cálculo de los ingresos anticipados que serán generados por el negocio o actividad. *Business Plan; Plan d'entreprise*

Plan de Trabajo: Documento elaborado por el administrador y el personal que cubre un período específico, enumera todas las actividades planeadas, la fecha en la cual éstas se completarán, los recursos que se requerirán y las personas responsables de su ejecución. *Work Plan; Plan de travail*

Plan de Visita del Supervisor (también conocido como Plan de Sesión): Lista de verificación utilizada por los supervisores en la cual se resumen los aspectos, habilidades y estadísticas que deben controlarse durante cada visita de supervisión. Dicho plan debe incluir también las actividades de apoyo del programa, tales como la recolección de formularios y el control de suministros además de cualquier otra actividad posterior a la sesión que debe llevar a cabo el supervisor. *Supervisor's Visit Plan; Plan de visite du superviseur*

Plan Estratégico: Documento que resulta de la planeación (estratégica) de largo plazo. Generalmente cubre un período mínimo de cinco años, plantea la misión y las metas del programa, fija prioridades para las estrategias y formula la base financiera para lograr dichas metas. *Strategic Plan; Plan stratégique*

Plan Operativo: A diferencia del plan estratégico (el cual plantea las estrategias o iniciativas generales que utilizará un programa para lograr sus objetivos), un plan operativo plantea los proyectos o actividades específicos (de acuerdo con el plan estratégico) que se llevarán a cabo y el cronograma y los recursos necesarios para completar dichos proyectos o actividades. (Ver también el **Plan de Acción.**) *Operational Plan; Plan opérationnel*

Planeación: Proceso continuo de análisis de datos, tomas de decisiones y formulación de planes para el futuro, con miras a lograr los objetivos del programa. *Planning; Planification*

Planeación de Actividades: Proceso de definición de las actividades, la planeación de la secuencia de las mismas y la identificación de los recursos (humanos, financieros y materiales) que se utilizarán para llevar a cabo dichas actividades a fin de lograr los resultados deseados. *Activity Planning; Planification des activités*

Planeación Estratégica: Proceso para planear a largo plazo, en un período de tres a cinco años. Este proceso incluye la fijación de objetivos generales, estrategias y objetivos específicos para el programa. *Strategic Planning; Planification stratégique*

Planilla de Actividades de Planificación Familiar: Formulario utilizado algunas veces en las clínicas con mayor movimiento a manera de formulario intermedio entre el Registro Diario de Actividades y el Resumen Mensual. Los totales del Registro Diario de Actividades se transfieren a la Planilla cada día, luego se suma el total del mes y se transfiere al Resumen Mensual de las Actividades de Planificación Familiar. *Family Planning Activities Worksheet; Fiche de calcul des activités de planification familiale*

Planilla de Proyecciones del Flujo de Fondos (también conocido como Estado de Flujo de Fondos): Proyección de los ingresos y desembolsos en efectivo utilizados para identificar los excedentes y déficits potenciales de efectivo. *Cash Flow Projection Worksheet; Formulaire de projection de l'état de la trésorerie*

Posición Financiera: El estado financiero de una organización en un momento determinado. La posición financiera indica la situación financiera general de la organización, tomando en cuenta los activos y pasivos actuales y los ingresos y gastos proyectados. *Financial Position; Situation financière*

Premio al Mérito: Ascensos o recompensas monetarias que se dan a los empleados en reconocimiento de su desempeño sobresaliente. *Merit Awards; Récompenses au mérite*

Presupuesto Consolidado: Documento que integra la información de los ingresos y egresos proyectados de todos los donantes, programas o instalaciones dentro de la misma institución. *Consolidated Budget; Budget consolidé*

Prevalencia de Uso de Anticonceptivos: Porcentaje de todas las mujeres en edad reproductiva (MER) o mujeres casadas en edad reproductiva (MCER), cuya edad fluctúa entre los 15 y los 49 años que están utilizando un método anticonceptivo. La prevalencia anticonceptiva generalmente se refiere al uso de todos los métodos, pero puede darse en forma separada para los métodos modernos (píldoras, DIUs, implantes, inyectables, condones, diafragmas, capuchones cervicales y esterilización voluntaria). La prevalencia se calcula dividiendo el número de MER o MCER que están utilizando un método (numerador) por el número total de MER o MCER (denominador). *Contraceptive Prevalence; Prévalence contraceptive*

Primera Visita o Primera Consulta de un Cliente: Ver **Cliente Nuevo**.

Primero en Expirar, Primero en Salir (PEPS): Sistema de administración de suministros en el cual los productos con las fechas de expiración más próximas, se distribuyen primero y los productos con fechas de expiración posteriores, sólo se distribuirán cuando se hayan agotado los de fecha de expiración más reciente. *First-to-Expire, First-Out (FEFO); Premier à périmer, premier sorti (PPPS)*

Privatización: Este término se refiere a la transferencia de funciones administrativas específicas, como la adquisición de productos anticonceptivos, la logística y la capacitación, a *organizaciones privadas sin o con fines de lucro* que están fuera de la estructura gubernamental.

A pesar de utilizarse frecuentemente para describir una forma de descentralización, algunos expertos creen que la privatización no es una forma de descentralización, porque, al privatizar, un gobierno se desliga de la responsabilidad en lugar de transferir el poder a los niveles inferiores. *Privatization; Privatisation*

Proceso de Mejoramiento Continuo de la Calidad (PMC): Técnica estructurada de uso cíclico para mejorar los sistemas y procesos de una organización o programa. El PMC incluye la identificación de un área donde existe una oportunidad de mejoramiento, la definición del problema identificado en dicha área, el resumen de la secuencia de actividades (el proceso) que ocurren en dicha área y la determinación de los resultados deseados del proceso y los requisitos necesarios para lograrlos. Asimismo, la selección de los pasos específicos para estudiar, recopilar y analizar los datos del proceso, adoptar medidas correctivas y controlar los resultados de dichas acciones. El PMC se basa en un enfoque de equipo y requiere del desarrollo de equipos compuestos por personal de diferentes áreas y niveles funcionales de la organización. El PMC asume que cualquier sistema puede ser mejorado siempre y por consiguiente, enfatiza un proceso de mejoramiento constante que requiere de un compromiso a largo plazo y un trabajo de grupo efectivo. *Continuous Quality Improvement (CQI); Amélioration continue de la qualité (ACQ)*

Proceso de Supervisión en Equipo: Cualquier sistema establecido para la supervisión del personal utilizando un enfoque participativo de equipo que vincule a los supervisores y al personal en todo el proceso. *Team Supervision Process; Processus de supervision en équipe*

Proceso de Trabajo: Secuencia de actividades que se llevan a cabo para completar una tarea. *Por ejemplo, el proceso de trabajo para el registro de un cliente en una clínica incluye el saludo al cliente, la anotación de su nombre, la verificación para determinar si se trata de un cliente nuevo o subsecuente, la apertura de un nuevo expediente y el llenado de los formularios necesarios, o la ubicación del expediente del cliente, el cobro de la cuota de ingreso (si fuese apropiado), el ofrecimiento de una silla al cliente para que espere hasta que pueda recibir atención y la notificación al personal encargado que el cliente está esperando ser atendido. Work Process; Processus de travail*

Programa de Cobro de Tarifas por Servicios: Programa que cobra una tarifa por cada servicio ofrecido por el programa o clínica. En un programa de cobro de tarifas por servicios, hay generalmente una tarifa diferente por cada tipo de servicio en base a su costo real. En dicho programa, una cliente nueva que recibe sus primeros ciclos de píldoras generalmente pagará más que una usuaria continua que regresa para reabastecerse. Esto se debe a que una cliente nueva recibe servicios más completos en su primera visita que una cliente subsecuente que solo acude a la clínica para reabastecerse de píldoras. *Fee-For-Service Program; Programme de paiement des prestations*

Programa para Aumentar la Tasa de Continuidad de Usuarios Activos: Enfoque sistemático desarrollado para aumentar la proporción de usuarios continuos (activos) en un sistema de servicios. Para establecer un programa para mejorar la continuación en servicios de planificación familiar debe determinarse para cada centro de servicios una tasa de continuación aceptable y hacer el seguimiento periódico tanto a los usuarios nuevos como a los activos. *User Continuity Program; Programme pour accroître le nombre d'utilisateurs actifs*

Protocolo de Supervisión: Sistema de supervisión del personal (clínico y no clínico). Un protocolo debe describir claramente los procedimientos y cronogramas de supervisión, la filosofía de la organización sobre la supervisión, las herramientas utilizadas para una supervisión efectiva (tales como las descripciones de trabajo y los objetivos de desempeño), los criterios para los ascensos y las técnicas para motivar y apoyar al personal. *Supervisory Protocol; Protocole de supervision*

Proyecciones Basadas en el Servicio: Cálculos basados en un análisis de los servicios de un programa y en el número proyectado de clientes que éste espera atender. *Service-Based Forecasts; Prévisions basées sur les prestations de services*

Proyecciones Basadas en Información Censual o en Encuestas Demográficas: Cálculos de necesidades de anticonceptivos que se basan en la proporción de la población objetivo que el programa piensa cubrir y el nivel proyectado de demanda para cada método anticonceptivo. *Population-Based Forecasts; Prévisions basées sur la population*

Proyecciones Basadas en la Distribución: Método para proyectar necesidades de anticonceptivos que permite conocer estimados sobre el número de anticonceptivos requeridos basándose en las cantidades previas distribuidas por la bodega a la clínica o centro de distribución. *Distribution-Based Forecasts; Prévisions basées sur la distribution*

Punto de Equilibrio: Volumen de actividad en el cuál los ingresos de las operaciones son iguales a los gastos de operación. *Break-Even Point; Seuil de rentabilité*

Razón: Proporción obtenida mediante la división de una cantidad entre otra cantidad. *Por ejemplo, 18 enfermeras de planificación familiar (numerador) dividas entre seis clínicas (denominador) da una razón de tres enfermeras por clínica.* **Ratio; *Ratio***

Recaudación de Fondos: Proceso para lograr apoyo financiero de los grupos comunitarios, unidades gubernamentales locales o centrales, organismos o individuos, donantes locales o internacionales y otros. ***Fund Raising; Mobilisation de fonds***

Reconocimiento del Desempeño: Procedimiento para evaluar el desempeño de un empleado, se efectúa en intervalos determinados, generalmente anuales o semianuales. ***Performance Appraisal; Evaluation de la performance***

Recursos: Medios disponibles para efectuar las actividades planeadas, tales como personal, equipos y dinero. ***Resources; Ressources***

Registro Diario de Actividades: Control diario del número de visitas de los clientes a una clínica, subdividido de acuerdo al tipo y a las cantidades de anticonceptivos suministrados a cada tipo de cliente (usuario nuevo o subsecuente). Debe obtenerse diariamente el número total de visitas de los clientes y el número total de cada tipo de anticonceptivo distribuido. ***Daily Activity Register; Registre journalier des activités***

Relaciones Públicas: Actividades para la promoción del programa, servicios e imagen de una organización ante el público. ***Public Affairs; Affaires publiques***

Remuneración: Pago por los servicios que se prestan a una institución. ***Remuneration; Rémunération***

Rendimiento de la Clínica: El rendimiento de la clínica se mide frecuentemente contando el número de clientes y/o el número de nuevos aceptantes y usuarios subsecuentes a los cuales la clínica presta servicios durante un período específico y cuya evaluación se efectúa en base a objetivos fijados previamente. ***Clinic Performance; Performance de la formation sanitaire***

Requisitos Previos («Benchmarks»): Objetivos o criterios establecidos que deben lograrse en un período específico. A menudo estos requisitos se fijan como incentivos para que un programa logre los objetivos a corto plazo los cuales, una vez logrados, califican al programa para recibir financiamiento adicional u otras formas de apoyo. ***Benchmarks; Jalons de performance progressifs***

Resolución de Problemas: Habilidad administrativa crítica que comprende la identificación objetiva de las causas de un problema y la propuesta de soluciones potenciales, a menudo creativas, que sean aceptables para varios individuos o entidades. *Problem Solving; Résolution de problèmes*

Responsabilidad Conjunta: Situación en la que diversas entidades o individuos son responsables en forma conjunta por los resultados de una actividad o actividades. *Mutually Accountable; Mutuellement responsable*

Responsabilidades del Personal: Las funciones específicas o el conjunto de actividades asumidas por los diferentes miembros del personal. Dichas responsabilidades generalmente pueden ser cuantificadas, como el número de sesiones de consejería a clientes durante un período específico, o el número de consultas médicas en una clínica distrital, tres veces a la semana. *Staff Responsibilities; Responsabilités du personnel*

Responsabilidades Funcionales: Tipo de compromisos de trabajo que una persona o grupo asume, tales como la planeación, monitoreo, evaluación, oferta de servicios médicos, capacitación, etc. *Functional Responsibilities; Responsabilités de fonction*

Resultados Intermedios: Los productos que son críticos para el logro de los resultados de largo plazo. *Por ejemplo, el número de talleres o cursos ofrecidos son un resultado intermedio crítico para lograr a largo plazo, la producción de personas calificadas. Intermediate Outputs; Résultats intermédiaires*

Resumen Mensual de Actividades de Planificación Familiar: Formulario utilizado para sintetizar los totales mensuales de todos los datos recopilados en los Registros Diarios de Actividades. Generalmente, el administrador de la clínica guarda una copia y la otra se envía al supervisor del programa el cual suma los datos mensuales de todas las clínicas de la región o distrito. *Monthly Summary of Family Planning Activities; Récapitulatif mensuel des activités de planification familiale*

Retroalimentación: Proceso que permite una comunicación fluida entre el campo y la oficina o entre un empleado y su supervisor, para modificar, corregir y fortalecer el desempeño y los resultados. *Feedback; Rétro-information*

S aldo Disponible: Ver Existencias Disponibles.

Salud Reproductiva: Un estado de bienestar físico, mental y social que no consiste solamente en la ausencia de enfermedades o dolencias en todos los aspectos referentes al sistema reproductivo, sus funciones y procesos. Por consiguiente la salud reproductiva implica que la gente pueda llevar una vida sexual segura y satisfactoria, teniendo la capacidad de reproducirse y la libertad de decidir cuándo y cuán a menudo hacerlo. En esta última condición está implícito el derecho de los varones y mujeres a mantenerse informados con respecto a los métodos anticonceptivos seguros, aceptables y al alcance de sus posibilidades, a elección suya, y a tener acceso a los mismos así como a otros métodos de planificación familiar para regular la fertilidad, que no sean contrarios a la ley, además del derecho de acceder a servicios apropiados de salud que permitirán que las mujeres tengan un embarazo y un parto seguros, proporcionando a las parejas las mejores oportunidades de tener un bebé sano.[1] (Ver **Servicios de Salud Reproductiva.**) *Reproductive Health; Santé reproductive*

Satisfacción del Cliente: Los beneficios o la apreciación del servicio (según la percepción del cliente) de un programa o clínica, determinados frecuentemente en base a la calidad de la interacción interpersonal del usuario con el personal, la gama de anticonceptivos y la eficiencia y grado de respuesta a las necesidades individuales de los clientes. *Client Satisfaction; Satisfaction des clients*

Sectores Desatendidos de la Población o Carentes de Servicios: Grupos de población que normalmente carecen de acceso a los servicios o que reciben servicios deficientes de los programas establecidos. En planificación familiar, los adolescentes, los varones, las mujeres de baja paridad, los residentes pobres de zonas urbanas, los solteros y la gente que habita áreas rurales remotas son ejemplos de estos sectores de la población. *Underserved Populations; Populations mal desservies (sous-servies)*

Servicios Adquiridos: Servicios o contratos de largo plazo suscritos con *instituciones* ajenas al proyecto para la oferta de servicios como el mantenimiento de vehículos, servicios de limpieza, vigilancia, propaganda o servicios de promoción. A pesar de ser similares, los convenios contractuales suscritos con *individuos* para la prestación de

---

[1] *Plan de Acción de la Conferencia Internacional de las Naciones Unidas sobre Población y Desarrollo, El Cairo, 23 de septiembre de 1994, párrafo 7.1.*

servicios especializados, tales como conferencias, capacitación y evaluación y se basan en el pago de honorarios por cada servicio prestado. (Ver **Honorarios Profesionales**.) *Purchased Services; Services achetés (ou sous-traitance)*

Servicios Comunitarios (SC): Información y servicios de salud y planificación familiar que se ofrecen a las mujeres y a las parejas en los lugares donde viven o a través de distribuidores locales. Los servicios se prestan mediante actividades comunitarias cuando los extensionistas de una clínica local o de la comunidad, ofrecen ciertos anticonceptivos selectos (generalmente píldoras y condones) a los clientes, realizan el seguimiento de los que desean formular preguntas o quejas o informar efectos colaterales y refieren a aquéllos que lo necesiten a las clínicas del área. *Community-Based Services (CBS); Services à base communautaire (SBC)*

Servicios de Almacén (o de Distribución Local): Tipo de servicio comunitario basado en una persona que se encuentra permanentemente en la comunidad y que está disponible para ofrecer información y anticonceptivos (generalmente píldoras y condones) a dicha comunidad cuando se necesitan. Dado que los clientes acuden generalmente a dicha persona para obtener servicios, esta modalidad reduce el número de personas que prestan servicios a nivel comunitario. *Depot Services; Services au dépôt communautaire*

Servicios de Salud Reproductiva: Variedad de métodos, técnicas y servicios que contribuyen a mantener o mejorar la salud reproductiva y el bienestar de una persona evitando y resolviendo los problemas de salud reproductiva.[2] (Ver **Salud Reproductiva**.) *Reproductive Health Care/Services; Prestations/services de santé reproductive*

Servicios Satélites: Servicios ofrecidos a una comunidad o a varias comunidades en un momento específico (generalmente una vez al mes) y en un lugar determinado. Los servicios satélites ofrecen frecuentemente servicios integrados de salud, atención materna e infantil y servicios de planificación familiar. (Ver también **Sistema de Cinco Mesas**.) *Satellite Services; Points de services périphériques*

---

[2] Adaptado del *Plan de Acción de la Conferencia Internacional de las Naciones Unidas sobre Población y Desarrollo*, El Cairo, 23 de septiembre de 1994, párrafo 7.1.

Servicios Verticales o Enfoque Vertical: Modalidad en la cuál la planificación familiar, la salud materna e infantil, nutrición, vacunación y otros servicios de salud reproductiva se ofrecen en centros separados que cuentan con un personal diferente que depende del nivel central de departamentos o ministerios separados que operan independientemente el uno del otro. *Vertical Services/Approach; Approche de services verticaux*

Servicios Voluntarios: Enfoque utilizado para apoyar un programa local público o privado en el cuál los miembros de la comunidad colaboran con los empleados del gobierno, o con los trabajadores de campo de las organizaciones no gubernamentales (ONGs), desempeñando funciones de motivación, suministro de anticonceptivos y actividades de seguimiento. Es posible pagar una pequeña compensación a los trabajadores, o reembolsarles sus gastos de viaje u otorgarles otras recompensas tangibles pero no un salario regular. *Volunteer Services; Services bénévoles (de volontaires)*

Sesión de Supervisión: Reunión con uno o más miembros del personal para revisar el trabajo realizado y hacer planes para el futuro, así como para posteriores sesiones de supervisión. *Supervisory Session; Session de supervision*

Sistema Bifurcado de Información: Sistema de información diseñado para obtener, en forma rutinaria, información de resultados y que a la vez requiere que los administradores recopilen información sobre el proceso con el fin de ayudar a determinar dónde podrían suscitarse problemas para corregirlos. *Two-Tier Information System; Système d'information à deux niveaux*

Sistema Contable: Sistema de recopilación, registro, procesamiento y reporte de todas las transacciones financieras. Dos sistemas comúnmente utilizados son la contabilidad de caja y la contabilidad sobre bases devengadas. *Accounting System; Système de comptabilité*

Sistema Continuo (Perpetuo) de Inventario (también conocido como Sistema de Pedidos de Intervalos Variables): Sistema de control de inventarios y reabastecimiento de suministros en el cual se revisan constantemente los niveles de existencias. Los pedidos se hacen cuando las existencias alcanzan o caen por debajo del nivel predeterminado de reabastecimiento. Mediante este sistema el reabastecimiento se hace sobre una base de cantidades estándar, sin regirse por un cronograma preestablecido. *Continuous (Perpetual) Review System; Système de revue continuelle ou perpétuelle*

Sistema de Administración de la Calidad: En planificación familiar, un sistema que reúne en forma armónica las diversas actividades que ayudan a asegurar y mejorar continuamente la calidad de los servicios de planificación familiar mediante una red de prestación de servicios. En un sistema efectivo de administración de la calidad los supervisores de todos los niveles deben contar con conocimientos y habilidades actualizados tanto en el área de prestación de servicios, como en temas administrativos. *Quality Management System; Système de gestion de la qualité*

Sistema de Asignación: Sistema de abastecimiento que entrega los anticonceptivos mediante envíos periódicos desde la bodega central o bodegas intermedias a los locales. Los centros o lugares de distribución reciben los anticonceptivos sin ordenarlos. *Push System; Système d'allocation*

Sistema de Cinco Mesas: Utilizado frecuentemente en los programas comunitarios móviles, el sistema de cinco mesas es un programa que presta servicios integrados de salud materno infantil y planificación familiar en un centro no permanente. Bajo este sistema, se organiza una mesa para cada uno de los cinco servicios: registro del niño; peso del niño; registro de los resultados en una cartilla de crecimiento; información sobre salud (nutrición, rehidratación oral, inmunización, lactancia, información sobre el espaciamiento de nacimientos/planificación familiar); y la entrega de cualquier tratamiento médico necesario, anticonceptivos o referencia a un centro permanente de salud si fuera necesario. *Five-Table System; Système des cinq tables*

Sistema de Incentivos: Política que recompensa a los empleados por su excelente desempeño o por logros especiales y los motiva a alcanzar sus objetivos y a mantener la calidad del programa. *Incentive System; Système de primes d'encouragement*

Sistema de Información: Sistema estandarizado de recopilación, registro, interpretación, análisis, y difusión de datos para que estén disponibles para la toma de decisiones administrativas críticas. En una clínica de planificación familiar, el sistema de información se refiere a la recopilación y distribución de la información programática y financiera referente a la prestación de servicios a los clientes y el funcionamiento de un centro. (Ver también **Sistema Bifurcado Información**.) *Information System; Système d'information*

Sistema de Información Gerencial (SIG): Sistema diseñado por una organización para recolectar y dar a conocer información de un programa, de manera que permita a los administradores planear, hacer el seguimiento (monitoreo) y evaluar las operaciones y resultados de todo el programa. *Management Information System (MIS); Système d'information de gestion (SIG)*

Sistema de Pagos de Terceros (Co-Pagos): Sistema mediante el cuál terceros (como un empleador, una compañía de seguros o un plan de salud) pagan el costo de los servicios ofrecidos al cliente. También pueden darse pagos compartidos en los cuales el cliente paga una parte de los servicios y el saldo se complementa por terceros. *Third-Party Payments; Paiements par un tiers (ou Co-paiements)*

Sistema de Pedidos de Intervalos Fijos: Ver **Sistema Periódico de Inventario.**

Sistema de Pedidos de Intervalos Variables: Ver **Sistema Continuo (Perpetuo) de Inventario.**

Sistema de Referencia: Sistema establecido que define cuando un cliente debe ser referido a otro centro para recibir servicios (frecuentemente para el tratamiento de complicaciones médicas o la entrega de métodos o para la prestación de procedimientos quirúrgicos), la forma como el cliente llegará a la clínica (por ejemplo, si un promotor lo acompañará hasta la clínica). Igualmente, con quién debe ponerse en contacto en el centro al que fue referido y qué documentación deberá presentarse o entregarse al cliente en dicho centro. Los sistemas efectivos de referencia mejoran el acceso a los servicios y a los métodos clínicos de largo plazo y sirven para mejorar la calidad de los servicios de una clínica satélite más pequeña. *Referral System; Système de référence*

Sistema de Requisición: Sistema de abastecimiento que requiere que los puntos de distribución pidan la cantidad de suministros que necesitan a las bodegas centrales de acuerdo al consumo. *Pull System; Système de commande (réquisition)*

Sistema de Supervisión: Métodos y procedimientos para dar seguimiento al volumen y a la calidad del trabajo desempeñado por el personal subordinado, así como para proporcionar el apoyo necesario a dicho personal. El sistema incluye visitas, reconocimientos de desempeño de los empleados, reuniones individuales y grupales del personal, revisión de informes, etc. *Supervisory System; Système de supervision*

Sistema Max/Min: Sistema eficiente que se usa para mantener la cantidad adecuada de anticonceptivos disponibles. Niveles máximo y mínimo de existencias son calculados para asegurar que un programa no agote sus suministros y al mismo tiempo evitar que tenga más de lo necesario. Los niveles máximo y mínimo se expresan en base a un cierto número de meses de suministros. *Max/Min (Maximum-Minimum) Stock Level; Système Max/Min (Maximum-Minimum)*

Sistema Periódico de Inventario (también conocido como Sistema de Pedidos de Intervalos Fijos): Sistema de control de inventarios y reabastecimientos en el cual se revisan los niveles de existencias a intervalos de tiempo predeterminados y los pedidos se basan en los niveles actuales de existencias, el nivel de reserva de emergencia y un máximo establecido. Mediante este método el reabastecimiento se hace sobre una base preestablecida, es decir, en una fecha fija. Sin embargo, la cantidad del pedido puede variar en cada ocasión. *Periodic Review System; Système de revue periodique*

Sistemas de Fiscalización: Todos los procedimientos y reglamentos que evitan la corrupción, el robo y el uso indebido de fondos u otros recursos. *Control Systems; Systèmes de contrôle*

Situación de Existencias: Número de meses de suministros disponibles en un momento dado para un solo tipo y marca de anticonceptivo o producto. La situación de existencias se calcula dividiendo la cantidad de existencias disponibles por el consumo mensual promedio de dicho anticonceptivo o producto. *Stock Position; Situation des stocks*

Subsidios Cruzados: Sistema que utiliza los ingresos generados por un servicio para apoyar el costo de otro servicio dentro del mismo programa. *Por ejemplo, utilizar el dinero generado por las ventas de anticonceptivos de una clínica para subsidiar el costo de los servicios a usuarios que no pueden pagar en la misma clínica o en otros lugares. Cross-Subsidization/Cross-Subsidies; Subvention croisée*

Subsistema: Sistema que forma parte de otro más grande que separa funcionalmente a una organización en divisiones tales como capacitación, prestación de servicios, infraestructura, etc. *Subsystem; Sous-système*

Suministros de Planificación Familiar: Todos los anticonceptivos, productos médicos y equipo que está disponible para dar servicios de planificación familiar. *Family Planning Commodities; Produits pour la planification familiale*

Supervisión Facilitadora: Enfoque de supervisión que enfatiza la consejería, la resolución conjunta de problemas y las comunicaciones fluidas entre el supervisor y el trabajador. *Facilitative Supervision; Supervision à but de facilitation*

Supervisión Selectiva: Procedimiento para supervisar los aspectos específicos sobre una base rotativa menos frecuenta, debido a restricciones de tiempo. *Selective Supervision; Supervision sélective*

Sustentabilidad: Habilidad que tiene un programa para prestar servicios de calidad a sus clientes, ampliar la cobertura de los servicios y la base de clientes, aumentar o mantener la demanda de servicios y generar ingresos mediante mecanismos locales de financiamiento, cuando disminuye su dependencia de los fondos de donantes externos. (Ver también **Autofinanciamiento** y **Autosuficiencia.**) *Sustainability; Viabilité*

T abla Comparativa: Ver **Matriz.**

Tabla de Análisis de Datos sobre Anticonceptivos: Formato utilizado (para cada método anticonceptivo) con el fin de controlar las existencias disponibles y la cantidad de suministros solicitados, recibidos y distribuidos mensualmente. Esta planilla ayuda a los administradores a supervisar los cambios en la cantidades mensuales de existencias y hace un resumen de las transacciones de los productos del inventario durante un año. *Contraceptive Data Analysis Chart; Tableau d'analyse des données sur les contraceptifs*

Tabla de Frecuencias: Tabla utilizada para registrar el número de veces que un evento u ocurrencia particular se repite durante un período específico, tal como el número de aceptantes nuevos y el de visitas mensuales subsecuentes el año anterior, o el número de personas que refieren los motivos por los cuáles no utilizan anticoncepción, etc. *Frequency Table; Tableau de fréquence*

Tabla del Flujo de Clientes: Tabla que resume la información obtenida del formulario de flujo de clientes. Muestra el tiempo total que el cliente pasa en la clínica, incluido el tiempo de espera y el que pasa con el personal, así como el porcentaje del tiempo total que los clientes pasan en la clínica esperando ser atendidos. *Client Flow Chart; Tableau du flux des clients*

Tabla para Control de Suministros: Planilla que se utiliza para calcular el consumo mensual promedio (CMP) y las cantidades mínima y máxima de existencias. La tabla para control de suministros permite a los administradores registrar en una misma gráfica la información sobre las cantidades mínima y máxima de existencias deseables de todos los tipos de anticonceptivos en base a patrones de consumo recientes. *Status of Supplies Chart; Tableau de la situation des stocks*

Tabulación Cruzada: Tabla o gráfica utilizada para mostrar simultáneamente los datos resumidos de dos o más conjuntos de variables. *Cross-Tabulation; Tableau croisée*

Tareas: Actividades divididas en acciones o responsabilidades específicas. *Tasks; Tâches*

Tarifas de Ingreso: Tarifa fija que se cobra a los clientes por cada visita que efectúan sin tomar en cuenta el tipo de servicio recibido. *Registration Fees; Droits d'inscription (ou d'admission)*

Tarifas para los Clientes: Cargos cobrados a un cliente como pago por los servicios prestados, tales como el suministro de anticonceptivos, consejería, servicios clínicos o de laboratorio y otros. Dichas tarifas incluyen el ingreso que se cobra en cada visita, los cobros por servicios individuales y las cuotas anuales de afiliación. Muchos programas cobran a los clientes una tarifa reducida para ayudar a cubrir parte del costo de la oferta de servicios y para motivar a los clientes que valoren los servicios que reciben. *Client Fees; Paiements effectués par les clients*

Tarifas por Servicios: Cargos cobrados a un cliente por cada servicio prestado, tales como consejería, exámenes médicos, análisis de laboratorio, y anticonceptivos. Algunos programas fijan una tarifa estándar para la visita inicial y para una subsecuente. Una visita inicial podría incluir el costo de un examen médico, una sesión de asesoría y un método anticonceptivo, mientras que la visita subsecuente podría cubrir el costo de un reabastecimiento de anticonceptivos y una consulta. *Service Fees; Paiements des prestations*

Tarjeta de Citas: Tarjeta que se distribuye a los clientes de planificación familiar en la que se detalla la fecha y hora de su próxima cita en la clínica, la dirección de la misma (y número de teléfono, si existe) y, frecuentemente, el nombre de una persona para contacto. El uso de un sistema de citas ayuda a los clientes a recordar cuándo deben regresar a la clínica para una visita de control, ayuda al personal de ésta a planear y ofrecer servicios en forma más eficiente y puede contribuir a la reducción del tiempo de espera de los clientes. *Appointment Card; Fiche de rendez-vous*

Tarjeta de Control de Inventario (conocida también como Tarjeta de Estiba o de Kardex): Formulario utilizado para registrar todas las transacciones del inventario (anticonceptivos recibidos o despachados) y las cantidades de anticonceptivos que se encuentran actualmente en el inventario o las que fueron ordenadas. Debería utilizarse una tarjeta separada para cada tipo y marca de anticonceptivo. *Stock Card; Fiche de stock*

Tarjeta de Referencia del Cliente: Tarjeta entregada al cliente o cliente potencial por un agente comunitario, extensionista o trabajador de la clínica que refiere al cliente a otro centro para que obtenga servicios específicos que generalmente no se ofrecen por dicho agente o clínica. La tarjeta de referencia contiene el nombre y ubicación del centro al cuál se está refiriendo al cliente, el programa o clínica que efectúa la referencia, el nombre del cliente y el motivo por el cuál se refiere. *Client Referral Card; Carte de référence du client*

Tasa: Medida de un evento (numerador) dividida por una población susceptible específica (denominador) en un período específico de tiempo. *Por ejemplo, la tasa de mortalidad infantil es el número de niños que se mueren en el primer año de vida (numerador) dividido entre el número de niños nacidos vivos (denominador) en un período específico de un año. Las tasas de mortalidad infantil se expresan generalmente como el número de muertes por cada 1.000 nacidos vivos. Rate; Taux*

Tasa de Abandono: Las tasas de abandono pueden medirse para cada método anticonceptivo, para varios métodos, o para todos los métodos ofrecidos por una clínica o programa. La tasa de abandono se calcula dividiendo el número de personas que dejan de usar un método o métodos (durante un período específico, tal como un año) entre el número total de usuarios de dicho método o métodos, incluyendo aquéllos que abandonaron el método o métodos, durante el mismo período. Al multiplicar el resultado por 100 se obtiene el porcentaje de abandono de dicho método o métodos para el período seleccionado. *Discontinuation Rate; Taux de discontinuation*

Tasa de Aceptación: Número de usuarios que han comenzado por primera vez a utilizar un método anticonceptivo, medido en relación a una población específica (comunidad, distrito, área del programa, usuarios del servicio) durante un período específico (mes, trimestre o año). La tasa de aceptación puede determinarse para todos los métodos o para un solo método en particular. *Por ejemplo, en una clínica, la tasa de aceptación de los anticonceptivos orales determinada a* *través de un período de tres meses (de enero a marzo) podría expresarse como 100 de cada 1.000 clientes, o el 10 por ciento de las clientes que aceptaron un suministro inicial de anticonceptivos orales, es decir una tasa de aceptación del 10 por ciento durante el primer trimestre de dicho año. Acceptance Rate; Taux d'acceptation*

Tasa de Continuación: Número de usuarios que continúan utilizando cualquier método anticonceptivo. Este indicador se determina para una población en particular (comunidad, distrito, área del programa), durante un período específico (mes, trimestre o año). La tasa de continuación puede medirse también para un método específico. *Continuation Rate; Taux de continuation*

Tasa de Inasistencia: Medida frecuentemente expresada como un porcentaje, se calcula más fácilmente en una clínica que utiliza un sistema de citas programadas, mediante el cuál puede saberse cuándo deben regresar los clientes a la clínica para recibir diferentes servicios. La tasa de inasistencia se calcula tomando el número total de clientes que acudieron a la clínica en busca de servicios (durante un período específico) dividido por el número de clientes que debían regresar a la clínica para recibir servicios durante ese mismo período. Al multiplicar el resultado por 100 se obtiene el porcentaje de inasistencia para dicho período. Este análisis puede también hacerse para un método anticonceptivo específico o para un grupo etáreo determinado de clientes. (Para mayor información sobre la determinación de las tasas de inasistencia, favor consultar al Volumen II, Número 3 de *Actualidad Gerencial,* «Reducción en el Abandono de los Métodos Anticonceptivos en los Programas de Planificación Familiar».) *No-Show Rate; Taux de clients non-assidus*

Técnica de Análisis de Casos Modelo («Benchmarking»): Técnica en la cual se establece un conjunto de indicadores y sub-indicadores (requisitos previos) con los cuales puede medirse el avance o progreso logrado frente a los objetivos. También puede utilizarse para comparar un servicio o proceso de una organización con servicios o procesos similares de otra organización parecida para mejorar la efectividad y eficiencia de un programa. *Benchmarking; Technique du modèle parfait*

Tiempo de Contacto: Lapso que un cliente pasa con el personal de la clínica durante una visita. Este elemento constituye uno de los aspectos que se estudia en el análisis del flujo de clientes. *Contact Time; Temps de contact*

Tiempo de Espera: Lapso (expresado generalmente en meses o semanas) que tarda un embarque en llegar, después de haberse hecho un pedido. *Lead Time; Délai de livraison*

Tiempo de Espera de Clientes: Tiempo que los clientes esperan antes de ser atendidos por el personal de una clínica. (Ver **Análisis del Flujo de Clientes.**) *Client Waiting Time; Temps d'attente des clients*

Tiempo de Espera Promedio: Lapso promedio que demora un embarque en llegar, después de efectuarse un pedido de anticonceptivos o de suministros. *Average Lead Time; Délai moyen de livraison*

Tipo de Organización: Definición estructural o legal de una organización, esto es una organización comercial, una organización privada sin fines de lucro, una agencia del sector público, una organización no gubernamental, o una afiliada o subsidiaria de una organización más grande. *Organization Type; Type d'organisation*

Tipo de Visita: Tipo de consulta efectuado por un cliente, tal como una visita inicial o primera visita, una consulta para la inserción de un DIU, una visita para reabastecerse de un anticonceptivo, una consulta por complicaciones, una visita para educación, una sesión de consejería, etc. Los tipos de visitas se definen generalmente con el objeto de determinar el costo promedio de cada una. *Visit-Type; Type de visite*

suario Nuevo: Ver Aceptante Nuevo.

Usuario Potencial (también conocido como Aceptante Potencial): En el caso de las mujeres, una usuaria potencial es cualquier mujer en edad reproductiva que esté en riesgo de quedar embarazada, que no utiliza la anticoncepción y que no desea embarazarse por el momento. En el caso de los hombres, un usuario potencial es cualquier hombre sexualmente activo que no utiliza ningún método anticonceptivo. *Potential User; Utilisateur potentiel*

Usuarios Continuos (también conocidos como Usuarios Activos, Regulares o Subsecuentes): Usuarios continuos son aquellos individuos que utilizan anticonceptivos y lo confirman en una fecha dada. Generalmente se cuentan y se reportan por separado de los clientes nuevos del programa y de los nuevos aceptantes de un método. *Continuing Users; Utilisateurs assidus*

Variación de Costos: La diferencia entre los gastos reales y los gastos esperados de un producto, servicio o programa. *Cost Variance; Variance des coûts*

Variaciones al Azar: Inconsistencias no sistemáticas o irregularidades identificadas en los datos. Al analizar los datos ciertas irregularidades (no sistemáticas) de menor importancia son frecuentemente insignificantes y pueden ser ignoradas. *Random Variations; Variations aléatoires*

Vida Util: Lapso durante el cuál puede almacenarse un anticonceptivo sin que éste pierda su eficacia. Las condiciones deficientes de almacenaje (tales como las temperaturas extremas) pueden acortar la vida útil de un producto. *Shelf Life; Durée de vie*

Visita de Control o Consecutiva: Ver Visita Subsecuente.

Visita de Inserción: Generalmente utilizada para describir una visita efectuada por una cliente para la inserción de un DIU o un implante. Frecuentemente un programa o clínica identifica los diferentes tipos de visitas para que puedan asignarse los costos específicos o las tarifas que se cobran por cada tipo de visita. *Insertion Visit; Visite pour insertion*

Visita de Procedimiento: Término generalmente utilizado para describir una visita efectuada por un cliente para someterse a un procedimiento médico específico, tal como la esterilización voluntaria o la inserción o extracción de un DIU o de implantes anticonceptivos. Los diferentes tipos de visitas son identificados frecuentemente por una clínica o programa para que puedan asignarse los costos específicos o puedan cobrarse las tarifas respectivas por cada tipo de atención prestada. *Procedure Visit; Visite pour intervention médicale*

Visita Subsecuente (también conocida como Visita de Control o Consecutiva): Visita efectuada por un cliente frecuentemente para verificar si éste se siente cómodo con el anticonceptivo que ha elegido o para tratar complicaciones médicas o efectos secundarios. Este término también se utiliza para describir una visita para el reabastecimiento de un anticonceptivo. *Revisit; Revisite*

Visitas de Observación-Estudio: Serie organizada de visitas a otros programas u organizaciones para estudiar y aprender sobre otros programas y compartir las experiencias exitosas para replicarlas o adecuarlas. *Observation-Study Visits; Visites d'observation et d'étude*

Lista de Términos y sus Equivalentes
en los Otros Idiomas

Español con equivalentes en inglés y francés:

«Abandono»	Discontinuer	Discontinuateur
Aceptante Nuevo	New Acceptor	Nouvel accepteur
Aceptante Potencial	Potential Acceptor	Accepteur potentiel
Actividades	Activities	Activités
Activo	Asset	Actifs
Activo Circulante (Activos a Corto Plazo)	Current or Short-Term Assets	Actifs courants ou à courte terme
Activos Fijos o Bien Duraderos	Fixed or Long-Term Assets	Immobilisations
Adiestramiento en Fases	Phased Training	Formation par étapes
Administración de la Calidad	Quality Management	Gestion de la qualité
Administración de la Clínica	Clinic Management	Gestion de la formation sanitaire
Administración de Recursos	Resource Management	Gestion des ressources
Administración de Suministros Anticonceptivos	Contraceptive Supply Management	Gestion des stocks de contraceptifs
Administración del Personal	Personnel Management	Gestion du personnel

Administración Estratégica	Strategic Management	Gestion stratégique
Administración Financiera	Financial Management	Gestion financière
Administración General	General Administration	Administration générale
Administración Logística	Logistics Management	Gestion de la logistique
Análisis de Costos	Cost Analysis	Analyse des coûts
Análisis de Datos	Data Analysis	Analyse des données
Análisis de Pareto	Pareto Analysis	Analyse de Pareto
Análisis de Tareas	Task Analysis	Analyse des tâches
Análisis de Tendencias	Trend Analysis	Analyse de tendances
Análisis del Flujo de Clientes	Client Flow Analysis	Analyse du flux des clients
Análisis del Flujo de Pacientes	Patient Flow Analysis	Analyse du flux des patients
Análisis del Mercado	Market Analysis	Analyse du marché
Análisis del Proceso	Process Analysis	Analyse de processus
Análisis FODA (Fortalezas, Oportunidades, Debilidades y Amenazas)	SWOT Analysis (Strengths, Weaknesses, Opportunities and Threats)	Analyse FFOM (Forces, Faiblesses, Opportunités et Menaces)
Análisis Situacional	Situation Analysis	Analyse de situation
Años Protección Pareja (APP)	Couple-Years of Protection (CYP)	Couple-années de protection (CAP)

Aprendizaje de Experiencias	Experiential Learning	Aprentissage par l'expérience
Arbol de Decisiones	Decision Tree	Arbre de décisions
Asignación de Costos	Allocation of Costs	Repartition des coûts
Auditoría Externa	External Audit	Audit externe
Auditoría Financiera	Financial Audit	Audit financier
Auditoría Interna	Internal Audit	Audit interne
Autosuficiencia	Self-Sufficiency	Autosuffisance
Balance de Fondos o Reserva	Fund Balance	Bilan des fonds (ou Réserves)
Balance General	Balance Sheet	Bilan
Barreras a los Servicios	Barriers to Services	Obstacles aux services
Bodega (almacén) Central	Central Warehouse	Magasin central
Bodega (almacén) Intermedia	Intermediate Warehouse	Magasin intermédiaire
Caja Chica	Petty Cash	Petite caisse
Calidad de los Servicios	Service Quality	Qualité des services
Canales para la Rendición de Informes	Reporting Channels	Voies de communication formelle
Cantidad Máxima	Maximum Quantity	Quantité maximum
Cantidad Mínima	Minimum Quantity	Quantité minimum

Cantidad para Cubrir el Tiempo de Espera	Lead Time Quantity	Quantité couvrant le délai de livraison
Capacidad del Servicio	Service Capacity	Capacité de service
Capacitación de Apoyo	Refresher Training	Recyclage
Capacitación en Servicio	Site Training	Formation sur le site
Capacitación Formal	Formal Training	Formation formelle
Capacitación Funcional (basada en la competencia)	Competency-Based Training	Formation basée sur les compétences
Capacitación Informal	Informal Training	Formation informelle
Capacitación Interfuncional	Cross-Training	Formation polyvalente
Capital Contable o Patrimonio	Equity	Capitaux propres
Capital de Trabajo	Working Capital	Fonds de roulement
Características del Cliente	Client Characteristics	Caractéristiques des clients
Catálogo de Cuentas	Chart of Accounts	Tableau des comptes
Categoría de Personal	Personnel Category	Catégorie de personnel
Centro de Costo	Cost Center	Centre de coût
Centro de Responsabilidad	Responsibility Center	Centre de responsabilité
Centro Operativo	Operating Center	Centre d'opérations

Cliente Nuevo	New Client	Nouveau client
Cliente Potencial	Potential Client	Client potentiel
Cliente que No Asiste	No-Show Client	Cliente non-assidu
Códigos de Identificación	Identification Codes	Codes d'identification
Colaboración entre Programas para la Reducción de Costos	Cost-Sharing	Partage des coûts
Combinación	Pooling	Regroupement
Comité del Personal	Personnel Committee	Comité du personnel
Componentes Administrativos	Management Components	Composantes de gestion
Componentes del Programa	Program Components	Volets du programme
Comprobantes	Paper Trail	Trace écrite
Conciliación Bancaria	Bank Reconciliation	Reconciliation (ou rapprochemente bancaire)
Conocimiento Interno («Inreach»)	Inreach	Diffusion interne
Consumo Mensual Promedio (CMP)	Average Monthly Consumption (AMC)	Consommation mensuelle moyenne (CMM)
Contabilidad Administrativa	Management Accounting	Comptabilité de gestion
Contabilidad de Caja	Cash Accounting	Comptabilité de caisse

Contabilidad de Costos	Cost Accounting	Comptabilité analytique
Contabilidad de Fondos	Fund Accounting	Comptabilité par fonds
Contabilidad en Base a Responsabilidades	Responsibility Accounting	Comptabilité par centres de responsabilité
Contabilidad sobre Bases Devengadas	Accrual Accounting	Comptabilité d'exercice
Contexto Externo	External Environment	Environnement externe
Contexto Interno	Internal Environment	Environnement interne
Contribuciones en Especie	In-Kind Contribution	Contribution en nature
Coordinación	Coordination	Coordination
Coordinación Externa	External Coordination	Coordination externe
Coordinación Interna	Internal Coordination	Coordination interne
«COPE» (Dirigido al Cliente, Eficiente para el Proveedor)	COPE (Client-Oriented, Provider Efficient)	COPE (Client orienté, prestation efficace)
Costo de Mantenimiento	Maintenance Cost	Coût d'entretien
Costo del Anticonceptivo	Contraceptive Product Cost	Coûts des produits contraceptifs
Costo del Personal (o Costo Total del Personal)	Personnel Cost (or Total Personnel Cost)	Coûts du personnel (ou Coûts totaux du personnel)

Costo del Personal por Tipo de Visita	Personnel Cost Per Visit-Type	Coût du personnel par type de visite
Costo-Efectividad	Cost-Effectiveness	Coût-efficacité
Costo por Año de Protección Pareja	Cost per Couple-Year of Protection	Coût par couple-année de protection
Costo por Año de Uso	Cost Per Year of Use	Coût par année d'utilisation
Costo Total por Visita	Total Visit Cost	Coût total par visite
Costo Unitario (de los Productos Anticonceptivos)	Unit Cost (of Contraceptive Products)	Coût unitaire (des produits contraceptifs)
Costos de Inversión (Gastos de Capital)	Capital Costs	Coûts d'investissement
Costos de Operación	Operating Costs	Coûts d'exploitation
Costos Directos	Direct Costs	Coûts directs
Costos Generales	Overhead Costs	Frais généraux
Costos Indirectos	Indirect Costs	Coûts indirects
Costos o Gastos Fijos	Fixed Costs or Expenses	Côuts (ou frais) fixes
Costos o Gastos Variables	Variable Costs or Expenses	Côuts (ou dépenses) variables
Costos Recurrentes	Recurrent Costs	Dépenses de fonctionnement (ou Coûts récurrents)
Cronograma	Chronogram	Chronogramme
Cronograma de Supervisión	Supervisory Schedule	Calendrier de supervision

Cuentas por Cobrar	Accounts Receivable	Comptes à recevoir (ou créances)
Cuentas por Pagar	Accounts Payable	Comptes à payer (ou dettes)
Cuotas de Afiliación	Membership Fees	Cotisations
Datos Históricos	Historical Data	Données rétrospectives
Datos sobre Clientes/ Clínica	Client/Clinic Data	Données sur les clients ou sur les formations sanitaires
De Punta	State-of-the-Art	Niveau de point
Declaración de Misión	Mission Statement	Enoncé de mission
Definición de Tareas	Task Definition	Définition des tâches
Delegación	Delegation	Délégation
Demanda no Cubierta o Necesidad no Cubierta	Unmet Demand or Unmet Need	Demande non satisfaite ou besoin non satisfait
Densidad Poblacional	Population Density	Densité de population
Depreciación	Depreciation	Amortissement
Desabastecimiento	Stockout	Rupture de stocks
Desarrollo del Personal	Staff Development	Perfectionnement du personnel
Desarrollo Profesional	Professional Development	Développement professionnel
Descentralización	Decentralization	Décentralisation

Desconcentración	Deconcentration	Déconcentration
Descripción del Cargo	Job Description	Description de poste
Desertor	Dropout	Abandon
Deuda Incobrable	Bad Debt	Créance irrécouvrable
Devolución	Devolution	Dévolution
Diagrama de Causa y Efecto	Cause-and-Effect Diagram	Diagramme de cause à effet
Diagrama de Flujo	Flowchart	Diagramme de processus
Diagrama Organizacional	Organizational Chart	Organigramme
Distribución de la Población	Population Distribution	Distribution de la population
Distribución Funcional	Functional Allocation	Répartition des fonctions
Donaciones	Grants	Subventions
Donaciones para Incentivar	Incentive Grants	Subventions qui contiennent des primes
Dotación	Endowment	Dotation
Efectividad	Effectiveness	Efficacité
Eficiencia	Efficiency	Efficience
Embarques Divididos	Split Shipments	Livraisons partielles
Embarques Incompletos	Short Shipments	Livraisons incomplètes

Encuesta a Clientes	Client Survey	Enquête auprès des clients
Encuesta a los Proveedores de Servicios de Planificación Familiar	Survey of Family Planning Providers	Enquête auprès des prestataires de planification familiale
Encuesta Basada en la Población	Population-Based Survey	Enquête auprès de la population
Encuesta de Base	Baseline Survey	Enquête de base
Encuesta de Grupos	Cluster Survey	Enquête par grappes
Encuesta de Hogares	Household Survey	Enquête auprès des ménages
Encuesta de la Comunidad	Community Survey	Enquête communautaire
Enfoque de Equipo	Team Approach	Approche d'équipe
Enfoque de la Prestación de Servicios	Service Delivery Approach	Approche de prestation de services
Entrevista de Salida	Exit Interview	Entretien à la sortie
Equipo Interfuncional	Cross-Functional Team	Equipe à fonctions multiples
Erogaciones	Expenditures	Dépenses
Escala Variable de Tarifas	Sliding Fee Scale	Echelle discriminatoire de tarifs
Esquema de Pagos Compartidos	Co-Payment Scheme	Système de co-paiement
Estabilidad Organizacional	Organizational Stability	Stabilité de l'organisation

Estaciones de Servicios	Service Stops	Postes de travail
Estado de Flujo de Fondos	Cash Flow Statement	Etat de la trésorerie
Estado de Ingresos y Egresos	Revenue and Expense Report	Etat des recettes et des dépenses
Estado de Pérdidas y Ganancias	Income Statement	Etat des revenus et des dépenses
Estados Financieros	Financial Statement	Etat financier
«Estancamiento»	Plateau Effect or "Plateauing"	Effet de plateau
Estilo Participativo	Participative Style	Style de participation
Estrategia	Strategy	Stratégie
Estructura de Supervisión	Supervisory Structure	Structure de supervision
Estructura Organizacional	Organizational Structure	Structure organisationnelle
Etapa de Consolidación	Consolidation Stage	Phase de consolidation
Etapa de Crecimiento	Growth Stage	Phase de croissance
Etapa de Madurez	Mature Stage	Phase de maturité
Etapa de Surgimiento (o Etapa Emergente)	Emergent Stage	Phase d'émergence
Etapas del Desarrollo de una Organización	Stages of Organizational Development	Phases de développement d'une organisation
Evaluación	Evaluation	Evaluation

Evaluación Rápida	Rapid Assessment	Evaluation rapide
Examen Post-Prueba	Post-test	Post-test
Examen Pre-Prueba	Pre-test	Pré-test
Existencias de Seguridad	Safety Stock	Stock de sécurité
Existencias Disponibles	Stock on Hand	Stock disponible
Existencias en Pedido	Stock on Order	Stock en commande
Exoneraciones/ Sistema de Exoneraciones y Excepciones	Waivers/Waiver System	Exonérations/Système de dérogation
Expediente del Cliente	Client Record	Dossier du client
Expediente Médico o Historia Clínica	Medical Record	Dossier médical
Extensión («Outreach»)	Outreach	Activités d'extension
Facilitador	Facilitator	Animateur
Fecha de Expiración	Expiration Date	Date de péremption
Fondo de Caja Chica	Imprest Fund	Caisse d'avance
Formulario de Flujo de Clientes	Client Flow Form	Formulaire de flux des clients
Formulario de Informe Trimestral	Quarterly Reporting Form	Fiche de rapport trimestriel
Formulario de Pedido y de Despacho	Requisition and Issue Voucher	Bon de commande et de sortie

Formularios Diarios de Retroalimentación	Daily Feedback Forms	Formulaires pour la rétro-information journalière
Funciones/Sistemas Administrativos	Management Functions/Systems	Fonctions/Systèmes de gestion
Funciones del Personal	Staff Roles	Rôle du personnel
Gastos	Expenses	Dépenses
Grado o Nivel	Grade	Grade
Gráfica	Graph	Graphique
Gráfica de Barras	Bar Chart	Graphique à colonnes
Gráfica de Flujo de Información	Information Flow Table	Tableau du circulation de l'information
Gráfica de Gantt	Gantt Chart	Tableau de Gantt
Gráfica de Sectores	Pie Chart	Graphique «camembert»
Gráfica Lineal	Line Graph	Graphique linéaire
Gratificación	Perquisites	Gratification
Grupo Focal	Focus Group	Groupe de discussion focalisée
Grupo Objetivo	Target Group	Groupe cible
Guías de Observación	Observation Guides	Grilles d'observation
«Hacer las Cosas Correctas»	"Doing the Right Things"	«Faire les choses nécessaires»
«Hacer las Cosas en Forma Correcta»	"Doing Things in the Right Way"	«Faire les choses correctement»

Histograma	Histogram	Histogramme
Hoja de Registro	Tally Sheet	Feuille de pointage (Liste des informations et données)
Honorarios Profesionales	Professional Fees	Honoraires
Impacto	Impact	Impact
Indicador	Indicator	Indicateur
Información de Desempeño	Performance Information	Information sur la performance
Información Operacional	Operational Information	Information opérationelle
Información sobre el Proceso	Process Information	Information sur les processus
Informe de Ejecución del Presupuesto	Budget Performance Report	Rapport de performance budgétaire
Informe de Ingresos	Revenue Report	Etat des recettes
Informe de Resultados	Output Information	Information sur les résultats
Informe por Uso de Vehículos	Vehicle Usage Report	Carnet de bord
Informes Financieros	Financial Reporting	Rapport financier
Informes Programáticos	Programmatic Reporting	Rapport programmatique
Ingresos, Entradas, Recibos	Revenues	Revenus
Institucionalización	Institutionalization	Institutionnalisation

Insumos	Inputs	Intrants
Integración/Servicios Integrados	Integration/Integrated Services	Intégration/Services intégrés
Integración Tipo «Embudo»	"Funnel" Approach	Approche de «l'entonnoir»
Integración Tipo «Reloj de Arena»	"Hourglass" Approach	Approche du «sablier»
Intervalo entre Pedidos	Order Interval	Intervalle entre les commandes
Inventario	Inventory	Stocks
Junta Administrativa	Managing Board	Comité de gestion
Junta de Asesores	Advisory Board	Conseil consultatif
Junta Directiva	Board of Directors	Conseil d'administration
Lista de «Asuntos Pendientes»	"To Do" Lists	Listes de choses «à faire»
Lista de Verificación para la Autoevaluación	Self-Assessment Tool or Checklist	Outil ou Liste aide-mémoire pour l'auto-évaluation
Lluvia de Ideas	Brainstorming	Lancement d'idées («Brainstorming»)
Local o Punto de Distribución	Outlet	Point de distribution (final)
Mantenimiento de la Cadena de Frío	Cold Chain Maintenance	Entretien de la chaîne du froid
Manual del Personal	Personnel Manual	Manuel du personnel
Mapa PAEL	ELCO Map	Carte ELCO

Mapeo	Mapping	Etablissement de cartes
Matriz	Matrix	Matrice
Mercadeo	Marketing	Marketing
Mercado de Servicios	Service Marketplace	Zone desservie
Mercadeo Social	Social Marketing	Marketing social
Meses de Suministros	Months of Supply	Mois d'approvi-sionnement
Metas	Targets	Cibles
Metodología	Methodology	Méthodologie
Métodos de Corto Plazo	Short-Term Methods	Méthodes à court terme
Métodos de Larga Duración	Long-Acting Methods	Méthodes de longue durée
Mezcla de Métodos	Method Mix	Gamme des méthodes
Micro-Administrar	Micro-Manage	Micro-gestion
Misión de la Organización	Organizational Mission	Mission de l'organisation
Monitoreo	Monitoring	Suivi
Motivación del Cliente	Client Motivation	Motivation des clients
Motivación del Personal	Staff Motivation	Motivation du personnel
Norma (o Guía) Clínica	Clinic Protocol	Protocole sanitaire

Normas de Auto-Evaluación	Self-Evaluation Guidelines	Directives pour l'auto-évaluation
Normas de Despidos	Termination policy	Procédure de rupture de contrat
Normas para Manejo de Quejas y Reclamos	Grievance Policy	Procédure de soumission de doléances
Núcleo del PMC (o Grupo Interno para el PMC)	CQI Core Group	Groupe-noyau pour l'ACQ
Número de Lote	Lot Number	Numéro de lot
Objetivos/Metas de Desempeño	Performance Targets and Objectives	Cibles et objectifs de performance
Objetivos Específicos	Objectives	Objectifs
Objetivos Generales	Goals	Buts
Oportunidad Perdida	Missed Opportunity	Occasion manquée
Organigrama	Organogram	Organigramme
Organización Incipiente (o de Arranque)	Start-Up Organization	Organisation qui démarre
Organización Interna	Internal Organization	Organisation interne
Paquete de Servicios	Managed Care	Système contrôlé de prestations sanitaires
Participación Comunitaria	Community Participation	Participation communautaire
Partida o Rubro	Line Item	Rubrique
Pasivos	Liabilities	Passif

Pedido de Emergencia	Emergency Order	Commande d'urgence
Pensamiento Estratégico	Strategic Thinking	Pensée stratégique
Perfil del Cliente	Client Profile	Profil des clients
Plan de Acción	Action Plan	Plan d'action
Plan de Negocios	Business Plan	Plan d'entreprise
Plan de Sesión	Session Plan	Plan des tournées de supervision
Plan de Trabajo	Work Plan	Plan de travail
Plan de Visita del Supervisor	Supervisor's Visit Plan	Plan de visite du superviseur
Plan Estratégico	Strategic Plan	Plan stratégique
Plan Operativo	Operational Plan	Plan opérationnel
Planeación	Planning	Planification
Planeación de Actividades	Activity Planning	Planification des activités
Planeación Estratégica	Strategic Planning	Planification stratégique
Planilla de Actividades de Planificación Familiar	Family Planning Activities Worksheet	Fiche de calcul des activités de planification familiale
Planilla de Proyecciones del Flujo de Fondos	Cash Flow Projection Worksheet	Formulaire de projection de l'état de la trésorerie
Posición Financiera	Financial Position	Situation financière
Premio al Mérito	Merit Awards	Récompenses au mérite

Presupuesto Consolidado	Consolidated Budget	Budget consolidé
Prevalencia de Uso de Anticonceptivos	Contraceptive Prevalence	Prévalence contraceptive
Primera Visita o Primera Consulta de un Cliente	First Visit or First Consultation of a Client	Première visite ou Première consultation d'un client
Primero en Expirar, Primero en Salir (PEPS)	First-to-Expire, First-Out (FEFO)	Premier à périmer, premier sorti (PPPS)
Privatización	Privatization	Privatisation
Proceso de Mejoramiento Continuo de la Calidad (PMC)	Continuous Quality Improvement (CQI)	Amélioration continue de la qualité (ACQ)
Proceso de Supervisión en Equipo	Team Supervision Process	Processus de supervision en équipe
Proceso de Trabajo	Work Process	Processus de travail
Programa de Cobro de Tarifas por Servicios	Fee-For-Service Program	Programme de paiement des prestations
Programa para Aumentar la Tasa de Continuidad de Usuarios Activos	User Continuity Program	Programme pour accroître le nombre d'utilisateurs actifs
Protocolo de Supervisión	Supervisory Protocol	Protocole de supervision
Proyecciones Basadas en el Servicio	Service-Based Forecasts	Prévisions basées sur les prestations de services

Proyecciones Basadas en Información Censual o en Encuestas Demográficas	Population-Based Forecasts	Prévisions basées sur la population
Proyecciones Basadas en la Distribución	Distribution-Based Forecasts	Prévisions basées sur la distribution
Punto de Equilibrio	Break-Even Point	Seuil de rentabilité
Razón	Ratio	Ratio
Recaudación de Fondos	Fund Raising	Mobilisation de fonds
Reconocimiento del Desempeño	Performance Appraisal	Evaluation de la performance
Recursos	Resources	Ressources
Registro Diario de Actividades	Daily Activity Register	Registre journalier des activités
Relaciones Públicas	Public Affairs	Affaires publiques
Remuneración	Remuneration	Rémunération
Rendimiento de la Clínica	Clinic Performance	Performance de la formation sanitaire
Requisitos Previos («Benchmarks»)	Benchmarks	Jalons de performance progressifs
Resolución de Problemas	Problem Solving	Résolution de problèmes
Responsabilidad Conjunta	Mutually Accountable	Mutuellement responsable
Responsabilidades del Personal	Staff Responsibilities	Responsabilités du personnel

Responsabilidades Funcionales	Functional Responsibilities	Responsabilités de fonction
Resultados Intermedios	Intermediate Outputs	Résultats intermédiaires
Resumen Mensual de Actividades de Planificación Familiar	Monthly Summary of Family Planning Activities	Récapitulatif mensuel des activités de planification familiale
Retroalimentación	Feedback	Rétro-information
Saldo Disponible	Balance on Hand	Stock résiduel
Salud Reproductiva	Reproductive Health	Santé reproductive
Satisfacción del Cliente	Client Satisfaction	Satisfaction des clients
Sectores Desatendidos de la Población o Carentes de Servicios	Underserved Populations	Populations mal desservies (sous-servies)
Servicios Adquiridos	Purchased Services	Services achetés (ou sous-traitance)
Servicios Comunitarios (SC)	Community-Based Services (CBS)	Services à base communautaire (SBC)
Servicios de Almacén (o de Distribución Local)	Depot Services	Services au dépôt communautaire
Servicios de Salud Reproductiva	Reproductive Health Care/Services	Prestations/services de santé reproductive
Servicios Satélites	Satellite Services	Points de services périphériques
Servicios Verticales o Enfoque Vertical	Vertical Services/ Approach	Approche de services verticaux

Servicios Voluntarios	Volunteer Services	Services bénévoles (de volontaires)
Sesión de Supervisión	Supervisory Session	Session de supervision
Sistema Bifurcado de Información	Two-Tier Information System	Système d'information à deux niveaux
Sistema Contable	Accounting System	Système de comptabilité
Sistema Continuo (Perpetuo) de Inventario	Continuous (Perpetual) Review System	Système de revue continuelle ou perpétuelle
Sistema de Administración de la Calidad	Quality Management System	Système de gestion de la qualité
Sistema de Asignación	Push System	Système d'allocation
Sistema de Cinco Mesas	Five-Table System	Système des cinq tables
Sistema de Incentivos	Incentive System	Système de primes d'encouragement
Sistema de Información	Information System	Système d'information
Sistema de Información Gerencial (SIG)	Management Information System (MIS)	Système d'information de gestion (SIG)
Sistema de Pagos de Terceros (Co-Pagos)	Third-Party Payments	Paiements par un tiers (ou Co-paiements)

Sistema de Pedidos de Intervalos Fijos	Fixed Order Interval System	Système de commande à intervalles fixes
Sistema de Pedidos de Intervalos Variables	Variable Order Interval System	Système de commande à intervalles variables
Sistema de Referencia	Referral System	Système de référence
Sistema de Requisición	Pull System	Système de commande (réquisition)
Sistema de Supervisión	Supervisory System	Système de supervision
Sistema Max/Min	Max/Min (Maximum-Minimum) Stock Level	Système Max/Min (Maximum-Minimum)
Sistema Periódico de Inventario	Periodic Review System	Système de revue periodique
Sistemas de Fiscalización	Control Systems	Systèmes de contrôle
Situación de Existencias	Stock Position	Situation des stocks
Subsidios Cruzados	Cross-Subsidization/ Cross-Subsidies	Subvention croisée
Subsistema	Subsystem	Sous-système
Suministros de Planificación Familiar	Family Planning Commodities	Produits pour la planification familiale
Supervisión Facilitadora	Facilitative Supervision	Supervision à but de facilitation
Supervisión Selectiva	Selective Supervision	Supervision sélective

Sustentabilidad	Sustainability	Viabilité
Tabla Comparativa	Comparison Table	Tableau de comparaison
Tabla de Análisis de Datos sobre Anticonceptivos	Contraceptive Data Analysis Chart	Tableau d'analyse des données sur les contraceptifs
Tabla de Frecuencias	Frequency Table	Tableau de fréquence
Tabla del Flujo de Clientes	Client Flow Chart	Tableau de flux des clients
Tabla para Control de Suministros	Status of Supplies Chart	Tableau de la situation des stocks
Tabulación Cruzada	Cross-Tabulation	Tableau croisée
Tareas	Tasks	Tâches
Tarifas de Ingreso	Registration Fees	Droits d'inscription (ou d'admission)
Tarifas para los Clientes	Client Fees	Paiements effectués par les clients
Tarifas por Servicios	Service Fees	Paiements des prestations
Tarjeta de Citas	Appointment Card	Fiche de rendez-vous
Tarjeta de Control de Inventario	Inventory Control Card or Bin Card	Fiche de contrôle des stocks
Tarjeta de Estiba o de Kardex	Stock Card	Fiche de stock
Tarjeta de Referencia del Cliente	Client Referral Card	Carte de référence du client
Tasa	Rate	Taux

Tasa de Abandono	Discontinuation Rate	Taux de discontinuation
Tasa de Aceptación	Acceptance Rate	Taux d'acceptation
Tasa de Continuación	Continuation Rate	Taux de continuation
Tasa de Inasistencia	No-Show Rate	Taux de clients non-assidus
Técnica de Análisis de Casos Modelo («Benchmarking»)	Benchmarking	Technique du modèle parfait
Tiempo de Contacto	Contact Time	Temps de contact
Tiempo de Espera	Lead Time	Délai de livraison
Tiempo de Espera de Clientes	Client Waiting Time	Temps d'attente des clients
Tiempo de Espera Promedio	Average Lead Time	Délai moyen de livraison
Tipo de Organización	Organization Type	Type d'organisation
Tipo de Visita	Visit-Type	Type de visite
Usuario Nuevo	New User	Nouvel utilisateur
Usuario Potencial	Potential User	Utilisateur potentiel
Usuarios Activos o Regulares	Active Users	Utilisateurs actifs
Usuarios Continuos o Subsecuentes	Continuing Users	Utilisateurs assidus
Variación de Costos	Cost Variance	Variance des coûts
Variaciones al Azar	Random Variations	Variations aléatoires
Vida Util	Shelf Life	Durée de vie

Visita de Control o Consecutiva	Follow-up Visit	Visite de suivi
Visita de Inserción	Insertion Visit	Visite pour insertion
Visita de Procedimiento	Procedure Visit	Visite pour intervention médicale
Visita Subsecuente	Revisit	Revisite
Visitas de Observación-Estudio	Observation-Study Visits	Visites d'observation et d'étude

Bibliografía de los Glosarios de Planificación Familiar

A continuación se encuentra una bibliografía de otros glosarios de población y planificación familiar impresos y actualmente disponibles en las organizaciones que trabajan en el campo de la población. Esta lista fue proporcionada en parte por JHPIEGO Corporation y el Grupo de Trabajo de Materiales de Salud Reproductiva de USAID.

Glosarios Publicados

AVSC International. *AVSC's Glossary of Terminology.* AVSC International, New York, NY, 1995. Producida en inglés.

Edmans, E. et al. *Glossary of Family Planning Terms.* INTRAH, School of Medicine, University of North Carolina, Chapel Hill, NC, 1987. Producida en inglés y en francés.

Haupt, A. y T. T. Kane. *Guía Rápida de Población.* The Population Reference Bureau, International Programs, Washington, DC, 1991. Producida en español, inglés, francés, portugués, y árabe.

Macció, G. *Diccionario Demográfico Multilingue.* Ordina Editions, Liège, Belgium, 1985. Producida en español, inglés, y francés.

Newman, C. y J. Birkmayer. *Glossary of Training Evaluation Terms.* INTRAH, School of Medicine, University of North Carolina, Chapel Hill, NC, 1992. Producida en inglés y en francés.

Population Resource Center. *Population Glossary.* Population Resource Center, Washington, DC, 1994. Producida en inglés.

Rodriguez-Garcia, R. et al. *Glosario de Terminos Utilizados en la Planificación Familiar.* Institute for Reproductive Health, Georgetown University, Washington, DC, 1989. Producida en español, inglés, francés, y portugués.

Veney, J. y P. Gorbach. *Definitions for Program Evaluation Terms.* The EVALUATION Project, Carolina Population Center, University of North Carolina, Chapel Hill, NC, 1993. Producida en inglés.

Wolff, J., J. Miller, y C. Bahamon, eds. «Desarrollo de un Vocabulario Común: Glosario de Téminos Gerenciales» *Actualidad Gerencial en Planificación Familiar.* Family Planning Management Development, Management Sciences for Health, Boston, MA. Vol. IV, No. 3, 1995. Producida en español, inglés, y francés.

Glosarios en las Publicaciones

Angle, M. y C. Murphy. *Guidelines for Clinical Procedures in Family Planning: A Reference for Trainers*. INTRAH, University of North Carolina, Chapel Hill, NC, 1993. Producida en inglés y en francés.

Garcia-Nunez, J. *Improving Family Planning Evaluation*. Kumarian Press, West Hartford, CT, 1992. Producida en inglés.

Hatcher, R. et al. *Contraceptive Technology*. Irvington Publishers, North Stratford, NH, 1994. Producida en inglés.

Johns Hopkins University, Center for Communication Programs. *Service Providers Guide to Family Planning*. Johns Hopkins University, Center for Communication Programs, Population Communications Services, Baltimore, MD, 1990. Producida en inglés.

Kent, M. *World Population: Fundamentals of Growth*. Population Reference Bureau, Washington, DC, 1995. Producida en inglés.

Wolff, J. et al. *Manual del Administrador de Planificación Familiar: Técnicas para Mejorar la Gestión de Programas*. Management Sciences for Health, Boston, MA, 1994. Producida en español, inglés, y francés.

Introduction

Le projet Family Planning Management Development (FPMD) travaille auprès de responsables de programmes de santé et planification familiale dans les secteurs public et privé des pays en voie de développement, en vue de perfectionner leurs capacités de gestion et d'accroître l'efficacité et la viabilité de leurs programmes.

En 1991 le projet a publié le *Guide des responsables des programmes de planification familiale*, le premier manuel rédigé exclusivement à l'intention des responsables de services de planification familiale. En 1992, le projet a entrepris la publication d'un bulletin bimestriel de formation en matière de gestion permanente en matière de gestion, *Management de la planification familiale*, dans lequel sont exposées certaines stratégies permettant d'améliorer la gestion des services de santé et de planification familiale. Ces documents ont par la suite été publiés en espagnol et en français. Au cours de ces dernières années, de nombreux responsables ont fait preuve d'un grand intérêt pour le glossaire figurant dans le *Guide* ainsi que pour un autre glossaire publié plus récemment comme numéro spécial du *Management de la planification familiale*. Le présent *Glossaire de poche* réunit les deux glossaires publiés précédemment, et fournit la traduction de chacun des termes en espagnol et en français.

Etant donné que les cadres de tous les pays participent de plus en plus à des travaux de coopération sud-sud, et que les nouveaux programmes prennent pour modèle ceux qui ont fait leurs preuves—tantôt dans les pays même, tantôt entre pays—il devient extrêmement important d'être bien informé des techniques de gestion de base, et de recourir à un vocabulaire commun. Le présent glossaire a pour but de perfectionner la compréhension des termes et des pratiques adoptés pour la gestion des programmes de planification familiale, et de promouvoir un vocabulaire de travail commun parmi les responsables du monde entier.

Chacune des sections du *Glossaire de poche* est organisée de façon semblable: premièrement, le glossaire complet fournissant, en ordre alphabétique, les termes et leurs définitions dans la langue concernée, et indiquant pour chaque terme le terme correspondant dans les langues étrangères. Vient ensuite une liste où figurent seuls les termes et leur équivalent dans les langues étrangères. Le glossaire se termine par une bibliographie des glossaires de planification familiale.

Nous espérons que ce *Glossaire de poche* rendra service aux responsables exerçant des responsabilités à divers niveaux des programmes de santé et planification familiale du monde entier, qu'il aidera à faire mieux comprendre et utiliser les bonnes méthodes de gestion, et que de ce fait il contribuera au succès des programmes qui s'efforcent de fournir des prestations de santé reproductive d'un haut niveau de qualité.

Glossaire des Termes

A bandon : Voir **Discontinuateur.**

Accepteur potentiel : Voir **Utilisateur potentiel.**

Actifs : C'est tout ce qui a une valeur pouvant aider une organisation à fournir ses services aux clients. Exemples d'actifs : argent en espèce, terrain, bâtiments, équipement, stock (de fournitures ou de biens à vendre), mobilier et argent dû à l'organisation (créances). Voir **Immobilisations** et **Actifs courants.** *Assets; Activos*

Actifs courants ou à court terme : Actifs ayant la particularité d'être utilisés dans un intervalle d'un an, tels que l'argent en espèce, les fournitures de bureau et les provisions médicales. *Current or Short-Term Assets; Activos circulantes (Activos a Corto Plazo)*

Activités d'extension : Activités concernant la fourniture d'informations (sensibilisation) et de services à la communauté hors de la formation sanitaire en travaillant généralement avec des groupes communautaires ou des volontaires. *Outreach; Extensión («Outreach»)*

Administration générale : Activités ou, dans le cas d'un budget, dépenses associées à la conduite des affaires telles que les frais de port, le transport, les photocopies, le téléphone, les frais bancaires, l'enregistrement des véhicules et tout autre coût administratif ordinaire et coutumier (à l'exclusion des coûts de personnel). *General Administration; Administración General*

Affaires publiques : Activités faisant la promotion du programme, des services et de l'image d'une organisation. *Public Affairs; Relaciones Públicas*

Amélioration continue de la qualité (ACQ) : Processus structuré cyclique d'amélioration des systèmes et activités dans une organisation ou un programme. Il s'agit d'identifier un domaine où l'on peut faire des améliorations, de définir un problème dans ce domaine, de mettre en relief la séquence des activités (le processus) dans ce domaine, d'établir les résultats souhaités du processus et les conditions nécessaires pour les atteindre, de sélectionner des étapes spécifiques à étudier dans le processus, de recueillir et d'analyser les données sur le processus, de prendre des mesures de correction et de contrôler les résultats de ces mesures. L'ACQ est basée sur une approche d'équipe et exige de former des équipes composées de personnel de divers secteurs et niveaux de l'organisation. Elle part de l'hypothèse que tout système peut toujours être amélioré et met, par conséquent, l'accent sur un processus d'amélioration constante qui exige un engagement à long terme de l'organisation et un travail en équipe efficace. *Continuous Quality Improvement (CQI); Proceso de Mejoramiento Continuo de la Calidad (PMC)*

Amortissement : Méthode comptable consistant à étaler le coût d'un bien immobilisé sur toute la durée de service prévue pour ce bien. L'amortissement peut se faire sous la forme d'une écriture comptable, ou bien il peut être «financé» grâce à des dépôts monétaires alimentant régulièrement un fonds destiné au remplacement du bien. *Par exemple, un camion valant 20.000 dollars et ayant une durée de service estimée à 10 ans fera l'objet d'une dotation annuelle de 2.000 dollars aux amortissements. Depreciation; Depreciación*

Analyse de Pareto : Basée sur le principe établi par l'économiste italien, Vilfredo Pareto, qui indique que seuls quelques facteurs sont responsables de la plupart des résultats (positifs ou négatifs), une analyse de Pareto aide à identifier les «quelques facteurs essentiels» qu'il faut améliorer pour atteindre les résultats souhaités. Cette analyse aide les responsables à concentrer leurs efforts sur quelques activités et par conséquent à utiliser leurs rares ressources de façon efficace et efficiente pour atteindre des résultats. (Pour savoir comment réaliser une analyse de Pareto, veuillez vous référer au Numéro 1 du Volume II du *Management de la planification familiale* intitulé «Utiliser l'ACQ pour renforcer les programmes de planification familiale» et le supplément *Boîte à outils du Manager pour ACQ.*) *Pareto Analysis; Análisis de Pareto*

Analyse de processus : Tout type d'analyse dans lequel on étudie un ou plusieurs processus, ou une séquence d'activités. Exemples d'analyses de processus : diagramme de processus, analyse avec arbres de décisions, et analyse du flux des clients. *Process Analysis; Análisis del Proceso*

Analyse de situation : Processus systématique d'analyse de l'environnement interne et des capacités d'une organisation, ainsi que de l'environnement politique, social, économique et programmatique dans lequel fonctionne le programme. On procède à cette analyse pour comparer la situation actuelle à une situation idéale afin de déterminer les mesures à prendre afin d'améliorer la gestion d'un programme, sa performance et sa viabilité. *Situation Analysis; Análisis Situacional*

Analyse de tendances : Représentation des données pour montrer une augmentation, une diminution ou l'absence de changement au cours d'une certaine période. On procède souvent à une analyse de tendances en créant un graphique linéaire à partir d'un ensemble de données. *Trend Analysis; Análisis de Tendencias*

Analyse des coûts : Etude des coûts (personnel, produits, matériel, etc.) associés à la mise en oeuvre d'un projet, d'un programme, d'un service ou d'autres activités. *Cost Analysis; Análisis de Costos*

Analyse des données : Processus d'examen de données et de recherche de tendances. Ceci donne aux responsables de nouvelles informations sur leurs programmes et services et les aide à prendre de meilleures décisions de gestion. *Data Analysis; Análisis de Datos*

Analyse des tâches : Examen de toutes les responsabilités et activités assumées par un employé ou une fonction en vue de déterminer les aptitudes, connaissances, attitudes et ressources nécessaires pour effectuer une tâche ainsi que les risques qui lui sont liés. *Task Analysis; Análisis de Tareas*

Analyse du flux des clients (également appelé Analyse du flux des patients) : Processus permettant de déterminer l'efficience des opérations de prestation de services dans une formation sanitaire. Elle est basée sur les observations du mouvement des clients à travers la formation sanitaire et enregistre, notamment, le temps que passe un client à attendre avant d'être vu par un prestataire et le temps de contact qu'il a avec chaque prestataire de service de la formation sanitaire. *Client Flow Analysis; Análisis del Flujo de Clientes*

Analyse du marché : Examen de l'environnement dans lequel une organisation ou un programme fournit ou vend des biens et services. Une analyse de marché comprend généralement une enquête des clients actuels (leurs besoins, leur satisfaction vis-à-vis des services, leur situation socio-économique, etc.), une enquête auprès de la communauté (afin d'apprendre davantage sur les clients potentiels et la demande existante de services), et une enquête auprès des autres prestataires de services de planification familiale de la zone (les types de services qu'ils fournissent, le coût et la qualité des services, etc.). Cette information donne à un programme ou à une organisation des renseignements primordiaux sur les populations maldesservies de leur zone, le niveau d'accès aux services, la rétro-information sur la satisfaction des clients, la capacité des clients de payer ou le montant qu'ils peuvent payer pour les services et autres informations sur le rôle que le programme doit jouer en relation avec les autres prestataires de services afin de maintenir une marge de compétitivité. Avoir la capacité de remédier à ces facteurs permet de renforcer la viabilité du programme. *Market Analysis; Análisis del Mercado*

Analyse FFOM (Forces, Faiblesses, Opportunités et Menaces) : C'est l'analyse des forces et faiblesses internes d'une institution, ainsi que des opportunités et menaces qui existent en dehors de l'institution ou du programme. *SWOT Analysis; Análisis FODA*

Animateur : Personne qui aide, encourage et appuie un groupe de personnes de façon à travailler ensemble de manière participative, prendre des décisions et résoudre des conflits afin d'atteindre un objectif commun. *Facilitator; Facilitador*

Apprentissage par l'expérience : Une méthode d'apprentissage qui, en plus des cours, utilise la participation active et met en application les nouvelles aptitudes par les jeux de rôles et l'expérience in situ. *Experiential Learning; Aprendizaje de Experiencias*

Approche d'équipe : Philosophie et technique qui s'appuient sur la création d'un groupe de personnes ayant des compétences et des perspectives différentes afin d'identifier et de discuter des questions, de définir les causes des problèmes (ou des réussites) et de trouver et de mettre en oeuvre des solutions afin d'atteindre un objectif commun. *Team Approach; Enfoque de Equipo*

Approche de «l'entonnoir» : Décrit une approche de prestation de services intégrée : elle représente un organisme ou une institution qui sépare les divers programmes verticalement au niveau national et de district mais intègre les programmes et services au niveau de la formation sanitaire ou de la communauté. (Voir **Approche du «sablier».**) *"Funnel" Approach; Integración Tipo «Embudo»*

Approche de prestation de services : Conçues pour atteindre et attirer différents groupes de clients, les méthodes de prestation de services comprennent les services à base communautaire, les services basés dans les formations sanitaires, les services basés sur les lieux de travail, les services basés dans les hôpitaux, les services à domicile ou dans les dépôts et les rassemblements communautaires d'information, éducation et communication (IEC) sur la planification familiale. *Service Delivery Approach; Enfoque de la Prestación de Servicios*

Approche de services verticaux : Approche selon laquelle les services tels que la planification familiale, la santé maternelle et infantile, la nutrition, les vaccinations et autres services de santé reproductive sont fournis par des formations sanitaires séparées ayant un personnel séparé, gérées au niveau central par des divisions ou ministères séparés et qui fonctionnent de manière indépendant les uns des autres. *Vertical Services/Approach; Servicios Verticales o Enfoque Vertical*

Approche du «sablier» : Utilisée pour décrire une méthode de prestation de services intégrés, elle décrit un programme à la fois vertical et intégré dans lequel le personnel du niveau national est réparti en divisions séparées pour la planification familiale, la vaccination, la lutte contre les maladies infectieuses, la nutrition et la santé maternelle. Au niveau régional ou du district cependant, les programmes sont coordonnés par un ou deux individus et au niveau des prestataires de services, le personnel est de nouveau réparti pour des programmes séparés. (Voir **Approche de «l'entonnoir».**) *"Hourglass" Approach; Integración Tipo «Reloj de Arena»*

Arbre de décisions : Une série de questions utilisées comme un outil pour vérifier si la formation est nécessaire pour résoudre les problèmes de performance. *Decision Tree; Arbol de Decisiones*

Audit externe : Vérification des déclarations comptables et financières d'un organisme, effectuée par une personne ou un groupement indépendant de cet organisme. *External Audit; Auditoría Externa*

Audit financier : Examen périodique formel des comptes et documents financiers d'une organisation ou d'un programme généralement dans le but de vérifier si les fonds ont été utilisés comme ils devaient l'être et conformément à des normes et pratiques de gestion financière. *Financial Audit; Auditoría Financiera*

Audit interne : Vérification des systèmes interne de contrôle et de la comptabilité d'un organisme, effectuée par des employés de cet organisme. *Internal Audit; Auditoría Interna*

Autosuffisance : Niveau de développement organisationnel atteint lorsqu'une organisation est capable de fonctionner indépendamment de l'assistance extérieure (des bailleurs de fonds). Les organisations autosuffisantes sont capables de mobiliser toutes sortes de ressources pour éviter de dépendre d'une source de crédit unique et avoir la capacité de gestion et de leadership pour adapter leurs programmes à un environnement en évolution. (Voir également **Viabilité**.) *Self-Sufficiency; Autosuficiencia*

B ilan : Etat financier résumant les valeurs en actif et en passif et les réserves d'une organisation à un moment précis. *Balance Sheet; Balance General*

Bilan des fonds ou Réserves (également appelé Capitaux propres) : Dans une organisation à but non lucratif, cela représente la valeur nette de l'organisme, calculée en soustrayant la valeur des charges du total des recettes. *Fund Balance; Balance de Fondos o Reserva*

Bon de commande et de sortie : Ce formulaire est utilisé par le responsable de la formation sanitaire pour demander de nouvelles fournitures, par le responsable de l'entrepôt pour remplir la commande et enregistrer les quantités envoyées et par le responsable de la formation sanitaire pour vérifier qu'il a bien reçu les quantités et types de fournitures commandées. Plus qu'un simple bon de commande, ce formulaire résume la consommation mensuelle moyenne de chaque contraceptif commandé, la quantité maximum souhaitée par la formation sanitaire et la quantité disponible au moment de la commande et sert par conséquent à justifier la quantité commandée. *Requisition and Issue Voucher; Formulario de Pedido y de Despacho*

Budget consolidé : Budget qui regroupe les informations sur les recettes et dépenses projetées recueillies auprès de divers donateurs ou programmes, ou qui facilite l'obtention d'une telle information au sein d'une même organisation. *Consolidated Budget; Presupuesto Consolidado*

Buts : Les bénéfices proposés au sens large à long terme du programme au profit des populations, définis de façon générale. *Goals; Objetivos Generales*

C aisse d'avance : Somme d'argent fixe mise de côté pour les dépenses de caisse immédiates et qui est périodiquement ravitaillée jusqu'à concurrence du montant dépensé. *Imprest Fund; Fondo de Caja Chica*

Calendrier de supervision : Plan écrit des tournées de supervision donnant le nom de l'employé concerné et la date, l'heure et le contenu des prochaines tournées de supervision. Un calendrier de supervision sert à planifier et à faire connaître aux employés les activités de supervision futures. *Supervisory Schedule; Cronograma de Supervisión*

Calendrier des activités du projet : Voir **Chronogramme.**

Capacité de service : Volume maximum de services qui peut être fourni moyennant un ensemble donné de ressources. *Par exemple, le nombre maximum de vasectomies pouvant être effectué*es par un médecin dans le cours d'une journée de travail. **Service Capacity; Capacidad del Servicio**

Capitaux propres (également appelés Bilan des fonds ou reserves) : Valeur nette d'une entreprise, calculée en soustrayant le total du passif du total des actifs. *Equity; Capital Contable o Patrimonio*

Caractéristiques des clients : Informations sur les particularités et les besoins des clients qui servent à analyser une base de clients du programme afin de fournir des soins de haute qualité répondant aux besoins des clients. Les caractéristiques des clients comprennent : l'âge, la situation matrimoniale, le nombre de grossesses, la présence de maladies sexuellement transmissibles (MST), l'alphabétisation, la préférence pour espacer les naissances ou limiter la fécondité, etc. *Client Characteristics; Características del Cliente*

Carnet de bord : Carnet qui retrace l'utilisation d'un véhicule. Il indique la date, la destination, le but du voyage, le kilométrage au départ et à l'arrivée, les achats de carburant et les réparations effectuées. Il sert à calculer le coût par kilomètre, ainsi qu'à contrôler et suivre les coûts d'utilisation des véhicules. *Vehicle Usage Report; Informe por Uso de Vehículos*

Carte de référence du client : Carte donnée au client ou au client potentiel par un agent basé dans la communauté, un agent d'extension des services ou un prestataire de formation sanitaire pour diriger le client vers une autre formation sanitaire pour certains services qui ne sont pas offerts par l'agent de santé ou la première formation sanitaire. Cette carte de référence donne le nom et l'adresse de la formation sanitaire à laquelle est envoyé le client, le nom du programme ou de la formation sanitaire d'où il vient, le nom du client et la raison de cette référence. *Client Referral Card; Tarjeta de Referencia del Cliente*

Carte ELCO : Représentation graphique de la situation dans une communauté ou un village des COuples ELigibles (ELCO sont en général des couples mariés en âge de procréer, mais la définition de couple éligible varie selon les pays) indiquant où ils habitent et le type de méthode contraceptive dont ils se servent actuellement. Utilisées en général par les agents de terrain, ces cartes permettent de suivre l'évolution de la procréation de chaque couple et tous les changements de méthode de contraception qu'ils utilisent. *ELCO Map; Mapa PAEL*

Catégorie de personnel : Les divers types de personnel. Dans un programme de planification familiale les catégories de personnel comprennent médecins, infirmières, pharmaciens, laborantins, conseillers, agents d'extension, chargés de l'enregistrement, etc. Les catégories de personnel sont souvent définies afin d'établir des niveaux de salaire homogènes et sont utiles lorsque l'on détermine les coûts du personnel associés aux types de services fournis. *Personnel Category; Categoría de Personal*

Centre d'opérations : Toute subdivision logique des activités d'un programme, tel qu'un département, une clinique ou un programme des services à base communautaire (SBC) d'une région. Beaucoup d'organisations estiment utile de produire des informations financières pour chaque centre d'opérations. *Operating Center; Centro Operativo*

Centre de responsabilité (également appelé Centre de coût) : Secteur fonctionnel placé sous l'autorité d'un responsable particulier, comme par exemple un laboratoire. *Responsibility Center; Centro de Responsabilidad*

Chronogramme (également appelé Tableau de Gantt ou Calendrier des activités du projet) : Outil de planification de projet qui récapitule les principales activités planifiées dans l'ordre chronologique, ainsi que le moment—mois ou trimestre—au cours duquel les activités auront lieu—ainsi que la ou les personne(s) responsable(s) de leur exécution. Il aide les responsables à contrôler les activités et les résultats à court terme, à réaliser le projet dans les délais et à gérer ses ressources. *Chronogram; Cronograma*

Cibles : Objectifs subdivisés en unités plus petites et reformulés en termes chiffrés. Ils appartiennent à un volet précis du programme, tel que le volet clinique ou Information, Education, Communication (IEC) et portent sur une unité précise de temps : un trimestre, un mois ou une semaine. *Targets; Metas*

Cibles et objectifs de performance : Les résultats finals qui doivent être atteints par une organisation ou un employé à la fin d'une période spécifique. Les cibles de performance concernent généralement une période courte (plusieurs mois) et visent des tâches très spécifiques. Les objectifs de performance concernent des périodes longues (une année) et déterminent le type et l'envergure des activités qu'une organisation, un programme ou un membre du personnel réalisera afin d'atteindre les résultats souhaités. *Performance Targets and Objectives; Objetivos/ Metas de Desempeño*

Client non-assidu : Un client qui ne se présente pas à un rendez-vous ou n'est pas revenu à la formation sanitaire pour des services depuis longtemps. *No-Show Client; Cliente que No Asiste*

Client potentiel : Personne en âge de procréer qui est sexuellement active, n'utilise pas actuellement les services d'une formation sanitaire ou d'un programme de planification familiale basé dans la communauté et n'a pas l'intention d'avoir des enfants dans le présent. Les clients potentiels comprennent également des couples qui ont des problèmes d'infertilité mais souhaitent avoir des enfants. Les programmes doivent essayer d'attirer ces personnes et de leur fournir des services appropriés. *Potential Client; Cliente Potencial*

Codes d'identification : Une série de chiffres ou de lettres utilisés dans un système d'information de gestion pour aider à différencier des points de service (ou types de formation sanitaire), types de visites (première visite, visite de suivi, visite de procédure), ou types de services ou de contraceptifs fournis (IEC, insertion de DIU, réapprovisionnement en pilules) et autres catégories de données. Pour être utiles, les mêmes codes d'identification doivent être employés systématiquement par toutes les personnes qui utilisent le système d'information intégré. *Identification Codes; Códigos de Identificación*

Comité de gestion : Groupe structuré de conseillers qui assurent une supervision stratégique et financière générale à une organisation et sont responsables du maintien et de la promotion de la stabilité et de la viabilité de l'organisation. *Managing Board; Junta Administrativa*

Comité du personnel : Il s'agit en général d'un sous-comité d'un plus grand groupe tel que le conseil d'administration qui s'intéresse aux questions, préoccupation et tendances du personnel et fait des recommandations au groupe plus important, au conseil d'administration ou à l'organisation sur les changements nécessaires. *Personnel Committee; Comité del Personal*

Commande d'urgence : Commande de contraceptifs ou de produits placée en dehors du calendrier normal de commande, en général lorsque les stocks sont extrêmement bas en raison d'une augmentation imprévue de la demande. Les commandes d'urgence sont généralement effectuées pour une quantité qui reconstituera les stocks à un niveau qui durera jusqu'au moment de la commande normale, et tiennent compte de la quantité qui sera distribuée dans l'intervalle. *Emergency Order; Pedido de Emergencia*

Composantes de gestion : Les éléments de base utilisés pour analyser la façon dont fonctionne une organisation. Les quatre composantes de base de la gestion sont la mission, la stratégie, la structure et les systèmes. (Voir également **Enoncé de mission, Stratégie, Structure organisationnelle et Fonctions/Systèmes de gestion**.) *Management Components; Componentes Administrativos*

Comptabilité analytique : Méthode comptable qui répartit les coûts entre des centres de responsabilité déterminés, correspondant par exemple à des programmes ou à des services distincts. *Cost Accounting; Contabilidad de Costos*

Comptabilité d'exercice : Système de comptabilité qui enregistre les recettes encaissées, les dépenses effectuées, ainsi que le coût d'utilisation des immobilisations telles que les bâtiments ou le matériel (par opposition à **Comptabilité de caisse**). *Accrual Accounting; Contabilidad sobre Bases Devengadas*

Comptabilité de caisse : Système de comptabilité qui n'enregistre les recettes qu'au moment où elles sont reçues et les dépenses qu'au moment où elles sont payées (par opposition à **Comptabilité d'exercice**). *Cash Accounting; Contabilidad de Caja*

Comptabilité de gestion : Collecte d'informations provenant du système de comptabilité financière et d'autres données financières (telles que les budgets), et combinaison de ces informations avec des données statistiques (telles que les résultats produits par les services) pour produire des informations qui serviront à prendre des décisions de gestion. *Management Accounting; Contabilidad Administrativa*

Comptabilité par centres de responsabilité : Enregistrement et classification des données comptables en fonction de centres de responsabilité prédéterminés. *Responsibility Accounting; Contabilidad en Base a Responsabilidades*

Comptabilité par fonds : Système de comptabilité qui suit les dépenses et les recettes des différents comptes de donateurs. *Fund Accounting; Contabilidad de Fondos*

Comptes à payer ou Dettes : Argent dû par l'organisation au titre des notes et factures déjà reçues. *Accounts Payable; Cuentas por Pagar*

Comptes à recevoir ou Créances : Argent dû à l'organisation au titre des notes ou factures qu'elle a émises. *Accounts Receivable; Cuentas por Cobrar*

Conseil consultatif : Groupe de spécialistes externes expérimentés chargés de conseiller les décideurs d'une organisation ou d'un programme. Un conseil consultatif est généralement structuré de façon plus informelle qu'un conseil d'administration, mais peut avoir des responsabilités similaires, telles qu'aider les décideurs à formuler la mission et la politique de l'organisation, définir les orientations stratégiques et donner un aperçu général sur la santé financière de l'organisation ou du programme. *Advisory Board; Junta de Asesores*

Conseil d'administration : La loi oblige souvent les organisations à but lucratif ou non à avoir un conseil d'administration composé généralement d'un groupe de cadres ayant des compétences et expériences diverses. Ce conseil est responsable de veiller à la stabilité de l'organisation. Comme les membres du conseil d'administration ne sont pas des employés de l'organisation, et que leur candidature obéit généralement au système de volontariat, les conseils peuvent guider une organisation de façon efficace et objective étant donné qu'ils n'ont rien à y gagner financièrement. Les domaines de responsabilité sont les suivants : mise au point d'un plan stratégique, appui au leadership et au développement de l'organisation, fourniture d'une supervision financière, maintien de relations avec la communauté et le gouvernement, assurer la fourniture de services de haute qualité et gérer les activités du conseil. *Board of Directors; Junta Directiva*

Consommation mensuelle moyenne (CMM) : Le nombre moyen d'unités d'un type ou d'une marque spécifique de contraceptifs distribués au cours d'un mois. Cette moyenne se base généralement sur les quantités qui ont été distribuées au cours d'une période de six mois. *Average Monthly Consumption (AMC); Consumo Mensual Promedio (CMP)*

Contribution en nature : Contribution non financière ou compensation sous forme de matériels, biens ou services. *In-Kind Contribution; Contribuciones en Especie*

Coordination : Collaboration planifiée des activités des divers individus, départements et organisations qui tentent d'atteindre un objectif commun. *Coordination; Coordinación*

Coordination externe : Le processus d'identification des buts et fonctions communs à différentes organisations et la collaboration pour la mise en oeuvre des activités visant ces buts. Le plus souvent, la répartition des activités et des responsabilités entre les organisations est déterminée par les points forts spécifiques à chaque organisation. *External Coordination; Coordinación Externa*

Coordination interne : L'organisation et la communication logiques concernant les activités d'une organisation de sorte que tout le personnel soit conscient des rôles et des responsabilités de chaque département et des interactions entre départements. *Internal Coordination; Coordinación Interna*

COPE (Client orienté, prestation efficace) : Il s'agit d'une méthode utilisant une technologie élémentaire visant à améliorer les services. COPE permet aux équipes locales de prestation de services d'évaluer leur travail afin d'identifier les problèmes de leur formation sanitaire et de leur trouver des solutions. *COPE (Client-Oriented, Provider Efficient); «COPE» (Dirigido al Cliente, Eficiente para el Proveedor)*

Cotisations : Droits fixes que paient les clients ou les membres d'une organisation, en général une fois par an, ce qui leur donne accès à toute une gamme de services. *Membership Fees; Cuotas de Afiliación*

Couple-années de protection (CAP) : Mesure représentant le nombre total d'années de protection contraceptive fournie par une méthode. Pour chaque méthode, le nombre de CAP s'obtient en divisant le nombre d'unités distribuées par un facteur qui représente le nombre d'unités (de cette méthode) nécessaires à la protection d'un couple pendant une année. *Couple-Years of Protection (CYP); Años Protección Pareja (APP)*

Coût d'entretien : Concerne en général le coût de l'entretien d'une installation y compris les réparations, le nettoyage, le loyer, les impôts, l'assurance, etc. *Maintenance Cost; Costo de Mantenimiento*

Coût du personnel par type de visite : Le coût d'un seul type de visite, telle qu'une visite pour insérer un DIU, en tenant compte uniquement du coût des divers membres du personnel qui participent à la prestation de ce service. *Personnel Cost Per Visit-Type; Costo del Personal por Tipo de Visita*

Coût-efficacité : Méthode permettant de mesurer l'efficience d'un programme en comparant le coût à l'impact sur la base d'un indicateur tel que le taux d'utilisation des contraceptifs. Une étude de coût-efficacité a pour but d'identifier les stratégies de programme et les modes opérationnels susceptibles d'assurer le maximum d'impact au moindre coût. *Cost-Effectiveness; Costo-Efectividad*

Coût par année d'utilisation (ou Coût par couple-année de protection) : Le coût moyen de la fourniture à un client d'un contraceptif pendant un an. Ce coût est calculé à partir du coût total par visite (coût du personnel plus fournitures), du nombre moyen de visites de suivi par an et de la durée moyenne d'emploi de cette méthode. Le coût d'utilisation par année est une mesure de résultat : le coût de la protection d'un couple pendant un an. *Cost Per Year of Use; Costo por Año de Uso*

Coût total par visite : Le coût de la fourniture des services pour différents types de services (par exemple, première visite pour la pilule, visite pour insertion d'un DIU, visite pour conseils), y compris les coûts directs de personnel et de la fourniture de contraceptifs ainsi qu'une partie des frais généraux. Est utilisé pour comparer le coût-efficacité et l'efficience des services et établir les tarifs. *Total Visit Cost; Costo Total por Visita*

Coût unitaire (des produits contraceptifs) : Le coût total d'une unité de produits contraceptifs tels qu'un cycle de pilules, une paire de gants chirurgicaux, un kit Norplant®, un seul condom, etc., y compris les coûts de transport, de douane, les taxes et autres coûts. *Unit Cost (of Contraceptive Products); Costo Unitario (de los Productos Anticonceptivos)*

Coûts d'exploitation (également appelés Dépenses de fonctionnement ou Coûts récurrents) : Dépenses ordinaires pour le fonctionnement des programmes, et la fourniture des services, qui sont encourues chaque année (par opposition aux **Coûts d'investissement**). *Operating Costs; Costos de Operación*

Coûts d'investissement : Coûts engendrés par l'acquisition, la construction ou la rénovation d'immobilisations telles que les terrains, les bâtiments et le gros équipement (par opposition aux **Coûts d'exploitation**). *Capital Costs; Costos de Inversión (Gastos de Capital)*

Coûts des produits contraceptifs : Utilisé en déterminant le coût des services, le coût des produits contraceptifs est le coût unitaire d'un produit contraceptif. Si les contraceptifs sont obtenus gratuitement, il faudra estimer leur coût. Ce coût inclut normalement toutes les dépenses de transport international et local, les droits de douane et les taxes. *Contraceptive Product Cost; Costo del Anticonceptivo*

Coûts directs : Ces coûts sont associés directement ou imputés à une activité ou à un département spécifique (coûts de formation ou d'inscription à un programme de formation, séminaire ou conférence; coûts des produits contraceptifs; salaires et traitements du personnel; coûts des services achetés; etc.). Ces coûts budgétisés doivent être clairement identifiables dans un plan d'activités. *Direct Costs; Costos Directos*

Coûts du personnel (ou Coûts totaux du personnel) : Le coût de la rémunération du personnel (y compris les avantages) pour le temps passé à réaliser un service spécifique ou plusieurs services ou un ensemble de services au cours d'une période de temps spécifique. *Personnel Cost (or Total Personnel Cost); Costo del Personal (o Costo Total del Personal)*

Coûts (ou frais) fixes : Coûts qui ne changent pas en fonction de la taille de la population servie ou des services offerts, tels que les principaux frais de bureau, l'assurance, le loyer ou les intérêts sur les hypothèques. *Fixed Costs or Expenses; Costos o Gastos Fijos*

Coûts indirects (également appelés Frais généraux) : Coûts d'exploitation d'une organisation qui sont partagés par plus d'une activité ou d'une département (par exemple, la maintenance des bâtiments et les dépenses d'eau et d'électricité). *Indirect Costs; Costos Indirectos*

Coûts récurrents : Voir **Coûts d'exploitation.**

Coûts (ou dépenses) variables : Dépenses qui varient selon le niveau des prestations de service ou la taille de la population servie. Par exemple, les dépenses en contraceptifs varient selon le nombre d'utilisateurs de chaque méthode. *Variable Costs or Expenses; Costos o Gastos Variables*

Créance irrécouvrable : Compte débiteur pour lequel le recouvrement est considéré comme impossible. *Bad Debt; Deuda Incobrable*

Créances : Voir **Comptes à recevoir.**

Date de péremption : La date déterminée par le fabricant au-delà de laquelle le contraceptif ou autre produit médical ne doit plus être administré ou utilisé pour les clients. *Expiration Date; Fecha de Expiración*

Décentralisation : Processus de transfert de la responsabilités, de l'autorité, et du contrôle de certaines fonctions de gestion précises ou générales à des niveaux inférieurs au sein d'une organisation, d'un système ou d'un programme. (Voir **Déconcentration, Délégation, Dévolution et Privatisation.**) *Decentralization; Descentralización*

Déconcentration : Dans un programme de décentralisation, la déconcentration signifie que certaines fonctions de gestion telles que la mise au point de budgets de programmes sont transférées du niveau central aux *unités sur le terrain au sein du même organisme ou de la même organisation,* mais que le contrôle global du programme reste au niveau central. *Deconcentration; Desconcentración*

Définition des tâches : Fonctions et activités qui sont spécifiquement la responsabilité d'un employé ou d'une fonction. *Task Definition; Definición de Tareas*

Délai de livraison : Le temps nécessaire (en général exprimé en mois ou en semaines) pour qu'une livraison arrive une fois la commande faite. *Lead Time; Tiempo de Espera*

Délai moyen de livraison : La période moyenne qui s'écoule entre le moment où l'on commande des contraceptifs ou des produits et leur livraison. *Average Lead Time; Tiempo de Espera Promedio*

Délégation : Lors de la décentralisation des programmes, la délégation signifie que le niveau central transfère la responsabilité de certaines fonctions de gestion spécifiques telles que la conception et la conduite de la formation en gestion à des *organisations ou agences se trouvant en dehors de la structure bureaucratique habituelle,* et ces fonctions ne sont ainsi contrôlées qu'indirectement par l'administration centrale. *Delegation; Delegación*

Demande non satisfaite ou besoin non satisfait : Ce terme décrit le nombre de personnes ou le pourcentage de la population qui désire utiliser les contraceptifs pour espacer ou limiter les naissances mais qui, pour toutes sortes de raisons, y compris la difficulté d'accès à l'information ou aux services, n'utilisent pas présentement de contraceptifs. *Unmet Demand or Unmet Need; Demanda no Cubierta o Necesidad no Cubierta*

Densité de population : Nombre total de personnes vivant dans une zone définie telle qu'une communauté, un district, une capitale, un pays, une région ou un kilomètre carré. *Population Density; Densidad Poblacional*

Dépenses : Tout déboursement effectif d'espèces ou de chèques en comptabilité. *Expenditures; Erogaciones*

Dépenses de fonctionnement : Voir **Coûts d'exploitation.**

Description de poste : Document qui donne au minimum le titre du poste et fournit une description des tâches et responsabilités de ce poste, les relations de supervision directe avec d'autres membres du personnel et les compétences et qualifications nécessaires pour le poste. *Job Description; Descripción del Cargo*

Dettes : Voir **Comptes à payer.**

Développement professionnel (également appelé Perfectionnement du personnel) : Processus consistant à accroître les capacités professionnelles du personnel en lui fournissant une formation et des possibilités d'éducation ou en lui y donnant accès. Il peut s'agir de formation en cours d'emploi, de formation en dehors de l'emploi ou d'observation du travail des autres. Le développement professionnel est une façon bien connue de maintenir le moral du personnel, de renforcer la capacité institutionnelle d'un programme et d'attirer et de garder du personnel de haute qualité. *Professional Development; Desarrollo Profesional*

Dévolution : Dans la décentralisation d'un programme, la dévolution consiste à transférer le pouvoir à des *cellules gouvernementales subnationales* nouvellement créées ou renforcées, dont les activités ne relèvent pas directement de l'administration centrale. Dans le cadre de cette approche, la responsabilité et l'autorité pour un programme sont généralement transférés à une administration provinciale ou municipale. *Devolution; Devolución*

Diagramme de cause à effet : Outil servant fréquemment dans un programme d'amélioration continue de la qualité à regrouper les idées des gens sur les causes d'un problème particulier de façon organisée. Cet outil est également appelé diagramme en «arête de poisson» en raison de sa forme lorsqu'il illustre les causes primaires et secondaires d'un problème. *Cause-and-Effect Diagram; Diagrama de Causa y Efecto*

Diagramme de processus : Graphique utilisé pour analyser un processus ou une activité; indique la séquence des activités, les étapes et les points de décisions qui se produisent dans un processus particulier donné tel que l'inscription d'un client dans une formation sanitaire. En définissant un point pour le commencement et un autre pour la fin de ce processus et en analysant chaque étape du processus, les responsables peuvent identifier les zones posant problème et les améliorations nécessaires afin d'atteindre le ou les résultats souhaités. *Flowchart; Diagrama de Flujo*

Diffusion interne : Dans la planification familiale, diffusion interne consiste à utiliser les ressources au sein d'une formation sanitaire pour améliorer la compréhension et les connaissances sur les services de planification familiale dans la formation sanitaire (par opposition aux **Activités d'extension**). Elle concerne les occasions manquées de fournir des informations sur les services de planification familiale au personnel, aux clients et aux clients potentiels de toutes les sections de la formation sanitaire. Ces activités de diffusion interne comprennent l'amélioration des rapports et des références entre sections, mettre des affiches sur les services dans toute la formation sanitaire et faire connaître au personnel des autres sections les services de planification familiale. *Inreach; Conocimiento Interno («Inreach»)*

Directives pour l'auto-évaluation (également appelées Outil ou Liste aide-mémoire pour l'auto-évaluation) : Directives ou séries de listes aide-mémoire qui posent des questions spécifiques pour évaluer les capacités du personnel, ou les performances ou le fonctionnement d'un programme. *Self-Evaluation Guidelines; Normas de Auto-Evaluación*

Discontinuateur (également appelé Abandon) : Quelqu'un qui utilisait auparavant une méthode de contraception mais qui, pour toutes sortes de raison ne s'en sert plus. Un discontinuateur d'un programme ou d'une formation sanitaire est quelqu'un qui ne vient plus y chercher de services. Bien que, dans certains cas, ceci puisse impliquer que le client a discontinué la contraception, il est possible qu'il reçoive des services dans une autre formation sanitaire. Afin de connaître le nombre de personnes ayant abandonné, il est important que chaque programme définisse (pour chaque type d'utilisateur d'une méthode) la durée de l'absence de la formation sanitaire après un rendez-vous (ou après la date où il le aurait dû se réapprovisionner en contraceptifs) avant d'être considéré comme discontinuateur. *Par exemple, on peut encore considérer qu'une femme qui prend la pilule est une discontinuatrice si trois mois se sont écoulés depuis la date où elle devait se réapprovisionner. Mais une femme qui a un DIU n'est pas considérée nécessairement comme ayant abandonné si elle ne se rend pas à la formation sanitaire même pendant une année entière, à moins qu'elle n'ait eu de rendez-vous ou qu'on lui ait demandé de se présenter. Discontinuer; «Abandono»*

Distribution de la population : Répartition de la population au plan géographique par zone définie telle qu'une communauté, un district, une capitale, un pays, une région, etc. Il est important que les responsables connaissent la répartition de la population lorsqu'ils font les plans de nouveaux programmes et décident où installer les formations sanitaires. *Population Distribution; Distribución de la Población*

Données rétrospectives : Données recueillies dans les rapports antérieurs telles que rapports sur la distribution des contraceptifs, registres journaliers des activités, fiches de stocks, etc. *Historical Data; Datos Históricos*

Données sur les clients ou sur les formations sanitaires : Informations récapitulatives sur les clients desservis par un programme à base communautaire ou une formation sanitaire. Les types de données sur les formations sanitaires ou les clients comprennent généralement : types de méthodes contraceptives utilisés par les clients d'un programme (gamme des méthodes), nombre d'utilisateurs assidus desservis par une formation sanitaire ou un programme par mois ou par an, nombre de nouveaux accepteurs d'une méthode de contraception dans une formation sanitaire ou un programme, nombre de discontinuateurs d'une méthode ou clients qui ont abandonné le programme, et informations récapitulatives sur l'âge moyen, la situation matrimoniale et le nombre d'enfants des clients. *Client/Clinic Data; Datos sobre Clientes/Clínica*

Dossier du client (également appelé Dossier médical) : La fiche ou le formulaire rempli pour chaque client contenant des informations sur l'histoire médicale et de la planification familiale du client, son état de santé et le résultat de ses examens de santé. Cette fiche doit inclure au minimum le nom, l'adresse, le sexe, l'âge, la parité, l'histoire de la santé reproductive et les méthodes contraceptives utilisées par le client. Cette fiche est gardée à la formation sanitaire et mise à jour chaque fois que le client revient. *Client Record; Expediente del Cliente*

Dotation : Don financier ou don ayant une valeur financière considérable qui peut être vendu ou investi pour produire des revenus supplémentaires sous forme d'intérêts, de rentes ou de dividendes puis utilisé plus tard pour les besoins de l'institution et dont l'usage doit se conformer aux stipulations du donateur. *Endowment; Dotación*

Droits d'inscription (ou d'admission) : Montant fixe que paient les clients à chaque visite quels que soient les types de services fournis. *Registration Fees; Tarifas de Ingreso*

Durée de vie : La durée pendant laquelle on peut entreposer un contraceptif dans les circonstances normales sans qu'il perde son efficacité. Les mauvaises conditions de stockage, telles que les changements de températures extrêmes, peuvent réduire la durée de vie d'un produit. *Shelf Life; Vida Util*

Echelle discriminatoire de tarifs : Système qui fait payer les clients en se basant sur le revenu des ménages et la taille de la famille et permet aux clients de payer ce qu'ils peuvent. *Sliding Fee Scale; Escala Variable de Tarifas*

Effet de plateau : Situation dans laquelle la performance d'un programme—nombre de personnes desservies et participant activement à la planification familiale—cesse de croître. Dans de nombreux cas, un programme qui arrive à un plateau a déjà atteint un niveau d'utilisation de contraceptifs de 40 à 50 pour cent, a la capacité de desservir davantage de clients et doit envisager de nouvelles façons d'attirer et de retenir les clients, de réduire les obstacles aux services, de réorganiser les programmes et systèmes qui fournissent des services et de prendre d'autres types de décisions stratégiques qui amélioreront sa performance. *Plateau Effect or "Plateauing"; «Estancamiento»*

Efficacité : Le degré auquel un programme a réalisé les changements désirés ou atteint les objectifs par la prestation de services. *Effectiveness; Efectividad*

Efficience : Le degré auquel un programme a utilisé les ressources de manière appropriée et a réalisé les activités à terme échu. *Efficiency; Eficiencia*

Enoncé de mission (également appelé Mission de l'organisation) : Une brève formulation générale définissant le type d'organisation, son objectif principal et ses valeurs. La mission d'une organisation fournit la raison d'être de la définition de ses buts et objectifs. *Mission Statement; Declaración de Misión*

Enquête auprès de la population : Enquête dans laquelle les informations proviennent directement d'un échantillon représentatif de la population ou d'un groupe de population intéressant le programme tel que les femmes en âge de procréer. On obtient généralement les informations au moyen d'entretiens plutôt qu'à partir de rapports ou autres sources indirectes (Voir également **Enquête par grappes**.) *Population-Based Survey; Encuesta Basada en la Población*

Enquête auprès des clients : Enquête menée souvent au moyen d'entretiens servant à déterminer les besoins des clients, si ces besoins sont satisfaits, quelles sont leur perception de la qualité des soins, leur capacité de payer les services et autres caractéristiques d'une population donnée de clients. *Client Survey; Encuesta a Clientes*

Enquête auprès des ménages : Enquête qui recueille des informations sur l'occupation ou les occupations d'un couple, la méthode contraceptive qu'il utilise ou a utilisé par le passé, si la femme est enceinte ou allaite, les naissances récentes, le nombre total de naissances et de décès et autres informations concernant la santé reproductive d'un couple et son passé en matière de planification familiale intéressant ce programme. Les enquêtes auprès des ménages servent à établir le repère où l'indicateur auquel on comparera les résultats futurs. *Household Survey; Encuesta de Hogares*

Enquête auprès des prestataires de planification familiale : Etude d'autres prestataires de planification familiale, travaillant en général dans le même secteur que le programme qui mène l'enquête. Cette information sert à comparer les types et la qualité des services offerts par les autres prestataires et à déterminer les domaines de coordination et de référence ou les nouvelles possibilités de services. *Survey of Family Planning Providers; Encuesta a los Proveedores de Servicios de Planificación Familiar*

Enquête communautaire : Enquête auprès d'une communauté cible d'un nouveau programme ou d'un programme de planification familiale existant. Dans ce type d'enquête, les enquêteurs/chercheurs recueillent souvent des informations sur les connaissances, attitudes et pratiques actuelles concernant la contraception. Des informations supplémentaires peuvent être recueillies selon les besoins sur la perception des services d'un programme (que les personnes interrogées utilisent ou non ces services), leurs sources de services, leur revenu et autres indicateurs socio-économiques qui aideront les responsables à planifier ou améliorer le programme. *Community Survey; Encuesta de la Comunidad*

Enquête de base : Enquête menée au début d'un projet pour déterminer le niveau des indicateurs clés avec lesquels on comparera les résultats futurs. *Baseline Survey; Encuesta de Base*

Enquête par grappes : Technique d'enquête sur les populations qui permet aux responsables et évaluateurs d'étudier de petits groupes de population et d'extrapoler les résultats pour représenter une proportion plus importante de la population totale, permettant ainsi d'obtenir une rétro-information plus rapide sur l'impact des activités du programme. Des techniques d'échantillonnage par stratification selon lesquelles la population est divisée en diverses catégories revêtant un certain intérêt pour le programme (telles que l'âge, la parité, le lieu de résidence et l'éducation) peuvent servir dans des enquêtes par grappes à affiner les résultats. *Cluster Survey; Encuesta de Grupos*

Entretien à la sortie : Entretien avec les clients qui quittent le centre de planification familiale pour recueillir leurs impressions au sujet des services qu'ils ont reçus. Cet entretien peut être une conversation informelle ou un questionnaire axé sur un aspect particulier des prestations de services. *Exit Interview; Entrevista de Salida*

Entretien de la chaîne du froid : Gestion d'un système de congélateurs, réfrigérateurs, transporteurs de neige carbonique et autre matériel servant à maintenir les vaccins à bonne température du point de fabrication au point d'administration. *Cold Chain Maintenance; Mantenimiento de la Cadena de Frío*

Environnement externe : Les conditions qui prévalent dans le pays ou la région qui affectent le développement et la mise en oeuvre des programmes de planification familiale. Ce sont entre autres, la démographie, la culture, la politique, l'économie, la santé, les caractéristiques du marché, les sources de financement et les produits de base. *External Environment; Contexto Externo*

Environnement interne : Leadership, politiques, systèmes, technologie, capacité financière, etc. qui influencent l'efficacité d'une organisation ou d'un programme. D'autres facteurs de l'environnement interne comprennent : structures de gestion, systèmes de gestion, capacités du personnel, etc. *Internal Environment; Contexto Interno*

Equipe à fonctions multiples : Groupe d'individus composé de personnel de différents programmes ou secteurs d'activités tels que soins, laboratoire, administration et activités d'extension, qui travaillent ensemble à atteindre un objectif commun. *Cross-Functional Team; Equipo Interfuncional*

Etablissement de cartes : Processus permettant de disposer sur un diagramme ou une représentation de la communauté, du village ou d'un autre territoire bien défini des informations ou des données afin de suivre leur évolution. *Mapping; Mapeo*

Etat de la trésorerie : Voir **Formulaire de projection de l'état de la trésorerie**.

Etat des recettes : Rapport quotidien, mensuel ou trimestriel, des sommes ou de l'équivalent reçu pour les ventes, services ou honoraires. Dans le système de comptabilité d'exercice, les recettes sont enregistrées au moment où elles sont gagnées et non pas lorsque l'argent ou les biens sont effectivement perçus. *Revenue Report; Informe de Ingresos*

Etat des revenus et des dépenses (également appelé **Etat des recettes et des dépenses ou pertes et profits**) : Résumé périodique des recettes et des dépenses indiquant un excédent (profit) ou un déficit (perte) pour la période consolidée. *Income Statement; Estado de Pérdidas y Ganancias*

Etat financier : Rapport financier couvrant une période déterminée (un mois ou une année) et récapitulant les recettes et les dépenses (Etats des recettes et des dépenses) ainsi que les actifs et les passifs (Bilans) à la fin de la période. *Financial Statement; Estado Financiero*

Evaluation : Etude d'un programme dans lequel des processus variés de collecte et d'analyse d'informations sont utilisés pour déterminer si le programme réalise les activités planifiées et jusqu'à quel point il atteint ses objectifs initialement établis (à travers ces activités). Les résultats de l'évaluation peuvent servir à identifier les aspects du programmes les plus efficaces et les modifications qu'il faut faire pour l'améliorer. *Evaluation; Evaluación*

Evaluation de la performance : Procédure établie pour l'évaluation des performances de l'employé, mise en oeuvre à des intervalles déterminés à l'avance, d'habitude chaque année ou tous les six mois. *Performance Appraisal; Reconocimiento del Desempeño*

Evaluation rapide : Mini-étude économe et de courte durée à partir d'un échantillon menée pour comprendre l'envergure ou les causes d'un problème ou déterminer les besoins spécifiques de clients ou de programmes qui ont été identifiés par des données du programme ou autres grandes études. *Rapid Assessment; Evaluación Rápida*

Exonérations/Système de dérogation : Système utilisé pour déterminer dans quelles conditions on ne fera pas payer un client ou quand on aura recours au fonds de réserve pour payer une partie de ce que doit le client. Un système de dérogation utilise un ensemble de critères pour déterminer les clients qui ont droit à cet appui financier. *Waivers/Waiver System; Exoneraciones/Sistema de Exoneraciones y Excepciones*

«**F**aire les choses correctement» : Devise moderne de gestion concernant les activités devant être exécutées de la façon la plus efficace et la plus efficiente. Les responsables sont tenus de «faire les choses correctement» lorsqu'ils s'occupent des opérations journalières des programmes. *"Doing Things in the Right Way"; «Hacer las Cosas en Forma Correcta»*

«**Faire les choses nécessaires**» : Devise moderne de gestion qui concerne la qualité de la programmation, de la stratégie et de l'éthique d'un programme. Les responsables qui sont tenus de «faire les choses nécessaires» sont concernés par la direction stratégique d'un programme ou d'une organisation et remettent en question la mission, les buts et les objectifs qui sont à la base de leurs décisions. *"Doing the Right Things"; «Hacer las Cosas Correctas»*

Feuille de pointage (ou Liste des informations et données) : Tableau conçu pour faciliter la collecte et l'organisation des données. Les fiches de pointage sont utilisées pour faire la liste des types de données qui seront recueillies et enregistrer le nombre de cas ou d'observations comptés dans chaque catégorie. *Tally Sheet; Hoja de Registro*

Fiche de calcul des activités de planification familiale : Formulaire utilisé dans certaines formations sanitaires très fréquentées comme formulaire intermédiaire entre le registre journalier des activités et le récapitulatif mensuel. Les totaux du registre journalier des activités sont reportés sur la fiche de calcul chaque jour puis totalisés pour le mois et reportés sur le récapitulatif mensuel. *Family Planning Activities Worksheet; Planilla de Actividades de Planificación Familiar*

Fiche de contrôle des stocks : Voir **Fiche de stock**.

Fiche de rapport trimestriel : Formulaire qui fournit des informations sur le nombre et le type de clients servis (nouveaux clients et clients assidus), la quantité de contraceptif (de chaque type et marque) en stock au début du trimestre, la quantité reçue et distribuée sur une période de trois mois, les quantités commandées pour le trimestre à venir, ainsi que tous ajustements ou pertes et les bilans de fin d'exercice. *Quarterly Reporting Form; Formulario de Informe Trimestral*

Fiche de rendez-vous : Fiche donnée aux clients de planification familiale indiquant la date et l'heure de leur prochaine visite à la formation sanitaire, l'adresse (et le cas échéant, le numéro de téléphone) de la formation sanitaire et souvent le nom de la personne à contacter. L'emploi d'un système de rendez-vous aide les clients à se souvenir de la date à laquelle ils doivent revenir pour une visite de suivi, aide le personnel de la formation sanitaire à planifier les services et à les fournir d'une façon plus efficace et peut aider à réduire le temps d'attente des clients. *Appointment Card; Tarjeta de Citas*

Fiche de stock (également appelée Fiche de contrôle des stocks) : Formulaire utilisé pour enregistrer toutes les transactions concernant les stocks (contraceptifs reçus ou dispensés) et les quantités de contraceptifs en stock actuellement et commandés. Il faut avoir une fiche de stock séparée pour chaque type et chaque marque de contraceptif. *Stock Card; Tarjeta de Control de Inventario*

Fonctions/Systèmes de gestion : Les fonctions de gestion de base : planification du programme, budgétisation, détermination des rôles et responsabilités du personnel, formation, supervision du personnel, gestion des ressources (y compris argent, contraceptifs et produits de base et autres matériels ou services du programme), suivi des activités du programme, évaluation des résultats du programme et gestion de la fourniture de services aux clients. *Management Functions/Systems; Funciones/Sistemas Administrativos*

Fonds de roulement : Montant des fonds disponibles à court terme pour l'exploitation, représentant la différence entre l'actif à court terme et les dettes à court terme. *Working Capital; Capital de Trabajo*

Formation basée sur les compétences : Une formation axée exclusivement sur l'apprentissage des aptitudes, des faits et attitudes liés à des postes spécifiques. L'idéal est que le contenu d'une telle formation soit prédéterminé par les stagiaires eux-mêmes. *Competency-Based Training; Capacitación Funcional (basada en la competencia)*

Formation formelle : Une formation qui a des objectifs spécifiques, en termes d'apprentissage, et qui est dispensée hors du lieu de travail. *Formal Training; Capacitación Formal*

Formation informelle : Une formation qui s'acquiert sur le tas et est souvent réalisée grâce à l'auto-formation, à l'orientation par le superviseur ou même à l'observation des collègues. *Informal Training; Capacitación Informal*

Formation par étapes : Une formation réalisée par étapes et comportant des périodes alternatives de formation en salle et d'expérience sur le terrain. *Phased Training; Adiestramiento en Fases*

Formation polyvalente : Formation du personnel à exercer les fonctions d'autres membres du personnel de façon à ce que si certains sont malades ou trop occupés, d'autres peuvent les remplacer. *Cross-Training; Capacitación Interfuncional*

Formation sur le site : Méthode de formation intégrée qui considère le site de la prestation de services comme un système et traite les membres du personnel comme les membres de l'équipe qui permettent au système de fonctionner. L'objectif de la formation sur le site est d'améliorer les systèmes dans un site local grâce à un travail d'équipe efficace et en assurant que tous les membres de l'équipe ont les connaissances et les compétences dont ils ont besoin pour jouer leur rôle dans l'équipe. *Site Training; Capacitación en Servicio*

Formulaire de flux des clients : Ce formulaire sert à enregistrer les informations nécessaires pour réaliser une analyse du flux des clientes. Il permet d'enregistrer le numéro du client, la méthode de planification familiale, le type de visite, l'heure d'arrivée à la formation sanitaire et le temps et la durée de chaque contact avec le personnel. *Client Flow Form; Formulario de Flujo de Clientes*

Formulaire de projection de l'état de la trésorerie (également appelé État de la trésorerie) : Projection des recettes et décaissements servant à identifier les excédents ou déficit potentiels de liquidités. *Cash Flow Projection Worksheet; Planilla de Proyecciones del Flujo de Fondos*

Formulaires pour la rétro-information (feedback) journalière : Des formulaires d'évaluation conçus pour être utilisés quotidiennement afin de donner aux formateurs et managers une rétro-information (feed-back) valable sur la satisfaction des stagiaires quant à la formation. *Daily Feedback Forms; Formularios Diarios de Retroalimentación*

Frais : Tous les coûts de fonctionnement d'un programme. Dans un système de comptabilité d'exercice, les frais sont comptabilisés dès qu'ils sont engagés, avant même que la dépense correspondante ne soit réellement effectuée. *Expenses; Gastos*

Frais généraux : Voir **Coûts indirects**.

G amme des méthodes : Récapitulatif, représenté en général en pourcentage, montrant la proportion de tous les utilisateurs (d'une population générale ou spécifique) pour chaque méthode contraceptive. *Method Mix; Mezcla de Métodos*

Gestion de la formation sanitaire : Tous les aspects de la gestion efficace d'une formation sanitaire, y compris la planification des activités et des services, l'organisation des locaux et du processus de travail pour servir les clients, la gestion des ressources financières et programmatiques (y compris les fournitures et les contraceptifs), la gestion de l'information, le suivi des progrès vers les objectifs et la supervision du personnel clinique et non-clinique. *Clinic Management; Administración de la Clínica*

Gestion de la logistique : Voir **Gestion des stocks de contraceptifs**.

Gestion de la qualité : La gestion de la qualité consiste à contrôler les produits ou services pour s'assurer que les fournisseurs et les prestataires suivent des normes acceptées afin d'atteindre les résultats souhaités, et en cas de problèmes, prennent les mesures nécessaires pour améliorer les produits ou services. *Quality Management; Administración de la Calidad*

Gestion des ressources : Les fonctions de gestion et de contrôle des ressources limitées nécessaires pour faire fonctionner un programme, telles que le personnel, les crédits et le matériel. (Certaines personnes considèrent également le temps comme une ressource.) *Resource Management; Administración de Recursos*

Gestion des stocks de contraceptifs (également appelée Gestion de la logistique) : Gestion de tous les aspects du cycle d'approvisionnement : sélection des produits, prévision, passation de marchés, entreposage et comptabilité matière, distribution et utilisation, de façon à ce que des contraceptifs non périmés soient à la disposition des clients en quantité suffisante lorsqu'elles en ont besoin. *Contraceptive Supply Management; Administración de Suministros Anticonceptivos*

Gestion du personnel : Responsabilités relatives à l'embauche et au licenciement et à la supervision, promotion, organisation, motivation et développement des capacités professionnelles du personnel. La gestion du personnel exige d'excellentes compétences en communication interpersonnelle ainsi qu'en animation de groupes, règlement de conflits et solution de problèmes. *Personnel Management; Administración del Personal*

Gestion financière : Processus de mise en oeuvre et de gestion des systèmes de contrôle financier, de collecte des données financières, d'analyse de rapports financiers et de prise de décisions financières saines se basant sur les analyses. La gestion financière exige de savoir comment lire et interpréter trois documents clés : formulaire de projection de l'état de la trésorerie, bilan et état des revenus et des dépenses. *Financial Management; Administración Financiera*

Gestion stratégique : Manière de gérer un programme en identifiant les services spécifiques que peut fournir au mieux une organisation et les groupes de population qu'elle peut desservir le plus efficacement tout en évaluant avec réalisme les ressources disponibles pour exécuter ses tâches. La gestion stratégique exige que les responsables pensent stratégiquement, en se posant des questions du type : «Le programme fait-il les choses nécessaires?» et prévoient les tendances externes qui peuvent affecter l'accomplissement des objectifs de l'organisation. *Strategic Management; Administración Estratégica*

Grade : Dans les descriptions de poste, le niveau ou rang typique sur lequel est basée la grille des salaires. Il est en partie déterminé par les compétences et qualifications nécessaires pour effectuer le travail demandé. *Grade; Grado*

Graphique : Utilisé dans l'analyse des données, un graphique illustre sous forme d'image les relations ou tendances existant entre des chiffres et ensembles de chiffres qu'il serait difficile autrement de voir en examinant les données brutes. (Voir **Graphique linéaire**, **Graphique à colonnes** et **Graphique «camembert»**.) *Graph; Gráfica*

Graphique à colonnes : Graphique représentant des données ou ensembles de données au moyen de colonnes verticales ou horizontales de façon à ce que l'on puisse interpréter plus facilement la relation entre les données. Les graphiques à colonnes servent à analyser la plupart des types de données de services et montrent la différence entre diverses catégories de données telles que le nombre d'utilisateurs, de non-utilisateurs et de discontinuateurs. *Bar Chart; Gráfica de Barras*

Graphique «camembert» : Graphique qui représente des données récapitulatives ou des pourcentages sous forme de portions de gâteau ou de camembert, ce qui permet de mieux voir et d'analyser la relation entre les données. Les graphiques «camembert» peuvent servir à analyser la gamme des méthodes de n'importe quel type de clients ou de tous les clients ou clientes dans un programme ou une formation sanitaire. Ils permettent aux responsables de comparer des proportions et de représenter des données récapitulatives pour une période de temps spécifique (un mois, un trimestre ou une année). *Pie Chart; Gráfica de Sectores*

Graphique linéaire : Graphique qui représente des données ou des ensembles de données qui ont été recueillies au cours d'une certaine période. Les données sont portées sur un graphique correspondant à des intervalles de temps standard et l'on tire un trait entre les points. La ligne de ce graphique permet aux responsables de connaître les tendances des données (augmentation, diminution ou pas de changement) au cours d'une période de temps. Les graphiques linéaires servent souvent à analyser les tendances chez les nouveaux accepteurs, les clients assidus, les discontinuateurs, les nouveaux accepteurs utilisant une méthode particulière et autres. Les graphiques linéaires (qui sont mis à jour régulièrement) aident les responsables à suivre les tendances au cours d'une certaine période et à prendre des mesures pour gérer ces tendances. *Line Graph; Gráfica Lineal*

Gratification : Récompenses en espèce ou en nature, qui s'ajoutent au salaire ou les remplacent, telles que : assurance maladie, adhésion à un club, repas ou stationnement gratuits. *Perquisites; Gratificación*

Grilles d'observation : Un formulaire conçu pour permettre au formateur ou au superviseur d'évaluer l'apprenant par l'observation. *Observation Guides; Guías de Observación*

Groupe cible : Le ou les groupe(s) de population spécifique(s) qui bénéficieront d'un programme. Il s'agit soit de tous les bénéficiaires soit d'un sous-groupe d'utilisateurs potentiels comme les adolescents, les femmes enceintes, les populations rurales ou les habitants d'une zone géographique donnée. *Target Group; Grupo Objetivo*

Groupe de discussion focalisée : Discussion planifiée et guidée au sein d'un groupe de participants afin d'examiner une ou plusieurs questions spécifiques. Il s'agit d'une méthode qualitative de collecte d'information. Aux résultats de ces discussions focalisées viennent souvent s'ajouter d'autres données qualitatives recueillies par des enquêtes ou autres méthodes quantitatives ces résultats. *Focus Group; Grupo Focal*

Groupe-noyau pour l'ACQ : Utilisé dans un programme d'amélioration continue de la qualité (ACQ), le groupe-noyau est un groupe de personnes chargées de diriger le processus ACQ. Ce groupe est responsable de la planification de la mise en oeuvre du processus, de son démarrage, de la mise au point des matériels de formation, de l'organisation et de la formation de tout personnel ainsi que de l'appui à tous les niveaux de l'organisation. *CQI Core Group; Núcleo del PMC (o Grupo Interno para el PMC)*

H istogramme : Type de graphique à colonnes utilisé pour présenter les données d'une seule *catégorie et des valeurs continues* telle que l'âge qui peut être regroupé en 20-24 ans, 25-29 ans, 30-34 ans, etc. On utilise un graphique à colonnes normal pour présenter *les données des diverses catégories* telles que les utilisateurs de contraceptifs, les non-utilisateurs, la résidence urbaine ou rurale, etc. (Pour plus d'informations sur les histogrammes et graphiques à colonnes, veuillez vous référer au Volume II, Numéro 1 du *Management de la planification familiale* intitulé «Utiliser l'ACQ pour renforcer les programmes de planification familiale» et son supplément *Boîte à outils du Manager pour ACQ*.) *Histogram; Histograma*

Honoraires : Coûts généralement encourus dans le cadre d'accords contractuels avec *des individus* pour des services spécialisés tels que conférences, formation et évaluation, par opposition à des coûts encourus dans le cadre d'accords contractuels à long terme avec des *institutions* extérieurs des services tels que l'entretien des véhicules et des bâtiments, la publicité ou les services de promotion, qui sont appelés *services achetés.* (Voir **Services achetés.**) *Professional Fees; Honorarios Profesionales*

Immobilisations : Actifs dont la durée d'utilisation dépasse un an, tels que terrain, bâtiments, mobilier et le gros équipement. *Fixed or Long-Term Assets; Activos Fijos o Bien Duraderos*

Impact : Mesure à quel point un programme a introduit des changements ou amélioré les connaissances, les attitudes, le comportement ou la santé de la population cible en matière de planification familiale et de santé reproductive. *Impact; Impacto*

Indicateur : Condition, capacité ou mesure chiffrée qui, lorsqu'elle est enregistrée, recueillie et analysée, permet de mesurer plus facilement des concepts complexes et donne aux responsables et évaluateurs la possibilité de comparer les résultats effectifs d'un programme avec les résultats attendus. *Indicator; Indicador*

Information opérationnelle : L'information dont on a besoin pour planifier les activités telles que l'utilisation du temps, du personnel, des ressources financières, et qui sert à évaluer la fonctionnalité d'un programme de planification familiale. *Operational Information; Información Operacional*

Information sur la performance : L'information nécessaire à la planification des objectifs et l'évaluation de l'impact des activités d'un programme sur la population cible. *Performance Information; Información de Desempeño*

Information sur les processus : Diffère de l'information sur les données qui identifie les produits, les résultats ou les réalisations (en termes numériques). Elle est qualitative et fournit des informations sur les façons dont les personnes et les matériels sont utilisés pour produire des résultats spécifiques. *L'information sur les processus permet, par exemple, aux responsable de déterminer la cause d'une rupture de stocks de contraceptifs (effet négatif), en analysant chaque étape du processus du système logistique. Process Information; Información sobre el Proceso*

Information sur les résultats : Information concernant les produits ou réalisations (en chiffre) des activités d'un individu ou d'un programme au cours d'une période donnée. *Output Information; Informe de Resultados*

Institutionnalisation : L'internalisation, par une organisation ou un programme, d'une activité, d'un système ou d'une pratique dans la mesure où l'activité, le système ou la pratique continuent d'opérer malgré la rotation du personnel et indépendamment des facteurs et implications externes. *Institutionalization; Institucionalización*

Intégration/Services intégrés : Il s'agit d'un programme combinant les services de planification familiale aux services de santé maternelle et infantile, de nutrition, de vaccination et autres services de santé reproductive tels que la lutte et le traitement des maladies sexuellement transmissibles. *Integration/Integrated Services; Integración/Servicios Integrados*

Intervalle entre les commandes : Nombre fixe de mois entre le moment où l'on effectue les commandes de contraceptifs. Cet intervalle doit être déterminé individuellement pour chaque méthode de contraception afin de correspondre aux niveaux de stock maximums et minimums souhaités. *Order Interval; Intervalo entre Pedidos*

Intrants: Les ressources utilisées pour un programme. *Inputs; Insumos*

J alons de performance progressifs : Objectifs ou critères établis qui doivent être atteints au cours d'une période donnée. On établit souvent ces jalons pour encourager un programme à atteindre ses objectifs à court terme, ce qui, une fois qu'ils ont été atteints, donne au programme le droit de recevoir des fonds supplémentaires ou d'autres formes d'appui. *Benchmarks; Requisitos Previos («Benchmarks»)*

L ancement d'idées («Brainstorming») : Activité de groupe qui permet aux participants de formuler rapidement des idées, de poser des questions et de proposer des solutions aux problèmes. *Brainstorming; Lluvia de Ideas*

Listes des choses «à faire» : Listes informelles d'activités et tâches à exécuter sur une courte période, en général inférieure à un mois. Les listes de choses «à faire» sont régulièrement révisées afin d'y incorporer de nouvelles activités en remplacement de celles déjà exécutées. *"To Do" Lists; Lista de «Asuntos Pendientes»*

Livraisons incomplètes : Lorsque les fournisseurs livrent des quantités incomplètes de contraceptifs. *Short Shipments; Embarques Incompletos*

Livraisons partielles : Sont généralement faites à la demande du destinataire, lorsqu'une importante livraison est divisée en plusieurs parties expédiées à des intervalles réguliers pour contourner les contraintes d'espace chez le destinataire. *Split Shipments; Embarques Divididos*

M agasin central : Une structure de stockage qui assure la manutention et le stockage de l'ensemble des produits reçus de l'extérieur. *Central Warehouse; Bodega (almacén) Central*

Magasin intermédiaire : Un dépôt de contraceptifs situé dans une région donnée d'un pays. Il ne distribue des produits que dans cette zone. *Intermediate Warehouse; Bodega (almacén) Intermedia*

Manuel du personnel : Document exposant dans le détail les politiques et procédures concernant le personnel d'une organisation, y compris une description de la structure administrative et des tâches du personnel-clé. *Personnel Manual; Manual del Personal*

Marketing : Activités liées à la conception et l'adoption des prix de biens et services de façon à ce qu'ils puissent être mis sur le marché et utilisés par le public, en informant le public des services disponibles et de leurs prix, et en faisant la promotion des biens et services afin de créer une demande. *Marketing; Mercadeo*

Marketing social : Approche pour la promotion, la distribution et la vente de produits contraceptifs à un prix relativement bas par le biais des points de distribution commerciale existants modelé sur le marketing des produits commerciaux. Le marketing social communique les messages de santé reproductive et de planification familiale aux diverses couches de la population en utilisant des entités commerciales comme la radio, la publicité dans les journaux et la télévision pour fournir information, éducation et communication sur la planification familiale. *Social Marketing; Mercadeo Social*

Matrice (également appelée Tableau de comparaison) : Tableau utilisé pour analyser deux ou plusieurs ensembles ou types d'information (tels que le nombre d'utilisateurs de chaque méthode de contraception par type de clients, tel que les nouveaux accepteurs et les visites de suivi). Une matrice peut aussi être utilisée pour comparer les processus ou activités de l'organisation à un ensemble de critères reflétant les priorités, ressources et contraintes de l'organisation afin d'aider les responsables à reclasser les domaines d'amélioration par ordre de priorité. *Matrix; Matriz*

Méthodes à court terme : Méthodes de contraception qui restent efficaces pendant une période de temps relativement courte. Les experts ne sont pas d'accord sur les méthodes que désigne ce terme. Certains experts incluent uniquement les spermicides, les diaphragmes, les condoms, alors que d'autres incluent également la pilule. *Short-Term Methods; Métodos de Corto Plazo*

Méthodes de longue durée (ou Méthodes à long terme) : Méthode contraceptives qui restent efficaces pendant une période de temps relativement longue. Les experts peuvent avoir des idées différentes sur les méthodes groupées sous cette appellation. Certains incluent uniquement les DIU, les implants, les injectables alors que d'autres comprennent également la pilule et même la stérilisation volontaire. *Long-Acting Methods; Métodos de Larga Duración*

Méthodologie : Les méthodes, les moyens et la procédure logique par lesquels un plan ou une approche de programme est mis en oeuvre : par exemple la formation sur le tas par opposition à la formation formelle. *Methodology; Metodología*

Micro-gestion : Le fait de fournir une supervision inutile et excessive dans le cadre de la gestion du personnel et de ses activités. *Micro-Manage; Micro-Administrar*

Mission de l'organisation : Voir **Enoncé de mission**.

Mobilisation de fonds : Processus permettant de rechercher un appui financier auprès de groupes locaux, d'unités gouvernementales, locales ou centrales, d'organisations de bailleurs de fonds ou d'individus au niveau local ou international et autres. *Fund Raising; Recaudación de Fondos*

Mois d'approvisionnement : Quantité d'un produit disponible (d'une contraceptif ou produit spécifique) en termes du nombre de mois d'approvisionnement si le produit est distribué au rythme actuel (moyen). Il s'agit de la quantité disponible (d'un contraceptif ou d'un produit de base spécifique) divisé par la consommation mensuelle moyenne de ce produit (CMM). *Months of Supply; Meses de Suministros*

Motivation des clients : Information, éducation, discussion ou activités de promotion qui servent à encourager un client ou un client potentiel à utiliser ou à continuer d'utiliser les contraceptifs et les services de santé reproductive régulièrement. *Client Motivation; Motivación del Cliente*

Motivation du personnel : Les activités concernant le personnel d'une organisation ou d'un superviseur qui sont conçues pour réaffirmer l'importance du travail du personnel quant aux accomplissements du programme et pour améliorer les compétences, la motivation et les qualifications des employés. Ces actions et activités comprennent formation, rétro-information positif et constructif constant, appréciation de leur travail et leur implication dans la résolution de problèmes. *Staff Motivation; Motivación del Personal*

Mutuellement responsable : Situation dans laquelle plusieurs parties ou individus sont conjointement responsables du ou des résultats d'une activité ou de plusieurs activités. *Mutually Accountable; Responsabilidad Conjunta*

Niveau de pointe : Le niveau actuel d'avancement d'une technologie donnée. *State-of-the-Art; De Punta*

Nouveau client (également appelé Première visite ou Première consultation d'un client) : Quelqu'un qui reçoit les services (d'un agent) d'un programme de planification familiale pour la première fois. Les programmes ont des définitions différentes de nouveaux clients. Certains programmes comprennent les personnes qui reçoivent n'importe quel type de services (y compris des conseils) et qui n'ont pas reçu auparavant de services de ce programme. D'autres programmes comptent uniquement les personnes qui acceptent une méthode de planification familiale pour la première fois et n'ont jamais utilisé auparavant de contraceptifs d'autres programmes. D'autres programmes encore distinguent entre les nouveaux clients (d'un programme) et les nouveaux accepteurs/utilisateurs (d'une méthode). Quelles que soient les définitions qu'utilisent un programme, il est essentiel qu'elles soient claires et comprises par tout le personnel de façon à ce que les données de service dans toutes les formations sanitaires soient recueillies et enregistrées de la même façon. *New Client; Cliente Nuevo*

Nouvel accepteur (également appelé **Nouvel utilisateur**) : Quelqu'un qui accepte une méthode de contraception pour la première fois. La définition de ce terme varie selon les programmes. Certains n'incluent que les personnes qui utilisent la contraception pour la première fois et qui n'ont jamais utilisé une forme de contraception auparavant. D'autres incluent également les personnes qui utilisent une méthode de contraception particulière pour la première fois (alors qu'elles utilisaient une autre méthode auparavant). D'autres encore peuvent inclure des personnes qui acceptent une méthode (d'un agent) de ce programme pour la première fois (alors qu'elles utilisaient une autre méthode fournie précédemment par un autre programme). Quelle que soit la définition qu'utilise un programme, il est essentiel qu'elle soit claire et bien comprise par tout le personnel, de façon à ce que les données de service soient recueillies et enregistrées de la même façon dans toutes les formations sanitaires. *New Acceptor; Aceptante Nuevo*

Numéro de lot : Se réfère à chaque lot distinct de contraceptifs au moment de la fabrication. *Lot Number; Número de Lote*

Objectifs : Les résultats ou rendements escomptés d'un programme, représentant les changements de connaissances, d'attitudes et de comportement des clients du programme; décrites d'une façon quantifiable tout en spécifiant la période pendant laquelle on doit atteindre ces résultats. Ces objectifs doivent être spécifiques, mesurables, appropriés, réalistes et programmés dans le temps. *Objectives; Objetivos Específicos*

Obstacles aux services : Lois ou politiques nationales ou locales, pratiques et procédures professionnelles, réglementation administrative ou tout autre règle officielle ou non qui empêchent les gens de recevoir des services à cause de leur âge, de leur sexe, de leur situation matrimoniale, de leur parité, de leur capacité financière, de leur lieu de résidence, etc. *Barriers to Services; Barreras a los Servicios*

Occasion manquée : Occasion qui aurait pu permettre la réalisation d'une activité bénéfique (prestation de service, rétro-information de l'employé, etc.) mais qui n'a pas été saisie. *Missed Opportunity; Oportunidad Perdida*

Organigramme : Diagramme montrant la relation de travail entre tous les postes au sein d'une organisation ou d'un programme et la structure de supervision formelle, ainsi que les relations entre les divers postes et fonctions de la direction et du personnel. *Organogram or Organizational Chart; Organigrama o Diagrama Organizacional*

Organisation interne : Structure et dispositions internes d'une organisation ou d'un programme en ce qui concerne l'affectation du personnel et les relations entre les divers domaines fonctionnels, tels que la planification, la budgétisation, la gestion financière, la supervision, etc. L'organisation interne d'un programme est particulièrement importante à mesure que les programmes se décentralisent et/ou plusieurs programmes se fusionnent en un programme unique. *Internal Organization; Organización Interna*

Organisation qui démarre : Il s'agit, en général, d'une petite organisation au cours des premières années de son développement. De nombreuses organisations qui démarrent sont caractérisées par un leadership très créatif, des initiatives extrêmement innovatrices et un personnel restreint, mais très engagé et motivé. *Start-Up Organization; Organización Incipiente (o de Arranque)*

Outil ou Liste aide-mémoire pour l'auto-évaluation: Voir **Directives pour l'auto-évaluation.**

Paiements des prestations : Montant que doit payer le client pour chaque service fourni, tels que les conseils, la consultation, les examens de laboratoire et les contraceptifs. Certains programmes établissent un tarif standard pour les visites initiales et les visites de suivi. Une visite initiale peut inclure le coût d'un examen, des conseils et d'une méthode contraceptive, alors qu'une visite de suivi peut ne couvrir que le coût du réapprovisionnement en contraceptifs et de la consultation. *Service Fees; Tarifas por Servicios*

Paiements effectués par les clients : Montants demandés aux clients en paiement des services qu'on leur assure, tels que fourniture de contraceptifs, conseils, services cliniques ou de laboratoires et autres. Les paiements des clients comprennent les droits d'inscription qui sont perçus à chaque visite, les paiements pour services recueillis lorsqu'ils reçoivent des services individuels et les cotisations recueillies chaque année. De nombreux programmes font payer aux clients un montant modeste pour aider à couvrir une partie des coûts de la prestation de services et encourager les clients à apprécier les services fournis. *Client Fees; Tarifas para los Clientes*

Paiements par un tiers (ou Co-paiements) : Système selon lequel un tiers (tel qu'un employeur, une compagnie d'assurance ou un plan de santé intégré) paie les services fournis au client. Il peut y avoir aussi des co-paiements, auquel cas le client paie une partie des frais. *Third-Party Payments; Sistema de Pagos de Terceros (Co-Pagos)*

Partage des coûts : Un système de réduction des coûts opérationnels basé sur la coordination avec d'autres organisations, comme par exemple l'achat en commun d'un grand volume de produit, le partage des infrastructures et des coûts de stockage, et le partage des coûts de transport. *Cost-Sharing; Colaboración entre Programas para la Reducción de Costos*

Participation communautaire : Composante essentielle des programmes de planification familiale, la participation communautaire peut prendre de nombreuses formes; elle existe lorsque les membres de la communauté et l'autorité locale jouent un rôle important dans la gestion du programme de planification familiale locale et la contribution en argent, matériels, ou bénévolat, ce qui leur donne le sentiment d'être responsables du programme et d'assumer les tâches nécessaires pour atteindre les objectifs fixés. *Community Participation; Participación Comunitaria*

Passif : Obligations ou dettes envers les fournisseurs, les employés, les banques ou l'Etat. *Liability; Pasivo*

Pensée stratégique : Compétence de gestion critique qui permet d'évaluer un programme, par rapport à sa mission, à ses buts futurs et au contexte externe dans lequel il fonctionne. La pensée stratégique exige que les responsables examinent si leurs programmes «font les choses nécessaires» pour réaliser leur mission. *Strategic Thinking; Pensamiento Estratégico*

Perfectionnement du personnel : Voir **Développement professionnel**.

Performance de la formation sanitaire : La performance de la formation sanitaire est souvent mesurée en comptant le nombre de clientes desservies par la formation et/ou le nombre de nouveaux accepteurs et utilisateurs assidus desservis par la formation au cours d'une période de temps donné et est évaluée par rapport aux objectifs établis pour cette formation sanitaire. *Clinic Performance; Rendimiento de la Clínica*

Petite caisse : Fonds de caisse à montant fixe avec une petite trésorerie fixe destinée à régler les petites dépenses au comptant, et qui est ravitaillée au fur et à mesure. *Petty Cash; Caja Chica*

Phase d'émergence : La première phase du développement d'une organisation dont l'objectif principal est de lancer la prestation de services. Cette étape est caractérisée par le fait que la mission de l'organisation est mal définie ou incomplète, que la structure de l'organization es simple, les programmes et les systèmes sont de base et que l'organisation est fortement tributaire du soutien financier externe. (Voir **Phases de développement d'une organisation**.) *Emergent Stage; Etapa de Surgimiento (o Etapa Emergente)*

Phase de consolidation : La troisième phase du développement d'une organisation pendant laquelle cette organisation se concentre sur le développement et le perfectionnement de ses systèmes afin d'accroître l'efficacité de sa gestion y compris ses capacités internes de mobiliser et de contrôler les ressources afin d'assurer la viabilité de l'organisation et du programme. (Voir **Phases de développement d'une organisation**.) *Consolidation Stage; Etapa de Consolidación*

Phase de croissance : Deuxième étape du développement de l'organisation. A ce stade, les organisations énoncent clairement leur mission, définissent les stratégies à suivre pour la réaliser, ont des buts et objectifs spécifiques et élaborent et utilisent des plans opérationnels pour atteindre les objectifs. A mesure que les activités et les services prennent rapidement de l'ampleur, l'organisation dépend de plus en plus des ressources externes pour appuyer ces programmes et services. (Voir **Phases de développement d'une organisation**.) *Growth Stage; Etapa de Crecimiento*

Phase de maturité : La quatrième et dernière étape de développement de l'organisation pendant laquelle une organisation renforce sa capacité de gérer efficacement et d'ajuster sa mission, sa stratégie, sa structure et ses systèmes pour répondre aux défis internes et externes afin d'améliorer ses chances de viabilité. (Voir **Phases de développement d'une organisation**.) *Mature Stage; Etapa de Madurez*

Phases de développement d'une organisation : Les quatre phases qui caractérisent le développement d'une organisation sont les suivants : émergence, croissance, consolidation et maturité. Ces phases sont basées sur le principe que les organisations se développent de façon systématique au cours du temps et prennent des caractéristiques différentes durant chaque étape compte tenu de leur mission, leur stratégie, leur structure et leur systèmes. (Voir **Phase d'émergence, Phase de croissance, Phase de consolidation** et **Phase de maturité**.) *Stages of Organizational Development; Etapas del Desarrollo de una Organización*

Plan d'action : Mis au point par un responsable et le personnel, un plan d'action fait la liste des buts et objectifs du programme et des activités qui seront mises en oeuvre pour atteindre ces objectifs. Un plan d'action couvre en général une période d'une année, indique la ou les personne(s) responsable(s) de la mise en oeuvre de chaque activité, montre comment chaque activité doit être réalisée et fait connaître les ressources financières nécessaires. (Voir **Plan opérationnel**.) *Action Plan; Plan de Acción*

Plan d'entreprise : Souvent mis au point afin de mobiliser des fonds pour un programme ou un projet, un plan d'entreprise précise les objectifs, les activités, les sources de revenu et autres ressources financières ainsi que les recettes prévisionnelles qui seront générées par l'entreprise ou les activités. *Business Plan; Plan de Negocios*

Plan de travail : Document élaboré par le responsable et le personnel pour une période précise qui dresse la liste des activités planifiées en précisant les dates auxquelles elles seront exécutées, les ressources nécessaires et les personnes chargées de les exécuter. *Work Plan; Plan de Trabajo*

Plan de visite du superviseur (également appelé **Plan des tournées de supervision**) : Etat descriptif ou liste des points à vérifier pendant une séance de supervision qui indique les rubriques, les techniques et les statistiques à contrôler au cours de chaque séance de supervision. Ce plan doit également comporter des activités de soutien au programme telles que la collecte des rapports et le réapprovisionnement en produits ainsi que toute autre activité post-tournée à être accomplie par le superviseur. *Supervisor's Visit Plan; Plan de Visita del Supervisor*

Plan opérationnel : Diffère d'un plan stratégique (qui établit les stratégies générales qu'un programme utilisera ou les initiatives qu'il prendra pour atteindre ses objectifs). Un plan opérationnel établit les projets ou activités spécifiques (qui s'inscrivent dans le plan stratégique) qui seront exécutés, et le calendrier et les ressources nécessaires pour mener à bien ces projets ou activités. (Voir également **Plan d'action**.) *Operational Plan; Plan Operativo*

Plan stratégique : Document qui est le résultat de la planification à long terme (ou planification stratégique). Il couvre au minimum une période de cinq ans, établit la mission et les objectifs du programme, classe les stratégies en ordre de priorité et établit la base financière qui permettra d'atteindre les objectifs. *Strategic Plan; Plan Estratégico*

Planification : Un processus continu pour analyser les données d'un programme, prendre des décisions et concevoir des plans de travail pour l'avenir. Elle vise la réalisation des objectifs du programme. *Planning; Planeación*

Planification des activités : Processus par lequel une organisation sélectionne les activités qui vont être menées, planifie la séquence de ces activités et identifie les ressources (humaines, financières et matérielles) qui seront utilisées pour exécuter ces activités afin d'atteindre les résultats souhaités. *Activity Planning; Planeación de Actividades*

Planification stratégique : Une planification à long terme couvrant une période de trois à cinq ans, qui consiste à déterminer les buts, stratégies et objectifs du programme. *Strategic Planning; Planeación Estratégica*

Point de distribution (final) : Le point final de distribution des contraceptifs aux clients (clinique, pharmacie, agents de distribution communautaire, etc.) *Outlet; Local o Punto de Distribución*

Points de services périphériques : Services qui sont fournis à une communauté ou à plusieurs communautés à un moment donné (une fois par mois en général), et à un endroit désigné. Les points de services périphériques assurent généralement des soins de santé intégrés, des soins de santé maternelle et infantile et des services de planification familiale. (Voir également *Système à cinq tables.) Satellite Services; Servicios Satélites*

Populations mal desservies (sous-servies) : Groupes de personnes qui normalement ne sont pas desservies ou sont mal desservies par les programmes de prestation de services établis. Dans le cadre de la planification familiale, il peut s'agir des adolescents, des hommes, des femmes à faible parité, des citadins pauvres, des célibataires et des personnes qui vivent dans des zones rurales éloignées. *Underserved Populations; Sectores Desatendidos de la Población o Carentes de Servicios*

Post-test : Test administré aux clients, employés, stagiaires ou à tout autre groupe de personnes que l'on désire évaluer à la fin ou pendant la mise en oeuvre d'un programme et qui a pour but de mesurer les progrès réalisés par rapport aux objectifs fixés. *Post-test; Examen Post-Prueba*

Postes de travail : Divers endroits ou étapes au sein d'une formation sanitaire où une cliente reçoit un type de service donné. Les postes de travail comprennent souvent l'inscription auprès du chargé de l'accueil, la pesée, la prise de la tension, l'entrevue avec une conseillère, l'examen par une infirmière ou un médecin et la sortie. *Service Stops; Estaciones de Servicios*

Premier à périmer, premier sorti (PPPS) : Système de gestion de l'approvisionnement selon lequel les contraceptifs portant la date de péremption la plus proche sont distribués les premiers et ceux portant la date d'expiration suivante après épuisement du stock précédent. *First-to-Expire, First-Out (FEFO); Primero en Expirar, Primero en Salir (PEPS)*

Première visite ou Première consultation d'un client : Voir **Nouveau client**.

Prestations/services de santé reproductive : Les diverses méthodes, techniques et prestations de services contribuant à entretenir ou à améliorer la santé et le bien-être reproductifs d'une personne grâce à la prévention et à la résolution des problèmes touchant à la santé reproductive.[1] (Voir **Santé reproductive**.) *Reproductive Health Care/ Services; Servicios de Salud Reproductiva*

Pré-test : Test administré aux clients, employés, stagiaires ou à tout autre groupe que l'on désire évaluer et qui a pour but de déterminer une base par rapport à laquelle les futurs résultats seront évalués. *Pretest; Examen Pre-Prueba*

Prévalence contraceptive : Le pourcentage de toutes les femmes en âge de reproduction (FAR) ou de femmes mariées en âge de reproduction (FMAR), en général de 15 à 49 ans, qui utilisent une méthode de contraception. La prévalence contraceptive concerne généralement l'emploi de toutes les méthodes mais doit être donné séparément pour les méthodes modernes (pilule, DIU, implants, injectables, condoms, diaphragmes, capes cervicales et stérilisation volontaire). On le calcule en divisant le nombre de femmes en âge de procréer ou de femmes mariées en âge de procréer qui utilisent une méthode (numérateur) par le nombre total de femmes en âge de procréer ou de femmes mariées en âge de procréer (dénominateur). *Contraceptive Prevalence; Prevalencia de Uso de Anticonceptivos*

Prévisions basées sur la distribution : Cette méthode de prévision des contraceptifs fournit une estimation du nombre de contraceptifs requis sur la base des quantités distribuées antérieurement au niveau du dépôt, du point de distribution ou de la clinique. *Distribution-Based Forecasts; Proyecciones Basadas en la Distribución*

---

[1]   D'après le *Programme d'action de la Conférence internationale des Nations unies sur la population et le développement*, Le Caire, 23 septembre 1994, paragraphe 7.1.

Prévisions basées sur la population : Les prévisions des besoins en approvisionnement qui se fondent sur la partie de la population cible que le programme veut servir ainsi que le niveau prévu de demande pour chaque méthode contraceptive. *Population-Based Forecasts; Proyecciones Basadas en Información Censual o en Encuestas Demográficas*

Prévisions basées sur les prestations de services : Ce sont les prévisions basées sur une analyse des statistiques existantes sur le programme et le nombre de clients qu'un programme compte servir. *Service-Based Forecasts; Prévisiones Basadas en el Servicio*

Privatisation : La privatisation concerne le transfert de fonctions spécifiques de gestion telles que la passation des marchés de contraceptifs, la logistique et la formation, à des *organisations privées à but non lucratif ou commerciales* externes à la structure gouvernementale. Bien que ce mot soit souvent utilisé pour décrire une forme de décentralisation, certains experts croient que la privatisation n'est pas un moyen de décentralisation parce que dans la privatisation, un gouvernement abandonne la responsabilité au lieu de la transférer à des échelons inférieurs. *Privatization; Privatización*

Procédure de rupture de contrat : Politique définie et mentionnée d'habitude dans le manuel du personnel, décrivant les motifs de licenciement et les droits de l'employé dans ce cas. *Termination Policy; Normas de Despidos*

Procédure de soumission de doléances : Politique définie et mentionnée dans le manuel du personnel, décrivant la procédure formelle de soumission, de traitement et de résolution des doléances du personnel. *Grievance Policy; Normas para Manejo de Quejas y Reclamos*

Processus de supervision en équipe : Tout processus conçu pour la supervision du personnel utilisant l'approche participative d'équipe qui implique les superviseurs et le personnel dans la totalité du processus. *Team Supervision Process; Proceso de Supervisión en Equipo*

Processus de travail : Le processus ou la séquence d'activités réalisées pour mener à bien une tâche. *Ainsi, le processus de travail nécessaire pour inscrire un client dans une formation sanitaire peut consister à bien accueillir le client, prendre son nom, vérifier s'il s'agit d'un client nouveau ou assidu, ouvrir un nouveau dossier et demander au client de remplir les papiers nécessaires ou retrouver le dossier existant du client, faire payer tout droit d'inscription (le cas échéant), prier le client de s'asseoir jusqu'à* *ce qu'il ou elle puisse être vu(e) par un prestataire de service et informer le prestataire que le client est prêt pour sa consultation.* **Work Process; Proceso de Trabajo**

Produits pour la planification familiale : Se réfère à tous les contraceptifs, matériel et produits pharmaceutiques et équipements nécessaires aux services de planification familiale. *Family Planning Commodities; Suministros de Planificación Familiar*

Profil des clients : Représentation en chiffres et/ou en pourcentage des principales caractéristiques des clients d'un programme. Un profil des clients permet aux responsables de mieux comprendre les types de clients que dessert le programme et (dans certains cas), les besoins prioritaires de ces clients de façon à ce que le programme puisse mieux satisfaire ses clients et peut-être en attirer de nouveaux qui ont des besoins similaires. *Client Profile; Perfil del Cliente*

Programme de paiement des prestations : Programme qui fait payer chaque service fourni par le programme ou la formation sanitaire. En général, dans un programme de ce type, chaque sorte de service a un prix différent basé sur le coût réel de la fourniture de ce service. Dans ce type de programme, une nouvelle cliente recevant sa première dose de pilules paiera en général davantage qu'une cliente qui vient se réapprovisionner. Ceci vient du fait que la nouvelle cliente reçoit des services plus complets pendant sa première visite qu'une cliente qui revient seulement pour se réapprovisionner en pilules. *Fee-For-Service Program; Programa de Cobro de Tarifas por Servicios*

Programme pour accroître le nombre d'utilisateurs actifs : Une approche systématique mise en oeuvre pour augmenter le nombre d'utilisateurs actifs dans un système de prestation de services. Pour instituer un programme permettant d'accroître le nombre d'utilisateurs actifs, on doit déterminer un taux ou un nombre acceptable d'utilisateurs pour chaque centre de services et mener régulièrement des activités de suivi. *User Continuity Program; Programa para Aumentar la Tasa de Continuidad de Usuarios Activos*

Protocole de supervision : Système établi pour superviser le personnel (clinique et non clinique). Un protocole de supervision doit décrire clairement les procédures et calendriers de supervision, la philosophie de l'organisation sur la supervision, les instruments nécessaires à une supervision efficace (tels que descriptions de poste et objectifs de performance), les critères de promotion et les techniques permettant de motiver et d'encourager le personnel. *Supervisory Protocol; Protocolo de Supervisión*

Protocole sanitaire : Liste des normes médicales que le personnel est appelé à suivre et qui décrivent en détail les procédures médicales et les normes sanitaires qui garantissent la sécurité et la santé des clients de planification familiale. *Clinic Protocol; Norma (o Guía) Clínica*

Qualité des services : La qualité des services dépend d'un certain nombre de facteurs liés entre eux, y compris la manière dont les clients sont traités par les prestataires, la gamme de services et le choix de méthodes contraceptives à la disposition des clients, le caractère complet de l'information fournie aux clients et la qualité des conseils donnés, l'encouragement du choix personnel, la compétence technique du prestataire et l'accessibilité et la continuité des services. *Service Quality; Calidad de los Servicios*

Quantité couvrant le délai de livraison : Quantité de contraceptifs qui seront distribués pendant la période allant du moment où une commande est faite jusqu'à la livraison de cette commande. On calcule cette quantité en se basant sur les données antérieures. *Lead Time Quantity; Cantidad para Cubrir el Tiempo de Espera*

Quantité maximum : La plus grande quantité de produits (contraceptifs) qu'un programme doit avoir en stock. Cette quantité doit être suffisamment élevée pour que les stocks ne s'épuisent pas entre les commandes et suffisamment faible pour éviter le surstockage et le gaspillage de produits périmés. Elle est calculée séparément pour chaque contraceptif et consiste de la quantité minimum nécessaire, plus la quantité utilisée entre les commandes ordinaires. (On trouvera aux pages 10 et 11 du Numéro 4 du Volume I du *Management de la planification familiale* intitulé «Améliorer la gestion des stocks de contraceptifs» une formule permettant de calculer les quantités maximum et minimum des stocks.) *Maximum Quantity; Cantidad Máxima*

Quantité minimum : Volume le plus faible (de chaque contraceptif) dont doit toujours disposer une formation sanitaire dans ses stocks. La quantité minimum doit être suffisamment élevée pour éviter les pénuries ou ruptures de stocks même en cas de livraisons en retard ou d'augmentation imprévue de la demande. La quantité minimum représente le stock de sécurité, plus la quantité de produits utilisée entre une commande et sa livraison. (On trouvera aux pages 10 et 11 du Numéro 4 du Volume I du *Management de la planification familiale* intitulé «Améliorer la gestion des stocks de contraceptifs» une formule permettant de calculer les niveaux minimum et maximum de stocks.) *Minimum Quantity; Cantidad Mínima*

R **apport de performance budgétaire** : Rapport comparant les recettes et dépenses réelles avec celles prévues par le budget. *Budget Performance Report; Informe de Ejecución del Presupuesto*

Rapport financier : Système établi de rapports périodiques sur les transactions financières et la situation financière d'une organisation ou d'un programme. *Financial Reporting; Informes Financieros*

Rapport programmatique : Système ou processus établi donnant des informations détaillées sur les activités entreprises pendant une période spécifique. Les rapports programmatiques prennent généralement une forme narrative et ne concernent que les informations non financières sur les activités et l'état d'avancement vers l'atteinte des objectifs. *Programmatic Reporting; Informes Programáticos*

Ratio : Promotion obtenue en divisant une quantité par une autre quantité. *Par exemple, dix-huit infirmières de planification familiale (numérateur) divisé par six formations sanitaires (dénominateur) est un ratio de trois infirmières par formation sanitaire. Ratio; Razón*

Récapitulatif mensuel des activités de planification familiale : Formulaire utilisé pour enregistrer les totaux mensuels de toutes les données recueillies dans le registre journalier des activités de planification familiale. En général, le responsable de la formation sanitaire en garde un exemplaire et un deuxième exemplaire est envoyé au superviseur du programme qui totalise les données mensuelles pour toutes les formations sanitaires de la région ou district. *Monthly Summary of Family Planning Activities; Resumen Mensual de Actividades de Planificación Familiar*

Récompenses au mérite : Promotions ou récompenses financières accordées aux agents en reconnaissance de leur brillante performance. *Merit Awards; Premios al Mérito*

Reconciliation (ou Rapprochement bancaire) : Opération consistant à reprendre le solde du compte bancaire en fonction du relevé bancaire afin de faire ressortir les dépôts effectués et les chèques tirés mais non encore débités ou crédités par la banque. *Bank Reconciliation; Conciliación Bancaria*

Recyclage : Formation périodique donnée au personnel en vue du renforcement d'une qualification ou de l'introduction de nouveaux concepts ou aptitudes. *Refresher Training; Capacitación de Apoyo*

Registre journalier des activités : Cahier qui répertorie quotidiennement le nombre de visites de clients à une formation sanitaire et indique les types et quantités de contraceptifs dispensés à chaque type de client, utilisateur nouveau ou assidu). Il faut calculer chaque jour le nombre de visites et le nombre de chaque type et marque de contraceptif dispensé. *Daily Activity Register; Registro Diario de Actividades*

Regroupement : Le fait de mettre ensemble les ressources, les compétences, l'équipement, etc. à utiliser pour atteindre un but commun. Cela aide à économiser les rares ressources, à réduire les possibilités de double emploi et à combler les lacunes au niveau des services. *Pooling; Combinación*

Rémunération : Paiement relatif à des produits livrés, des services rendus ou des pertes encourues. *Remuneration; Remuneración*

Répartition des coûts : C'est le fait, dans un système de comptabilité de caisse ou de comptabilité par fonds, d'assigner des coûts à des programmes, centres d'opérations, ou types de services différents. *Par exemple, le système de comptabilité peut affecter 50 pour cent du salaire du Coordinateur de la Formation aux frais généraux, et les 50 autres pour cent à cinq programmes différents, à raison de 10 pour cent par programme. Allocation of Costs; Asignación de Costos*

Répartition des fonctions : Une activité qui présente, sous forme de tableau, le nom des organisations qui collaborent et les principales responsabilités de chacune dans différents domaines d'intervention. Elle a pour but de révéler les cas de double emploi et les lacunes au niveau des services. *Functional Allocation; Distribución Funcional*

Résolution de problèmes : Compétence de gestion essentielle qui consiste à identifier objectivement les causes d'un problème et à proposer des solutions potentielles—souvent innovatrices—qui seront agréablement accueillies par plusieurs groupes ou individus. *Problem Solving; Resolución de Problemas*

Responsabilités de fonction : Les types de fonctions dont est responsable une personne ou un groupe tel que planification, suivi, évaluation, fourniture de services médicaux, formation, etc. *Functional Responsibilities; Responsabilidades Funcionales*

Responsabilités du personnel : Les responsabilités spécifiques ou l'ensemble des responsabilités des divers membres du personnel dont il est responsable. Ces responsabilités peuvent être en général quanti-fiées : fourniture de conseils, par exemple, à un certain nombre de clients au cours d'une période de temps donnée ou de services médicaux à une formation sanitaire de district trois jours par semaine. *Staff Responsibilities; Responsabilidades del Personal*

Ressources : Moyens disponibles pour la mise en oeuvre des activités planifiées, tels que les personnes, les objets et l'argent. *Resources; Recursos*

Résultats intermédiaires : Résultats à moyen terme qui sont essentiels pour obtenir des résultats à long terme. *Ainsi, le nombre d'ateliers ou de cours organisés est un résultat à moyen terme essentiel pour atteindre le résultat à long terme qu'est la formation de prestataires qualifiés. Intermediate Outputs; Resultados Intermedios*

Rétro-information : Procédé permettant une double communication entre le terrain et l'administration, ou entre un employé et son superviseur, et ayant pour objet de modifier, rectifier, et renforcer les performances et les résultats obtenus. *Feedback; Retroalimentación*

Revenus : Sommes d'argent ou leur équivalent reçues à l'occasion des ventes des services; il s'y ajoute les dons et des subventions. Dans le cas des subventions, seule la partie dépensée est effectivement considérée comme revenu. Il est possible que le solde doive être retourné au donateur. Dans les systèmes de comptabilité de caisse, on enregistre les revenus dès qu'ils sont acquis, sans attendre que les fonds ou les biens soient effectivement reçus. *Revenues; Ingresos, Entradas, Recibos*

Revisite (également appelée Visite de suivi) : Visite faite par un client à une formation sanitaire dans le but généralement de vérifier si le client est satisfait de sa méthode de contraception ou de traiter les complications médicales ou les effets secondaires. Ce terme est également utilisé pour décrire une visite pour se réapprovisionner en contraceptifs. *Revisit; Visita Subsecuente*

Rôle du personnel : L'ensemble des responsabilités attachées à différents postes. *Par exemple, le rôle des responsables comprend le leadership, la compréhension, la résolution de problèmes, les conseils et les encouragements. Staff Roles; Funciones del Personal*

Rubrique : Subdivision d'un budget, d'un tableau de comptes, ou d'un état financier représentant un compte où l'on enregistre les transactions d'un type déterminé de recette, dépense, actif ou dette. *Line Item; Partida o Rubro*

Rupture de stocks : Situation pendant laquelle un programme ou une formation sanitaire n'a plus assez d'une ou de plusieurs produits contraceptifs (ou autre médicament ou fourniture) et ne peut répondre à la demande. *Stockout; Desabastecimiento*

S anté reproductive : Etat de bien-être physique, mental et social— allant au-delà de l'absence de maladies et d'infirmités—pour tout ce qui se rapporte à l'appareil reproducteur, à ses fonctions et à ses activités. Un bon état de santé reproductive indique donc que l'on est en mesure d'avoir une vie sexuelle satisfaisante et dépourvue de risques, et que l'on possède la capacité de procréer ainsi que la liberté de décider si et quand et avec quelle fréquence on désire le faire. Il découle de cette dernière affirmation que les hommes et les femmes ont le droit d'être informés des méthodes de planification familiale qui sont sûres, efficaces, abordables et acceptables, et ont le droit de choisir parmi ces méthodes et d'y avoir accès, ainsi qu'à d'autres méthodes de régulation de la fécondité de leur choix qui ne soient pas interdites par la loi; ils ont également le droit d'accéder aux prestations sanitaires indispensables pour que la grossesse de la femme et l'accouchement puissent se dérouler sans danger, et que le couple ait les meilleures chances d'avoir un nouveau-né en bonne santé.[2] (Voir **Prestations/services de santé reproductive**.) *Reproductive Health; Salud Reproductiva*

Satisfaction des clients : Les bénéfices ou la valeur des services (tels que perçus par les clients) fournis par un programme ou une formation sanitaire, et mesurés souvent en termes de qualité de l'interaction personnelle avec les prestataires, la gamme de contraceptifs disponibles et l'efficience et la façon de répondre aux besoins individuels des clients. *Client Satisfaction; Satisfacción del Cliente*

Services à base communautaire (SBC) : Information et services de santé et de planification familiale fournis aux femmes et aux couples à l'endroit où ils vivent ou par le biais de dépôts basés dans la communauté. Les services sont organisés dans le cadre d'activités communautaires où des agents d'extension des services d'une formation sanitaire locale ou de la communauté fournissent aux clients certains contraceptifs (en général, la pilule et les condoms), conseillent les clientes qui ont des questions, des plaintes ou des effets secondaires, et les dirigent selon les besoins vers les formations sanitaires de la région. *Community-Based Services (CBS); Servicios Comunitarios (SC)*

---

[2]   D'après le *Programme d'action de la Conférence internationale des Nations unies sur la population et le développement,* Le Caire, 23 septembre 1994, paragraphe 7.1.

Services achetés (ou sous-traitance) : Services ou accords contractuels à long terme avec des *institutions* externes pour les services tels que l'entretien des véhicules et des bâtiments, la publicité ou les services de promotion. Bien que semblables, les accords contractuels avec des *individus* sont souvent passés pour services spécialisés tels que conférences, formation et évaluation, auxquels cas on parle de prestation payée à l'acte. (Voir **Honoraires**.) *Purchased Services; Servicios Adquiridos*

Services au dépôt communautaire : Type de services basés dans la communauté pour lequel une personne résidant dans la communauté fournit des informations et des contraceptifs (en général pilule et condoms) aux membres de la communauté selon leurs besoins. Comme les clients viennent généralement s'approvisionner au dépôt, cette méthode réduit le nombre de personnes travaillant à la prestation des services au niveau communautaire. *Depot Services; Servicios de Almacén (o de Distribución Local)*

Services bénévoles (de volontaires) : Méthode utilisée pour appuyer un programme local du secteur public ou du secteur privé dans lequel les membres de la communauté aident les fonctionnaires ou agents de terrain employés par des organisations non gouvernementales (ONG) à mettre en oeuvre des activités de motivation, de réapprovisionnement en contraceptifs et de suivi. Il arrive que ces agents reçoivent une petite compensation, le remboursement de leurs frais de déplacement ou autre rémunération réelle mais ils ne touchent pas de salaire régulier. *Volunteer Services; Servicios Voluntarios*

Session de supervision : Une réunion avec un ou plusieurs membres du personnel afin d'examiner le travail accompli et de faire le plan des tâches futures et des prochaines sessions de supervision. *Supervisory Session; Sesión de Supervisión*

Seuil de rentabilité : Niveau d'activité auquel le chiffre des recettes et celui des frais de fonctionnement sont à égalité. *Break-Even Point; Punto de Equilibrio*

Situation des stocks : Nombre de mois d'approvisionnement disponibles à un moment précis pour un type et une marque donnée de contraceptifs ou de produits. On calcule la situation des stocks en divisant le nombre d'unités disponibles par la consommation mensuelle moyenne de ce contraceptif ou produit. *Stock Position; Situación de Existencias*

Situation financière : Etat financier d'une organisation à un moment donné. Elle indique la position financière de l'organisation en tenant compte de l'actif et du passif actuel, ainsi que des dépenses et des recettes prévues. *Financial Position; Posición Financiera*

Sous-système : Un système compris dans un autre plus vaste qui sépare les divisions fonctionnelles du programme d'une institution telles que : les produits, la formation, la prestation de services, etc. *Subsystem; Subsistema*

Stabilité de l'organisation : La capacité d'une organisation d'utiliser efficacement les systèmes et contrôle de gestion pour prévenir toute perturbation majeur concernant les services malgré des changements inattendus relatifs à l'environnement externe ou à la rotation du personnel, particulièrement ceux touchant les responsables. *Organizational Stability; Estabilidad Organizacional*

Stock de sécurité : La quantité de produits (nombre de mois d'approvisionnement) en deça du niveau minimal prévue pour pallier aux fluctuations majeures de la demande de contraceptifs ou aux retards imprévus dans la livraison. *Safety Stock; Existencias de Seguridad*

Stock disponible (également appelé Stock résiduel) : La quantité de chaque contraceptif ou produit en stock à un moment donné. *Stock on Hand; Existencias Disponibles*

Stock en commande (ou en attente) : La quantité de chaque contraceptif qui a été commandée mais n'a pas encore été reçue (par le centre ou la formation sanitaire). *Stock on Order; Existencias en Pedido*

Stock résiduel : Voir **Stock Disponible**.

Stocks : La quantité de produits (contraceptifs, produits de base et autres fournitures) disponibles que peut utiliser un programme ou une formation sanitaire à un moment donné. *Inventory; Inventario*

Stratégie : L'ensemble des approches que l'organisation va adopter pour remplir la mission afin d'atteindre ses buts ou ceux du programme. *Strategy; Estrategia*

Structure de supervision : La structure officielle qui régit le système de communication formelle et le contexte relationnel entre les différentes fonctions et postes de direction, d'une part, et le personnel, d'autre part. *Supervisory Structure; Estructura de Supervisión*

Structure organisationnelle : Les lignes internes d'autorité et de communication au sein d'une organisation qui définissent comment les programmes et sections sont gérés, quels types d'activités ont été exécutés par quels programmes ou sections, et la relation fonctionnelle et de supervision entre le personnel et le responsable de ces sections. (Voir également **Organigramme**.) *Organizational Structure; Estructura Organizacional*

Style de participation : Type de gestion dans laquelle le superviseur ou le responsable travaille activement avec son personnel et écoute leurs idées, tient compte de leurs points de vue et de ce qu'ils ont accompli, encourage les discussions sur les questions et les problèmes, et cherche ensemble des solutions. *Participative Style; Estilo Participativo*

Subvention croisée : Système utilisant les recettes générées dans un service pour subventionner le coût d'un autre service du même programme. *Par exemple, les recettes provenant de la vente de contraceptifs dans une formation sanitaire peuvent servir à subventionner le coût de la fourniture de services à des clients qui ne sont pas capables de payer les services ou les contraceptifs dans la même formation sanitaire ou dans d'autres sites du programme. Cross-Subsidization/Cross-Subsidies; Subsidios Cruzados*

Subventions : Fonds ou donations donnés à une organisation ou un programme pour lui permettre d'exécuter des programmes ou services spécifiques. Les subventions sont généralement offerts par les gouvernements et les bailleurs de fonds nationaux ou internationaux. *Grants; Donaciones*

Subventions qui contiennent des primes : Fonds utilisés pour récompenser la performance d'un programme, l'atteinte d'objectifs ou pour encourager les programmes à lancer de nouvelles initiatives. Les primes servent à motiver les programmes et les employés à (continuer d') atteindre leurs objectifs et maintenir ou améliorer la qualité du programme. *Incentive Grants; Donaciones para Incentivar*

Suivi : Processus consistant à vérifier régulièrement la situation d'une programme en observant si les activités planifiées sont exécutées comme prévu. *Monitoring; Monitoreo*

Supervision à but de facilitation : Méthode de supervision qui met l'accent sur le parrainage, la résolution de problèmes en collaboration et la communication à double sens entre le superviseur et l'employé. *Facilitative Supervision; Supervisión Facilitadora*

Supervision sélective : Une procédure de supervision des rubriques spécifiques sur une base moins fréquente et rotative, en raison des contraintes de temps. *Selective Supervision; Supervisión Selectiva*

Système contrôlé de prestations sanitaires : Système résultant d'un accord passé entre un acheteur et un fournisseur de prestations de santé et planification familiale, et prévoyant une certaine série de prestations à fournir pour un prix prédéterminé (généralement un tarif mensuel fixe appliqué à chaque membre du groupe servi). *Managed Care; Paquete de Servicios*

Système d'allocation : Un procédé par lequel les contraceptifs sont fournis par le dépôt central ou intermédiaire au point de distribution sans que ces derniers ne les aient commandés. *Push System; Sistema de Asignación*

Système d'information : Système standardisé de collecte, d'enregistrement, d'interprétation, d'analyse, d'établissement de rapports et de diffusion de données de façon à ce qu'on puisse utiliser les données pour prendre des décisions de gestion capitales. Dans une formation sanitaire de planification familiale, il s'agit normalement de la collecte et de la diffusion de l'information programmatique et financière liée à la prestation de services aux clients et au fonctionnement d'un centre. (Voir également **Système d'information à deux niveaux**.) *Information System; Sistema de Información*

Système d'information à deux niveaux : Système d'information conçu pour recueillir régulièrement des informations sur les résultats et qui demande aux responsables de recueillir aussi des informations sur le processus pour les aider à déterminer là où un problème a pu apparaître pour pouvoir le corriger. *Two-Tier Information System; Sistema Bifurcado de Información*

Système d'information de gestion (SIG) : Un système conçu par une institution et ayant pour objet de collecter et rapporter l'information sur un programme donné, et qui permet aux responsables de planifier, de contrôler et d'évaluer les opérations et les performances de l'ensemble du programme. *Management Information System (MIS); Sistema de Información Gerencial (SIG)*

Système de commande (réquisition) : Un procédé par lequel les points de distribution commandent les quantités de produits dont ils ont besoin à un niveau de stockage supérieur. *Pull System; Sistema de Requisición*

Système de commande à intervalles fixes : Voir **Système de revue périodique**.

Système de commande à intervalles variables : Voir **Système de revue continuelle ou perpétuelle**.

Système de comptabilité : Système de collecte, d'enregistrement, de traitement et d'établissement de rapports pour toutes les transactions ayant des connotations financières. Deux systèmes utilisés fréquemment sont la comptabilité de caisse et la comptabilité d'exercice. *Accounting System; Sistema Contable*

Système de co-paiement : Un système de paiement pour des services rendus où le client paie une partie de la facture avec l'aide d'un tiers tel que l'employeur, une compagnie d'assurance, ou une police de couverture médicale payée d'avance. *Co-Payment Scheme; Esquema de Pagos Compartidos*

Système de gestion de la qualité : Dans le domaine de la planification familiale, il s'agit d'un système qui lie de façon harmonieuse et synergique les différentes activités qui aident à assurer et à améliorer continuellement la qualité des services de planification familiale dans le cadre d'un réseau de prestation de services. Dans un système efficace de gestion de la qualité, les superviseurs à tous les niveaux doivent mettre leurs connaissances et leurs compétences à jour aussi bien dans les domaines de la prestation de services que de la gestion. *Quality Management System; Sistema de Administración de la Calidad*

Système de primes d'encouragement : Un système de récompense des employés pour leurs excellentes performances ou réalisations exceptionnelles afin de les encourager à continuer d'oeuvrer pour l'atteinte des objectifs et le maintien de la qualité du programme. *Incentive System; Sistema de Incentivos*

Système de référence : Système établi qui définit le moment où un client doit être dirigé vers une autre formation sanitaire pour y recevoir des services (souvent pour le traitement de complications médicales ou la fourniture de méthodes cliniques ou de procédures chirurgicales), comment le client se rendra à la formation sanitaire (si, par exemple, un agent d'extension des services l'accompagnera), qui le client doit contacter au site où il a été envoyé et quels documents il doit présenter ou, au contraire, on doit lui donner dans cette autre formation sanitaire. Les systèmes de référence efficaces donnent davantage d'accès aux services et aux méthodes cliniques de longue durée et améliorent la qualité des services fournis par une petite formation sanitaire satellite. *Referral System; Sistema de Referencia*

Système de revue continuelle ou perpétuelle (également appelé Système de commande à intervalles variables) : Système de contrôle des stocks et de réapprovisionnement par lequel les niveaux de stocks sont examinés à des intervalles déterminés et les commandes effectuées lorsque les stocks atteignent un certain niveau ou descendent au-dessous d'un niveau de réapprovisionnement prédéterminé. Avec ce système, les nouvelles commandes sont généralement faites en fonction de normes de quantité et non selon un calendrier établi. *Continuous (Perpetual) Review System; Sistema Continuo (Perpetuo) de Inventario*

Système de revue périodique (également appelé Système de commande à intervalle fixe) : Un système de contrôle d'inventaire et de réapprovisionnement par lequel les niveaux de stock sont revus à des intervalles déterminés et les commandes sont faites sur la base des niveaux effectifs de stock, celui du stock de sécurité et selon une quantité maximale établie. Par cette méthode, le réapprovisionnement est programmé mais la quantité de produits peut varier à chaque commande. *Periodic Review System; Sistema Periódico de Inventario*

Système de supervision : Les méthodes et procédures utilisées pour contrôler le volume et la qualité du travail effectué par le personnel et lui apporter l'appui et le soutien dont il a besoin. Le système comporte des visites sur le terrain, des évaluations de performance de l'agent, des réunions individuelles ou de groupes avec le personnel, ainsi que l'examen des formulaires de rapport, etc. *Supervisory System; Sistema de Supervisión*

Système des cinq tables : Utilisé fréquemment pour les approches communautaires mobiles, ce système est un programme qui fournit des services intégrés de santé maternelle et infantile, et de planification familiale dans un site unique temporaire. Dans le cadre de ce système, on établit un table pour chacun des cinq services : inscription de l'enfant, pesage de l'enfant, enregistrement des résultats sur une fiche de croissance; éducation sanitaire (nutrition, réhydratation orale, vaccination, allaitement au sein, espacement des naissances et planification familiale); et fourniture de tout traitement médical nécessaire, de contraceptifs ou référence vers une formation sanitaire fixe selon les besoins. *Five-Table System; Sistema de Cinco Mesas*

Système Max/Min (maximum-minimum) : Niveaux de stock maximum et minimum prévus pour éviter les ruptures de stock de contraceptifs ou au contraire qu'il y ait des sur-stocks. Les niveaux minimum et maximum sont exprimés en nombre de mois d'approvisionnement. *Max/Min (Maximum-Minimum) Stock Level; Sistema Max/Min*

Systèmes de contrôle : Toutes les procédures et règles visant à prévenir la corruption, le vol et l'utilisation inappropriée des fonds ou autres ressources. *Control Systems; Sistemas de Fiscalización*

Tableau croisée (ou tabulation à multi-paramètres) : Tableau ou graphique utilisé pour montrer simultanément des données récapitulatives concernant deux ou plusieurs ensembles de variables. *Cross-Tabulation; Tabulación Cruzada*

Tableau d'analyse des données sur les contraceptifs : Fiche de travail utilisée (pour chaque méthode de contraception) pour garder la trace des stocks disponibles et de la quantité de fournitures commandées, reçues et distribuées chaque mois. Cette fiche de travail aide les responsables à contrôler les mouvements des stocks chaque mois et donne un résumé des transactions concernant les stocks au cours d'une période d'un an. *Contraceptive Data Analysis Chart; Tabla de Análisis de Datos sobre Anticonceptivos*

Tableau de circulation de l'information : Un tableau qui illustre les types d'information (indicateurs) qui seront collectés et rapportés, les agents chargés de la collecte, ainsi que les destinataires, l'utilisation qui en sera faite et le niveau de détail nécessaire. L'objet de ce tableau est d'assurer une circulation correcte et adéquate de l'information et la communication au personnel du fonctionnement du système. *Information Flow Table; Gráfica de Flujo de Información*

Tableau de comparaison : Voir **Matrice**.

Tableau de fréquence : Graphique utilisé pour enregistrer le nombre de fois où se produit un événement pendant une période de temps donnée tel que le nombre de nouveaux accepteurs et de visites de suivi pendant chaque mois de l'année précédente ou, pour chaque raison citée pour ne pas utiliser la contraception, le nombre de personnes donnant ces raisons, etc. *Frequency Table; Tabla de Frecuencias*

Tableau de Gantt : Voir **Chronogramme**.

Tableau de la situation des stocks (ou des approvisionnements) : Fiche de travail permettant de calculer la consommation mensuelle moyenne (CMM) et les quantités minimum et maximum de stock. Ce tableau permet aux responsables d'enregistrer sur un seul tableau les renseignements sur les quantités minimum et maximum qu'ils désirent avoir en stock pour tous les types de contraceptifs en se basant sur les profils de consommation récents. *Status of Supplies Chart; Tabla para Control de Suministros*

Tableau des comptes : Plan faisant partie du système de comptabilité et dressant la liste des programmes, centres d'opérations, et catégories dans lesquels seront enregistrées les recettes et les dépenses, dans des rubriques numérotées. *Chart of Accounts; Catálogo de Cuentas*

Tableau du flux des clients : Ce tableau résume les informations obtenues sur un formulaire de flux des clients. Il montre le temps total passé à la formation sanitaire, y compris le temps passé à attendre et le temps en consultation avec le personnel, et donne le pourcentage de temps total passé à la formation sanitaire pendant lequel les clients ont attendu les services. *Client Flow Chart; Tabla del Flujo de Clientes*

Tâches : Activités découpées en responsabilités précises attribuées à un agent. *Tasks; Tareas*

Taux : Mesure d'un événement (numérateur) au sein d'une population déterminée (dénominateur) à un moment défini. *Par exemple, le taux de mortalité infantile représente le nombre de nourrissons qui meurent avant d'atteindre un an (numérateur) parmi toutes les naissances vivantes (dénominateur) pendant une période d'une année donnée. Les taux de mortalité infantile sont généralement exprimés comme le nombre de décès pour 1.000 naissances vivantes. Rate; Tasa*

Taux d'acceptation : Nombre de nouveaux utilisateurs qui ont commencé à utiliser une méthode contraceptive, mesuré parmi une population donnée (communauté, district, zone du programme), couvrant une période de temps (mois, trimestre ou année). On peut mesurer le taux d'acceptation pour toutes les méthodes ou pour une seule méthode spécifique. *Par exemple, dans une formation sanitaire le taux d'acceptation des contraceptifs oraux mesuré au cours de la période de trois mois (janvier à mars) peut être exprimé comme 100 clientes sur 1000, soit 10 % des clientes venues consulter, ont accepté un cycle initial de contraceptifs oraux—ce qui représente un taux d'acceptation de 10 % pendant le premier trimestre de l'année. Acceptance Rate; Tasa de Aceptación*

Taux de clients non-assidus : Souvent exprimé en pourcentage, ce taux peut être calculé plus facilement dans une formation sanitaire qui utilise un système de rendez-vous qui permet de savoir combien de clients doivent revenir à la formation sanitaire pour y obtenir des services et à quelle date. Le taux de clients non-assidus est calculé en prenant le nombre total de clients qui se sont présentés à la formation sanitaire (pendant une période spécifique) pour des services et en le divisant par le nombre de clients qui devaient venir à la formation sanitaire pendant la même période. En multipliant ce résultat par 100, on obtient le pourcentage des clients que ne reviennent pas pendant la période considérée. On peut aussi procéder à cette analyse pour une méthode de contraception spécifique ou selon le groupe d'âge du client. (Pour plus de renseignements sur la façon de mesurer les taux de clients non-assidus, veuillez vous référer au Numéro 3 du Volume II du *Management de la planification familiale* intitulé «Réduire la discontinuation dans les programmes de planification familiale».) *No-Show Rate; Tasa de Inasistencia*

Taux de continuation : Le nombre d'utilisateurs qui continuent à se servir d'une méthode de contraception, mesuré dans la population sélectionnée (communauté, district, zone du programme) pendant une période de temps donné (mois, trimestre ou année). On peut également mesurer le taux de continuation pour une méthode spécifique. *Continuation Rate; Tasa de Continuación*

Taux de discontinuation : Ces taux se mesurent pour chaque méthode contraceptive offerte par une formation sanitaire, pour plusieurs méthodes ou pour toutes les méthodes offertes par une formation sanitaire ou un programme. On obtient ce taux en divisant le nombre de personnes qui abandonnent une méthode ou des méthodes (pendant une période de temps donnée, un an par exemple) par le nombre total d'utilisateurs de cette méthode ou de ces méthodes, y compris ceux qui les ont abandonnées pendant la même période. En multipliant le résultat par 100, on obtient le pourcentage de discontinuation de cette ou de ces méthodes pour la période donnée. *Discontinuation Rate; Tasa de Abandono*

Technique du modèle parfait : Technique par laquelle on établit un ensemble d'indicateurs et de sous-indicateurs qui permettront de mesurer les performances ou les progrès vers l'atteinte des objectifs. Cette technique peut également servir à comparer un service ou processus dans une organisation à des services ou processus semblables dans d'autres organisations ou programmes similaires, afin d'améliorer l'efficacité et l'efficience d'un programme. *Benchmarking; Técnica de Análisis de Casos Modelo («Benchmarking»)*

Temps d'attente des clients : Le temps que les clients passent à attendre avant d'être vus par les prestataires d'une formation sanitaire. (Voir **Analyse du flux des clients**.) *Client Waiting Time; Tiempo de Espera de Clientes*

Temps de contact : Le temps que passe un client avec le personnel de la formation sanitaire au cours d'une visite. C'est un des éléments examinés dans l'analyse du flux des clients. *Contact Time; Tiempo de Contacto*

Trace écrite : Relevé de tout mouvement de ressources (humaine, financière et matérielle) conservé afin de pouvoir retrouver et suivre le mouvement et comptabiliser les ressources. *Paper Trail; Comprobantes*

Type d'organisation : La structure ou définition légale d'une organisation telle que : organisation privée commerciale, privée à but non lucratif, organisme public, organisation non gouvernementale ou affiliée ou filiale d'une organisation plus importante. *Organization Type; Tipo de Organización*

Type de visite : Catégorie de visite faite par un client à une formation sanitaire telle que la première visite ou visite initiale, visite pour insertion, visite pour retrait, visite de réapprovisionnement, visite à la suite de complications, visite pour éducation ou conseils, etc. On établit en général des types de visites afin de déterminer le coût moyen de la fourniture de chaque type de services. *Visit-Type; Tipo de Visita*

Utilisateur potentiel (également appelé Accepteur potentiel) : Pour les femmes, une acceptrice potentielle est toute femme en âge de procréer, capable d'avoir un enfant qui, sans vouloir être enceinte à cette période n'utilise pas la contraception. Pour les hommes, l'accepteur potentiel est tout homme sexuellement actif qui n'utilise pas actuellement la contraception. *Potential User; Usuario Potencial*

Utilisateurs assidus (également appelés Utilisateurs actifs ou Utilisateurs continus) : Il s'agit des utilisateurs de contraception qui pratiquent la planification familiale à une date donnée. Généralement on les compte et on les déclare séparément de nouveaux clients d'un programme et de nouveaux utilisateurs d'une méthode. *Continuing Users; Usuarios Continuos o Subsecuentes*

Variance des coûts : La différence entre les dépenses prévues et les dépenses réelles pour un produit, un service ou un programme. *Cost Variance; Variación de Costos*

Variations aléatoires : Irrégularités non systématiques ou irrégularités dans les données. Lors de l'analyse des données, des irrégularités faibles (non systématiques) sont souvent insignifiantes et il n'est pas nécessaire d'en tenir compte. *Random Variations; Variaciones al Azar*

Viabilité : La capacité d'un programme de fournir des services de qualité à ses clients, d'étendre la gamme des services et la base de clients, d'accroître ou de maintenir la demande pour les services et de générer des revenus dans le cadre du programme et par des mécanismes locaux de financement tout en réduisant sa dépendance vis-à-vis des crédits venant des bailleurs de fonds. (Voir également **Autosuffisance**.) *Sustainability; Sustentabilidad*

Visite de suivi : Voir **Revisite**.

Visite pour insertion : Décrit en général une visite d'une cliente pour l'insertion d'un DIU ou d'un implant contraceptif. On établit souvent différents types de visites dans un programme ou une formation sanitaire de façon à pouvoir imputer à chaque type de visite des coûts spécifiques. *Insertion Visit; Visita de Inserción*

Visite pour intervention médicale : Terme utilisé généralement pour décrire une visite faite par un client pour une intervention médicale spécifique telle que la stérilisation volontaire ou l'insertion ou le retrait d'un DIU ou d'un implant contraceptif. Les programmes ou formations sanitaires classent ces visites en différentes catégories de façon à leur assigner des coûts spécifiques ou à établir un tarif pour chaque type de visite. *Procedure Visit; Visita de Procedimiento*

Visites d'observation et d'étude : Une série organisée de visites à d'autres sites du programme ou à d'autres organisations dans le but d'étudier l'autre programme et de mettre en commun les expériences bien réussies qui seront dupliquées ou adaptées. *Observation-Study Visits; Visitas de Observación-Estudio*

Voies de communication formelle : Système établi au sein d'une structure de supervision pour rendre compte des informations et des données. Il est essentiel de disposer de moyens de transmettre les rapports, surtout lorsque les divers types de services deviennent plus intégrés et/ou la gestion des programmes devient plus décentralisée. *Reporting Channels; Canales para la Rendición de Informes*

Volets du programme : Unités fonctionnelles d'une organisation de prestation de services visant la réalisation de buts organisationnels; par exemple un volet des services à base communautaire, un volet clinique ou encore un volet IEC. *Program Components; Componentes del Programa*

Zone desservie : La zone ou la région cible qu'un programme a l'intention d'attendre en fournissant ses services à la population. *Service Marketplace; Mercado de Servicios*

Liste des termes avec leurs équivalents dans les langues étrangères

Français avec les équivalents en anglais et en espagnol:

Abandon	Dropout	Desertor
Accepteur potential	Potential Acceptor	Aceptante Potencial
Actifs	Assets	Activos
Actifs courants ou à court terme	Current or Short-Term Assets	Activos circulantes (Activos a Corto Plazo)
Activités d'extension	Outreach	Extensión («Outreach»)
Administration générale	General Administration	Administración General
Affaires publiques	Public Affairs	Relaciones Públicas
Amélioration continue de la qualité (ACQ)	Continuous Quality Improvement (CQI)	Proceso de Mejoramiento Continuo de la Calidad (PMC)
Amortissement	Depreciation	Depreciación
Analyse de Pareto	Pareto Analysis	Análisis de Pareto
Analyse de processus	Process Analysis	Análisis del Proceso
Analyse de situation	Situation Analysis	Análisis Situacional
Analyse de tendances	Trend Analysis	Análisis de Tendencias
Analyse des coûts	Cost Analysis	Análisis de Costos
Analyse des données	Data Analysis	Análisis de Datos

Analyse des tâches	Task Analysis	Análisis de Tareas
Analyse du flux des clients	Client Flow Analysis	Análisis del Flujo de Clientes
Analyse du flux des patients	Patient Flow Analysis	Análisis del Flujo de Pacientes
Analyse du marché	Market Analysis	Análisis del Mercado
Analyse FFOM	SWOT Analysis	Análisis FODA
Animateur	Facilitator	Facilitador
Apprentissage par l'expérience	Experiential Learning	Aprendizaje de Experiencias
Approche d'équipe	Team Approach	Enfoque de Equipo
Approche de «l'entonnoir»	"Funnel" Approach	Integración Tipo «Embudo»
Approche de prestation de services	Service Delivery Approach	Enfoque de la Prestación de Servicios
Approche de services verticaux	Vertical Services/ Approach	Servicios Verticales o Enfoque Vertical
Approche du «sablier»	"Hourglass" Approach	Integración Tipo «Reloj de Arena»
Arbre de décisions	Decision Tree	Arbol de Decisiones
Audit externe	External Audit	Auditoría Externa
Audit financier	Financial Audit	Auditoría Financiera
Audit interne	Internal Audit	Auditoría Interna
Autosuffisance	Self-Sufficiency	Autosuficiencia
Bilan	Balance Sheet	Balance General

Bilan des fonds ou Réserves	Fund Balance	Balance de Fondos o Reserva
Bon de commande et de sortie	Requisition and Issue Voucher	Formulario de Pedido y de Despacho
Budget consolidé	Consolidated Budget	Presupuesto Consolidado
Buts	Goals	Objetivos Generales
Caisse d'avance	Imprest Fund	Fondo de Caja Chica
Calendrier de supervision	Supervisory Schedule	Cronograma de Supervisión
Calendrier des activités du projet	Project Activity Timeline	Cronograma de Actividades del Proyecto
Capacité de service	Service Capacity	Capacidad del Servicio
Capitaux propres	Equity	Capital Contable o Patrimonio
Caractéristiques des clients	Client Characteristics	Características del Cliente
Carnet de bord	Vehicle Usage Report	Informe por Uso de Vehículos
Carte de référence du client	Client Referral Card	Tarjeta de Referencia del Cliente
Carte ELCO	ELCO Map	Mapa PAEL
Catégorie de personnel	Personnel Category	Categoría de Personal
Centre d'opérations	Operating Center	Centro Operativo
Centre de coût	Cost Center	Centro de Costo

Centre de responsabilité	Responsibility Center	Centro de Responsabilidad
Chronogramme	Chronogram	Cronograma
Cibles	Targets	Metas
Cibles et objectifs de performance	Performance Targets and Objectives	Objetivos/Metas de Desempeño
Client non-assidu	No-Show Client	Cliente que No Asiste
Client potentiel	Potential Client	Cliente Potencial
Codes d'identification	Identification Codes	Códigos de Identificación
Comité de gestion	Managing Board	Junta Administrativa
Comité du personnel	Personnel Committee	Comité del Personal
Commande d'urgence	Emergency Order	Pedido de Emergencia
Composantes de gestion	Management Components	Componentes Administrativos
Comptabilité analytique	Cost Accounting	Contabilidad de Costos
Comptabilité d'exercice	Accrual Accounting	Contabilidad sobre Bases Devengadas
Comptabilité de caisse	Cash Accounting	Contabilidad de Caja
Comptabilité de gestion	Management Accounting	Contabilidad Administrativa
Comptabilité par centres de responsabilité	Responsibility Accounting	Contabilidad en Base a Responsabilidades

Comptabilité par fonds	Fund Accounting	Contabilidad de Fondos
Comptes à payer ou Dettes	Accounts Payable	Cuentas por Pagar
Comptes à recevoir ou Créances	Accounts Receivable	Cuentas por Cobrar
Conseil consultatif	Advisory Board	Junta de Asesores
Conseil d'administration	Board of Directors	Junta Directiva
Consommation mensuelle moyenne (CMM)	Average Monthly Consumption (AMC)	Consumo Mensual Promedio (CMP)
Contribution en nature	In-Kind Contribution	Contribuciones en Especie
Coordination	Coordination	Coordinación
Coordination externe	External Coordination	Coordinación Externa
Coordination interne	Internal Coordination	Coordinación Interna
COPE (Client orienté, prestation efficace)	COPE (Client-Oriented, Provider Efficient)	«COPE» (Dirigido al Cliente, Eficiente para el Proveedor)
Cotisations	Membership Fees	Cuotas de Afiliación
Couple-années de protection (CAP)	Couple-Years of Protection (CYP)	Años Protección Pareja (APP)
Coût d'entretien	Maintenance Cost	Costo de Mantenimiento
Coût du personnel par type de visite	Personnel Cost Per Visit-Type	Costo del Personal por Tipo de Visita
Coût-efficacité	Cost-Effectiveness	Costo-Efectividad

Coût par année d'utilisation	Cost Per Year of Use	Costo por Año de Uso
Coût par couple-année de protection	Cost per Couple-Year of Protection	Costo por Año de Protección Pareja
Coût total par visite	Total Visit Cost	Costo Total por Visita
Coût unitaire (des produits contraceptifs)	Unit Cost (of Contraceptive Products)	Costo Unitario (de los Productos Anticonceptivos)
Coûts d'exploitation	Operating Costs	Costos de Operación
Coûts d'investissement	Capital Costs	Costos de Inversión (Gastos de Capital)
Coûts des produits contraceptifs	Contraceptive Product Cost	Costo del Anticonceptivo
Coûts directs	Direct Costs	Costos Directos
Coûts du personnel	Personnel Cost	Costo del Personal
Coûts (ou frais) fixes	Fixed Costs or Expenses	Costos o Gastos Fijos
Coûts indirects	Indirect Costs	Costos Indirectos
Coûts (ou dépenses) variables	Variable Costs or Expenses	Costos o Gastos Variables
Créance irrécouvrable	Bad Debt	Deuda Incobrable
Date de péremption	Expiration Date	Fecha de Expiración
Décentralisation	Decentralization	Descentralización
Déconcentration	Deconcentration	Desconcentración
Définition des tâches	Task Definition	Definición de Tareas
Délai de livraison	Lead Time	Tiempo de Espera

Délai moyen de livraison	Average Lead Time	Tiempo de Espera Promedio
Délégation	Delegation	Delegación
Demande non satisfaite ou besoin non satisfait	Unmet Demand or Unmet Need	Demanda no Cubierta o Necesidad no Cubierta
Densité de population	Population Density	Densidad Poblacional
Dépenses	Expenditures	Erogaciones
Dépenses de fonctionnement ou Coûts récurrents	Recurrent Costs	Costos Recurrentes
Description de poste	Job Description	Descripción del Cargo
Développement professionnel	Professional Development	Desarrollo Profesional
Dévolution	Devolution	Devolución
Diagramme de cause à effet	Cause-and-Effect Diagram	Diagrama de Causa y Efecto
Diagramme de processus	Flowchart	Diagrama de Flujo
Diffusion interne	Inreach	Conocimiento Interno («Inreach»)
Directives pour l'auto-évaluation	Self-Evaluation Guidelines	Normas de Auto-Evaluación
Discontinuateur	Discontinuer	«Abandono»
Distribution de la population	Population Distribution	Distribución de la Población

Données rétrospectives	Historical Data	Datos Históricos
Données sur les clients ou sur les formations sanitaires	Client/Clinic Data	Datos sobre Clientes/ Clínica
Dossier du client	Client Record	Expediente del Cliente
Dossier médical	Medical Record	Expediente o Historia Clínica
Dotation	Endowment	Dotación
Droits d'inscription (ou d'admission)	Registration Fees	Tarifas de Ingreso
Durée de vie	Shelf Life	Vida Util
Echelle discriminatoire de tarifs	Sliding Fee Scale	Escala Variable de Tarifas
Effet de plateau	Plateau Effect or "Plateauing"	«Estancamiento»
Efficacité	Effectiveness	Efectividad
Efficience	Efficiency	Eficiencia
Enoncé de mission	Mission Statement	Declaración de Misión
Enquête auprès de la population	Population-Based Survey	Encuesta Basada en la Población
Enquête auprès des clients	Client Survey	Encuesta a Clientes
Enquête auprès des ménages	Household Survey	Encuesta de Hogares

Enquête auprès des prestataires de planification familiale	Survey of Family Planning Providers	Encuesta a los Proveedores de Servicios de Planificación Familiar
Enquête communautaire	Community Survey	Encuesta de la Comunidad
Enquête de base	Baseline Survey	Encuesta de Base
Enquête par grappes	Cluster Survey	Encuesta de Grupos
Entretien à la sortie	Exit Interview	Entrevista de Salida
Entretien de la chaîne du froid	Cold Chain Maintenance	Mantenimiento de la Cadena de Frío
Environnement externe	External Environment	Contexto Externo
Environnement interne	Internal Environment	Contexto Interno
Equipe à fonctions multiples	Cross-Functional Team	Equipo Interfuncional
Etablissement de cartes	Mapping	Mapeo
Etat de la trésorerie	Cash Flow Statement	Estado de Flujo de Fondos
Etat des recettes	Revenue Report	Informe de Ingresos
Etat des recettes et des dépenses	Revenue and Expense Report	Estado de Ingresos y Egresos
Etat des revenus et des dépenses	Income Statement	Estado de Pérdidas y Ganancias
Etat financier	Financial Statement	Estado Financiero
Evaluation	Evaluation	Evaluación

Evaluation de la performance	Performance Appraisal	Reconocimiento del Desempeño
Evaluation rapide	Rapid Assessment	Evaluación Rápida
Exonérations/Système de dérogation	Waivers/Waiver System	Exoneraciones/ Sistema de Exoneraciones y Excepciones
«Faire les choses correctement»	"Doing Things in the Right Way"	«Hacer las Cosas en Forma Correcta»
«Faire les choses nécessaires»	"Doing the Right Things"	«Hacer las Cosas Correctas»
Feuille de pointage (Liste des informations et données)	Tally Sheet	Hoja de Registro
Fiche de calcul des activités de planification familiale	Family Planning Activities Worksheet	Planilla de Actividades de Planificación Familiar
Fiche de contrôle des stocks	Inventory Control Card or Bin Card	Tarjeta de Control de Inventario
Fiche de rapport trimestriel	Quarterly Reporting Form	Formulario de Informe Trimestral
Fiche de rendez-vous	Appointment Card	Tarjeta de Citas
Fiche de stock	Stock Card	Tarjeta de Estiba o de Kardex
Fonctions/Systèmes de gestion	Management Functions/Systems	Funciones/Sistemas Administrativos
Fonds de roulement	Working Capital	Capital de Trabajo

Formation basée sur les compétences	Competency-Based Training	Capacitación Funcional (basada en la competencia)
Formation formelle	Formal Training	Capacitación Formal
Formation informelle	Informal Training	Capacitación Informal
Formation par étapes	Phased Training	Adiestramiento en Fases
Formation polyvalente	Cross-Training	Capacitación Interfuncional
Formation sur le site	Site Training	Capacitación en Servicio
Formulaire de flux des clients	Client Flow Form	Formulario de Flujo de Clientes
Formulaire de projection de l'état de la trésorerie	Cash Flow Projection Worksheet	Planilla de Proyecciones del Flujo de Fondos
Formulaires pour la rétro-information (feedback) journalière	Daily Feedback Forms	Formularios Diarios de Retroalimentación
Frais	Expenses	Gastos
Frais généraux	Overhead Costs	Costos Generales
Gamme des méthodes	Method Mix	Mezcla de Métodos
Gestion de la formation sanitaire	Clinic Management	Administración de la Clínica
Gestion de la logistique	Logistics Management	Administración Logística
Gestion de la qualité	Quality Management	Administración de la Calidad

Gestion des ressources	Resource Management	Administración de Recursos
Gestion des stocks de contraceptifs	Contraceptive Supply Management	Administración de Suministros Anticonceptivos
Gestion du personnel	Personnel Management	Administración del Personal
Gestion financière	Financial Management	Administración Financiera
Gestion stratégique	Strategic Management	Administración Estratégica
Grade	Grade	Grado
Graphique	Graph	Gráfica
Graphique à colonnes	Bar Chart	Gráfica de Barras
Graphique «camembert»	Pie Chart	Gráfica de Sectores
Graphique linéaire	Line Graph	Gráfica Lineal
Gratification	Perquisites	Gratificación
Grilles d'observation	Observation Guides	Guías de Observación
Groupe cible	Target Group	Grupo Objetivo
Groupe de discussion focalisée	Focus Group	Grupo Focal
Groupe-noyau pour l'ACQ	CQI Core Group	Núcleo del PMC (o Grupo Interno para el PMC)
Histogramme	Histogram	Histograma

Honoraires	Professional Fees	Honorarios Profesionales
Immobilisations	Fixed or Long-Term Assets	Activos Fijos o Bien Duraderos
Impact	Impact	Impacto
Indicateur	Indicator	Indicador
Information opérationnelle	Operational Information	Información Operacional
Information sur la performance	Performance Information	Información de Desempeño
Information sur les processus	Process Information	Información sobre el Proceso
Information sur les résultats	Output Information	Informe de Resultados
Institutionnalisation	Institutionalization	Institucionalización
Intégration/Services intégrés	Integration/Integrated Services	Integración/Servicios Integrados
Intervalle entre les commandes	Order Interval	Intervalo entre Pedidos
Intrants	Inputs	Insumos
Jalons de performance progressifs	Benchmarks	Requisitos Previos («Benchmarsk»)
Lancement d'idées («Brainstorming»)	Brainstorming	Lluvia de Ideas
Listes des choses «à faire»	"To Do" Lists	Lista de «Asuntos Pendientes»

Livraisons incomplètes	Short Shipments	Embarques Incompletos
Livraisons partielles	Split Shipments	Embarques Divididos
Magasin central	Central Warehouse	Bodega (almacén) Central
Magasin intermédiaire	Intermediate Warehouse	Bodega (almacén) Intermedia
Manuel du personnel	Personnel Manual	Manual del Personal
Marketing	Marketing	Mercadeo
Marketing social	Social Marketing	Mercadeo Social
Matrice	Matrix	Matriz
Méthodes à court terme	Short-Term Methods	Métodos de Corto Plazo
Méthodes de longue durée	Long-Acting Methods	Métodos de Larga Duración
Méthodologie	Methodology	Metodología
Micro-gestion	Micro-Manage	Micro-Administrar
Mission de l'organisation	Organizational Mission	Misión de la Organización
Mobilisation de fonds	Fund Raising	Recaudación de Fondos
Mois d'approvi-sionnement	Months of Supply	Meses de Suministros
Motivation des clients	Client Motivation	Motivación del Cliente
Motivation du personnel	Staff Motivation	Motivación del Personal

Mutuellement responsable	Mutually Accountable	Responsabilidad Conjunta
Niveau de pointe	State-of-the-Art	De Punta
Nouveau client	New Client	Cliente Nuevo
Nouvel accepteur	New Acceptor	Aceptante Nuevo
Nouvel utilisateur	New User	Usuario Nuevo
Numéro de lot	Lot Number	Número de Lote
Objectifs	Objectives	Objetivos Específicos
Obstacles aux services	Barriers to Services	Barreras a los Servicios
Occasion manquée	Missed Opportunity	Oportunidad Perdida
Organigramme	Organogram or Organizational Chart	Organigrama o Diagrama Organizacional
Organisation interne	Internal Organization	Organización Interna
Organisation qui démarre	Start-Up Organization	Organización Incipiente (o de Arranque)
Outil ou Liste aide-mémoire pour l'auto-évaluation	Self-Assessment Tool or Checklist	Lista de Verificación para la Autoevaluación
Paiements des prestations	Service Fees	Tarifas por Servicios
Paiements effectués par les clients	Client Fees	Tarifas para los Clientes
Paiements par un tiers (ou Co-paiements)	Third-Party Payments	Sistema de Pagos de Terceros (Co-Pagos)

Partage des coûts	Cost-Sharing	Colaboración entre Programas para la Reducción de Costos
Participation communautaire	Community Participation	Participación Comunitaria
Passif	Liability	Pasivo
Pensée stratégique	Strategic Thinking	Pensamiento Estratégico
Perfectionnement du personnel	Staff Development	Desarrollo del Personal
Performance de la formation sanitaire	Clinic Performance	Rendimiento de la Clínica
Petite caisse	Petty Cash	Caja Chica
Phase d'emergence	Emergent Stage	Etapa de Surgimiento (o Etapa Emergente)
Phase de consolidation	Consolidation Stage	Etapa de Consolidación
Phase de croissance	Growth Stage	Etapa de Crecimiento
Phase de maturité	Mature Stage	Etapa de Madurez
Phases de développement d'une organisation	Stages of Organizational Development	Etapas del Desarrollo de una Organización
Plan d'action	Action Plan	Plan de Acción
Plan d'entreprise	Business Plan	Plan de Negocios
Plan de travail	Work Plan	Plan de Trabajo
Plan de visite du superviseur	Supervisor's Visit Plan	Plan de Visita del Supervisor

Plan des tournées de supervision	Session Plan	Plan de Sesión
Plan opérationnel	Operational Plan	Plan Operativo
Plan stratégique	Strategic Plan	Plan Estratégico
Planification	Planning	Planeación
Planification des activités	Activity Planning	Planeación de Actividades
Planification stratégique	Strategic Planning	Planeación Estratégica
Point de distribution (final)	Outlet	Local o Punto de Distribución
Points de services périphériques	Satellite Services	Servicios Satélites
Populations mal desservies (sous-servies)	Underserved Populations	Sectores Desatendidos de la Población o Carentes de Servicios
Post-test	Post-test	Examen Post-Prueba
Postes de travail	Service Stops	Estaciones de Servicios
Premier à périmer, premier sorti (PPPS)	First-to-Expire, First-Out (FEFO)	Primero en Expirar, Primero en Salir (PEPS)
Première visite ou Première consultation d'un client	First Visit or First Consultation of a Client	Primera Visita o Primera Consulta de un Cliente
Prestations/services de santé reproductive	Reproductive Health Care/Services	Servicios de Salud Reproductiva
Pré-test	Pre-test	Examen Pre-Prueba

Prévalence contraceptive	Contraceptive Prevalence	Prevalencia de Uso de Anticonceptivos
Prévisions basées sur la distribution	Distribution-Based Forecasts	Proyecciones Basadas en la Distribución
Prévisions basées sur la population	Population-Based Forecasts	Proyecciones Basadas en Información Censual o en Encuestas Demográficas
Prévisions basées sur les prestations de services	Service-Based Forecasts	Prévisiones Basadas en el Servicio
Privatisation	Privatization	Privatización
Procédure de rupture de contrat	Termination Policy	Normas de Despidos
Procédure de soumission de doléances	Grievance Policy	Normas para Manejo de Quejas y Reclamos
Processus de supervision en équipe	Team Supervision Process	Proceso de Supervisión en Equipo
Processus de travail	Work Process	Proceso de Trabajo
Produits pour la planification familiale	Family Planning Commodities	Suministros de Planificación Familiar
Profil des clients	Client Profile	Perfil del Cliente
Programme de paiement des prestations	Fee-For-Service Program	Programa de Cobro de Tarifas por Servicios

Programme pour accroître le nombre d'utilisateurs actifs	User Continuity Program	Programa para Aumentar la Tasa de Continuidad de Usuarios Activos
Protocole de supervision	Supervisory Protocol	Protocolo de Supervisión
Protocole sanitaire	Clinic Protocol	Norma (o Guía) Clínica
Qualité des services	Service Quality	Calidad de los Servicios
Quantité couvrant le délai de livraison	Lead Time Quantity	Cantidad para Cubrir el Tiempo de Espera
Quantité maximum	Maximum Quantity	Cantidad Máxima
Quantité minimum	Minimum Quantity	Cantidad Mínima
Rapport de performance budgétaire	Budget Performance Report	Informe de Ejecución del Presupuesto
Rapport financier	Financial Reporting	Informes Financieros
Rapport programmatique	Programmatic Reporting	Informes Programáticos
Ratio	Ratio	Razón
Récapitulatif mensuel des activités de planification familiale	Monthly Summary of Family Planning Activities	Resumen Mensual de Actividades de Planificación Familiar
Récompenses au mérite	Merit Awards	Premios al Mérito
Reconciliation (ou Rapprochement bancaire)	Bank Reconciliation	Conciliación Bancaria

Recyclage	Refresher Training	Capacitación de Apoyo
Registre journalier des activités	Daily Activity Register	Registro Diario de Actividades
Regroupement	Pooling	Combinación
Rémuneration	Remuneration	Remuneración
Répartition des coûts	Allocation of Costs	Asignación de Costos
Répartition des fonctions	Functional Allocation	Distribución Funcional
Résolution de problèmes	Problem Solving	Resolución de Problemas
Responsabilités de fonction	Functional Responsibilities	Responsabilidades Funcionales
Responsabilités du personnel	Staff Responsibilities	Responsabilidades del Personal
Ressources	Resources	Recursos
Résultats intermédiaires	Intermediate Outputs	Resultados Intermedios
Rétro-information	Feedback	Retroalimentación
Revenus	Revenues	Ingresos, Entradas, Recibos
Revisite	Revisit	Visita Subsecuente
Rôle du personnel	Staff Roles	Funciones del Personal
Rubrique	Line Item	Partida o Rubro
Rupture de stocks	Stockout	Desabastecimiento

Santé reproductive	Reproductive Health	Salud Reproductiva
Satisfaction des clients	Client Satisfaction	Satisfacción del Cliente
Services à base communautaire (SBC)	Community-Based Services (CBS)	Servicios Comunitarios (SC)
Services achetés (ou sous-traitance)	Purchased Services	Servicios Adquiridos
Services au dépôt communautaire	Depot Services	Servicios de Almacén (o de Distribución Local)
Services bénévoles (de volontaires)	Volunteer Services	Servicios Voluntarios
Session de supervision	Supervisory Session	Sesión de Supervisión
Seuil de rentabilité	Break-Even Point	Punto de Equilibrio
Situation des stocks	Stock Position	Situación de Existencias
Situation financière	Financial Position	Posición Financiera
Sous-système	Subsystem	Subsistema
Stabilité de l'organisation	Organizational Stability	Estabilidad Organizacional
Stock de sécurité	Safety Stock	Existencias de Seguridad
Stock disponible	Stock on Hand	Existencias Disponibles
Stock en commande	Stock on Order	Existencias en Pedido
Stock résiduel	Balance on Hand	Saldo Disponible

Stocks	Inventory	Inventario
Stratégie	Strategy	Estrategia
Structure de supervision	Supervisory Structure	Estructura de Supervisión
Structure organisationnelle	Organizational Structure	Estructura Organizacional
Style de participation	Participative Style	Estilo Participativo
Subvention croisée	Cross-Subsidization/ Cross-Subsidies	Subsidios Cruzados
Subventions	Grants	Donaciones
Subventions qui contiennent des primes	Incentive Grants	Donaciones para Incentivar
Suivi	Monitoring	Monitoreo
Supervision à but de facilitation	Facilitative Supervision	Supervisión Facilitadora
Supervision sélective	Selective Supervision	Supervisión Selectiva
Système contrôlé de prestations sanitaires	Managed Care	Paquete de Servicios
Système d'allocation	Push System	Sistema de Asignación
Système d'information	Information System	Sistema de Información
Système d'information à deux niveaux	Two-Tier Information System	Sistema Bifurcado de Información

Système d'information de gestion (SIG)	Management Information System (MIS)	Sistema de Información Gerencial (SIG)
Système de commande (réquisition)	Pull System	Sistema de Requisición
Système de commande à intervalles fixes	Fixed Order Interval System	Sistema de Pedidos de Intervalos Fijos
Système de commande à intervalles variables	Variable Order Interval System	Sistema de Pedidos de Intervalos Variables
Système de comptabilité	Accounting System	Sistema Contable
Système de co-paiement	Co-Payment Scheme	Esquema de Pagos Compartidos
Système de gestion de la qualité	Quality Management System	Sistema de Administración de la Calidad
Système de primes d'encouragement	Incentive System	Sistema de Incentivos
Système de référence	Referral System	Sistema de Referencia
Système de revue continuelle ou perpétuelle	Continuous (Perpetual) Review System	Sistema Continuo (Perpetuo) de Inventario
Système de revue périodique	Periodic Review System	Sistema Periódico de Inventario
Système de supervision	Supervisory System	Sistema de Supervisión
Système des cinq tables	Five-Table System	Sistema de Cinco Mesas

Système Max-Min (maximum-minimum)	Max/Min (Maximum-Minimum) Stock Level	Sistema Max/Min
Systèmes de contrôle	Control Systems	Sistemas de Fiscalización
Tableau croisée	Cross-Tabulation	Tabulación Cruzada
Tableau d'analyse des données sur les contraceptifs	Contraceptive Data Analysis Chart	Tabla de Análisis de Datos sobre Anticonceptivos
Tableau de circulation de l'information	Information Flow Table	Gráfica de Flujo de Información
Tableau de comparaison	Comparison Table	Tabla Comparativa
Tableau de fréquence	Frequency Table	Tabla de Frecuencias
Tableau de Gantt	Gantt Chart	Gráfica de Gantt
Tableau de la situation des stocks	Status of Supplies Chart	Tabla para Control de Suministros
Tableau des comptes	Chart of Accounts	Catálogo de Cuentas
Tableau du flux des clients	Client Flow Chart	Tabla del Flujo de Clientes
Tâches	Tasks	Tareas
Taux	Rate	Tasa
Taux d'acceptation	Acceptance Rate	Tasa de Aceptación
Taux de clients non-assidus	No-Show Rate	Tasa de Inasistencia
Taux de continuation	Continuation Rate	Tasa de Continuación

Taux de discontinuation	Discontinuation Rate	Tasa de Abandono
Technique du modèle parfait	Benchmarking	Técnica de Análisis de Casos Modelo («Benchmarking»)
Temps d'attente des clients	Client Waiting Time	Tiempo de Espera de Clientes
Temps de contact	Contact Time	Tiempo de Contacto
Trace écrite	Paper Trail	Comprobantes
Type d'organisation	Organization Type	Tipo de Organización
Type de visite	Visit-Type	Tipo de Visita
Utilisateur potentiel	Potential User	Usuario Potencial
Utilisateurs actifs	Active Users	Usuarios Activos o Regulares
Utilisateurs assidus	Continuing Users	Usuarios Continuos o Subsecuentes
Variance des coûts	Cost Variance	Variación de Costos
Variations aléatoires	Random Variations	Variaciones al Azar
Viabilité	Sustainability	Sustentabilidad
Visite de suivi	Follow-up Visit	Visita de Control o Subsecuente
Visite pour insertion	Insertion Visit	Visita de Inserción
Visite pour intervention médicale	Procedure Visit	Visita de Procedimiento
Visites d'observation et d'étude	Observation-Study Visits	Visitas de Observación-Estudio

Voies de communication formelle	Reporting Channels	Canales para la Rendición de Informes
Volets du programme	Program Components	Componentes del Programa
Zone desservie	Service Marketplace	Mercado de Servicios

Bibliographie des glossaires de planification familiale

On trouvera ci-dessous une liste d'autres glossaires de population et de planification familiale disponibles actuellement auprès d'organisations travaillant dans le domaine de la population. Une partie de cette liste a été fournie par la société JHPIEGO et le Groupe de travail de l'USAID chargé des matériels sur la santé reproductive.

Glossaires publiés

AVSC International. *AVSC's Glossary of Terminology*. AVSC International, New York, NY, 1995. Publié en anglais.

Edmans, E. et al. *Glossaire de termes de planification familiale/Glossary of Family Planning Terms*. INTRAH, School of Medicine, University of North Carolina, Chapel Hill, NC, 1987. Publié en français et en anglais dans un seul volume.

Haupt, A. et T. T. Kane. *Guide de démographie*. The Population Reference Bureau, International Programs, Washington, DC, 1990. Publié en français, anglais, espagnol et arabe.

Newman, C. et J. Birkmayer. *Glossaire des termes utilisé en évaluation des formations*. INTRAH, School of Medicine, University of North Carolina, Chapel Hill, NC, 1987. Publié en français et en anglais.

Population Resource Center. *Population Glossary*. Population Resource Center, Washington, DC, 1994. Publié en anglais.

Rodriguez-Garcia, R. et al. *Glossaire sur la planification familiale naturelle*. Institute for Reproductive Health, Georgetown University, Washington, DC, 1989. Publié en français, anglais, espagnol et portugais.

Vandewalle, E. *Dictionnaire démographique multilingue*. Ordina Editions, Liège, Belgique, 1982. Publié en français, anglais et espagnol.

Veney, J. et P. Gorbach. *Definitions for Program Evaluation Terms*. The EVALUATION Project, Carolina Population Center, University of North Carolina, Chapel Hill, NC, 1993. Publié en anglais.

Wolff, J., J. Miller, et C. Bahamon, eds. «A la recherche d'un vocabulaire commun : Glossaire des termes de gestion» *Management de la planification familiale*. Family Planning Management Development, Management Sciences for Health, Boston, MA. Vol. IV, No. 3, 1995. Publié en français, anglais et espagnol.

Glossaires faisant partie de publications

Angle, M. et C. Murphy. *Lignes directrices pour les procédures en planification familiale : une référence pour les formateurs.* University of North Carolina, Chapel Hill, NC, 1993. Publié en français et en anglais.

Garcia-Nunez, J. *Improving Family Planning Evaluation.* Kumarian Press, West Hartford, CT, 1992. Publié en anglais.

Hatcher, R. et al. *Contraceptive Technology.* Irvington Publishers, North Stratford, NH, 1994. Publié en anglais.

Johns Hopkins University, Center for Communication Programs. *Service Providers Guide to Family Planning.* Johns Hopkins University, Center for Communication Programs, Population Communications Services, Baltimore, MD, 1990. Publié en anglais.

Kent, M. *World Population: Fundamentals of Growth.* Population Reference Bureau, Washington, DC, 1995. Publié en anglais.

Wolff, J. et al. *Guide des responsables des programmes de planification familiale : Aptitudes et outils essentiels pour la conduite des programmes de planification familiale.* Kumarian Press, West Hartford, CT, 1994. Publié en français, anglais et espagnol. Disponible de Kumarian Press en West Hartford CT, et de Management Sciences for Health en Boston, MA.

About Management Sciences for Health and the FPMD Project

Management Sciences for Health (MSH) is a private, non-profit organization dedicated to closing the gap between what is known about public health problems and what is done to solve them. Through technical assistance, training, systems development, and applied research, MSH helps decision makers throughout the world use techniques of modern management to improve the delivery of primary health care and family planning services.

MSH collaborates with public- and private-sector counterparts in population, maternal and child health, management information systems, drug management, health care financing, and management training. Since its founding in 1971, MSH has provided assistance in these areas to managers in over 100 countries. MSH's staff of 217 is based in its headquarters in Boston, Massachusetts; 21 field offices; and Washington, D.C.

The **Family Planning Management Development** (FPMD) project, implemented by MSH and funded by the United States Agency for International Development, provides management assistance to national family planning programs and organizations to improve the effectiveness of service delivery and program sustainability. Working in over 30 countries, FPMD provides technical assistance to public- and private-sector programs in: strategic planning; business planning; operational work planning; financial management; marketing, pricing, and costing; human resources management; management information systems; program evaluation; and coordination and collaboration between public and private sectors.

FPMD has published award-winning publications, which have been used in over 175 countries worldwide. In addition to this *Pocket Glossary*, FPMD has produced the following publications:

> *The Family Planning Manager* bi-monthly
> management series
> (Available in English, Spanish, and French)

> *The Family Planning Manager's Handbook: Basic Skills and Tools for Managing Family Planning Programs*
> (Available in English, French, Spanish, Bangla, and Arabic)

> *Beyond the Clinic Walls: Case Studies in Community-Based Distribution*
> (Available in English)

For more information about Management Sciences for Health, please contact:

> Management Sciences for Health
> 400 Centre Street
> Newton, Massachusetts 02158
> Telephone: (617) 527-9202
> Fax: (617) 965-2208
> E-Mail: development@msh.org

Acerca de Management Sciences for Health y el Proyecto FPMD

Management Sciences for Health (MSH) es una organización privada sin fines de lucro que se dedica a cerrar la brecha existente entre lo que se sabe acerca de los problemas de salud pública y lo que se está haciendo para solucionarlos. A través de la asistencia técnica, la capacitación, el desarrollo de sistemas y los trabajos de investigación aplicada, MSH ayuda a las personas encargadas de tomar decisiones a nivel mundial a utilizar técnicas gerenciales modernas para mejorar la prestación de servicios de salud primaria y planificación familiar.

MSH colabora con contrapartes del sector público y privado en las áreas de población, salud materna e infantil, sistemas de información gerencial, administración de medicamentos, financiamiento de servicios de salud y capacitación gerencial. Desde su fundación en 1971, MSH ha proporcionado asistencia en dichas áreas a de administradores en más de 100 países. El personal de MSH consta de 217 personas que trabajan en la oficina principal ubicada en Boston, Massachusetts; en 21 oficinas adentro de diversos países; y en Washington D.C.

El Proyecto **Family Planning Management Development (FPMD)**, implementado por MSH y financiado por la Agencia de los Estados Unidos para el Desarrollo Internacional (USAID), presta asistencia gerencial a los programas de planificación familiar y a las organizaciones nacionales con el objeto de mejorar la prestación de servicios y la sustentabilidad del programa. Al trabajar en más de 30 países, FPMD proporciona asistencia técnica a los programas del sector público y privado en las áreas de: planificación estratégica; planificación de negocios; planificación operativa del trabajo; administración financiera; mercadeo, fijación de precios y determinación de costos; manejo de recursos humanos; sistemas de información gerencial; evaluación de programas y coordinación y colaboración entre el sector público y privado.

FPMD ha lanzado publicaciones que han sido merecedoras de premios y que se han utilizado en más de 175 países a nivel mundial. Además del presente *Glosario de Bolsillo*, el proyecto ha publicado los siguientes:

Actualidad Gerencial en Planificación Familiar,
una serie bi-mensual
(Disponible en español, inglés y francés)

Manual del Administrador de Planificación Familiar:
Técnicas para Mejorar la Gestión de Programas
(Disponible en español, inglés, francés, bangla y árabe)

Beyond the Clinic Walls: Case Studies in Community-Based
Distribution
(Disponible solamente en inglés)

Para mayor información acerca de Management Sciences for Health, favor ponerse en contacto con:

Management Sciences for Health
400 Centre Street
Newton, Massachusetts 02158
Teléfono: (617) 527-9202
Fax: (617) 965-2208
E-Mail: development@msh.org

Note concernant Management Sciences for Health et le Projet FPMD

Management Sciences for Health (MSH) est un organisme privé à but non lucratif dont la mission est de franchir le pas entre l'étude et la résolution des problèmes de santé publique. Grâce à ses prestations en matière d'assistance technique, de formation, de mise au point de systèmes et de recherche appliquée, MSH aide les décideurs du monde entier à appliquer les techniques modernes de gestion à l'amélioration des prestations de services de santé primaire et de planification familiale.

MSH travaille en collaboration avec des responsables de services publics et privés dans une série de domaines: population, santé maternelle et infantile, systèmes d'information de gestion, gestion des médicaments, financement des services de santé, formation à la gestion. Depuis sa création en 1971, MSH a prêté son concours, dans ces divers domaines, à des responsables appartenant à plus de 100 pays. MSH emploie actuellement 217 collaborateurs, répartis entre le siège social de Boston, Massachusetts; 21 bureaux à l'étranger; et le bureau de Washington.

Le Projet **FPMD (Family Planning Management Development)**, exécuté par MSH et financé par l'Agence des Etats-Unis pour le développement international (USAID), fournit à des programmes et organismes nationaux de planification familiale des prestations d'assistance à la gestion destinées à accroître l'efficacité de leurs prestations de services et la viabilité de leurs programmes. Dans plus de 30 pays, le Projet FPMD fournit aux programmes publics et privés des prestations techniques dans des domaines tels que planification stratégique, organisation et planification des travaux, gestion financière; commercialisation, calcul des prix et des coûts; gestion des ressources humaines, systèmes d'information de gestion, évaluation des programmes; coordination et collaboration entre secteurs public et privé.

Le Projet FPMD a publié un certain nombre d'ouvrages qui ont été couronnés, et ont été utilisés dans plus de 175 pays. Outre le présent *Glossaire de poche*, le Projet a publié les ouvrages suivants :

Management de la planification familiale,
bulletin bimestriel concernant la gestion
(disponible en français, en anglais et en espagnol)

Guide des responsables des programmes de planification familiale : Aptitudes et outils essentiels pur la conduite des programmes de planification familiale
(disponible en français, en anglais, en espagnol, en bangla et en arabe)

Beyond the Clinic Walls: Case Studies in Community-Based Distribution
(disponible en anglais)

Pour tous renseignements complémentaires concernant Management Sciences for Health, prière de s'adresser à :

Management Sciences for Health
400 Centre Street
Newton, Massachusetts 02158
Téléphone: (617) 527-9202
Fax: (617) 965-2208
E-Mail: development@msh.org

Notes